THE MIKIRS

THE MIKIRS

EDWARD STACK

GYAN

Published by

Gyan Publishing House
5, Ansari Road
Daryaganj, New Delhi-110002
Phone: 011-47034999, 9811692060
E-mail: books@gyanbooks.com

Distribution Network
gyanbooks.com
India, USA, Canada, UK, Australia

ISBN: 978-93-6280-828-8 (PB)
First Published, 1908

2nd Impression 2024

Printed at: Gyan Press, Delhi.

THE MIKIRS
Author: EDWARD STACK

THE MIKIRS

Frontispiece

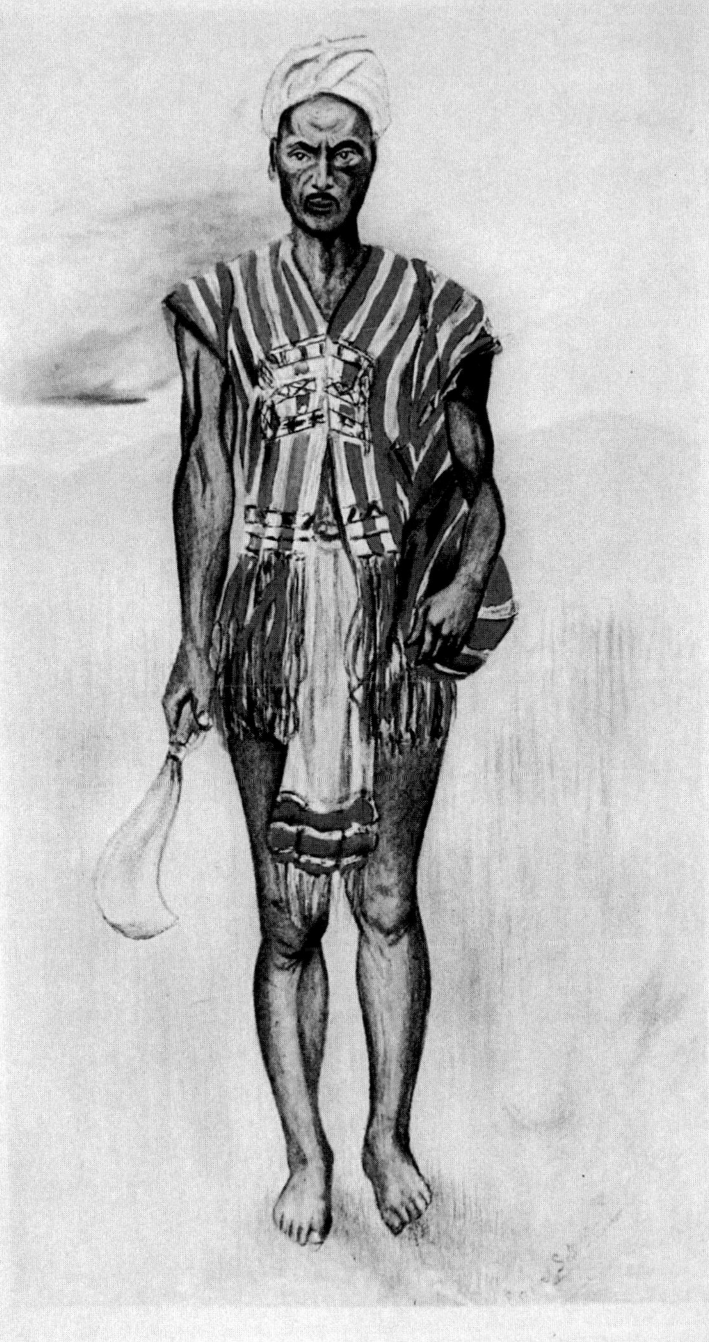

MIKIR MAN.

THE MIKIRS

FROM THE PAPERS OF THE LATE

EDWARD STACK

INDIAN CIVIL SERVICE

SOMETIME DIRECTOR OF LAND RECORDS AND AGRICULTURE, AND

SECRETARY TO THE CHIEF COMMISSIONER, ASSAM

EDITED, ARRANGED AND SUPPLEMENTED

BY

SIR CHARLES LYALL

UNITED PUBLISHERS

PAN BAZAR, GAUHATI

To

M. R. L.-J.

In Memoriam

INTRODUCTORY NOTE.

In 1882 Edward Stack, appointed the first Director of the newly-created Department of Land Records and Agriculture in Assam, entered upon his duties in that province, and applied himself with ardour to the study of its people. He had passed just ten years in the Indian Civil Service, which he joined in 1872 at the head of his year. These ten years had been fruitful in varied interest and activity: the strenuous life of a District and Settlement officer in the North-Western Provinces; secretariat employment in his own province and the Government of India; and, just before his translation to Assam, six months spent in travel in Persia.* Activity of mind and body, and keen interest in the people and speech of all the countries he lived in, were his strongest characteristics. During the cold season of 1882–83 he spent several months in moving up and down the Brahmaputra Valley, learning, observing, and noting. He acquired a working knowledge of Assamese with surprising rapidity; with this as his foundation and instrument, he attacked the multitude of tribal languages which he found impinging on the Aryan pale. To him, more than to any one else, is due the honourable distinction of the Assam

* The record of these travels, under the name *Six Months in Persia* (two vols.), was published in 1882; "A really clever and trustworthy, readable, book," was the judgment on it of the late Sir Frederic Goldsmid—the best of all judges.

Province in the grammars, vocabularies, and phrase-books of nearly all the most important of its multitudinous varieties of Indo-Chinese speech, which have been drawn up by officers and others who have served there. In 1883 the Report on the Census of 1881 in Assam was published; and in this Report, mainly the work of the Chief Commissioner, Sir Charles Elliott, the chapter on Castes and Tribes was written by Edward Stack. Paragraphs 131–136 deal with the Mikirs, and much in these represents the result of his careful personal inquiries among them. His interest in this tribe gradually grew. In 1884 he was called to take up the work of Secretary to the Chief Commissioner, and while thus employed he occupied his leisure in studying Mikir. He became acquainted with a bright young Mikir lad, a convert of the American Baptist Mission at Nowgong, named Sārdokā, to which he was accustomed to add the names of his sponsor at baptism, Perrin Kay. With the help of Mr. Neighbor's *Vocabulary of English and Mikir, with illustrative sentences*,* Stack and Sārdokā worked together at the language, correcting and largely supplementing the material contained in their text-book. From this they went on to folk-tales, which were written down, with a careful attention to systematic orthography, by Stack from Sārdokā's dictation, each day's work being provided with a series of notes elucidating every difficulty in it. Thus material gathered; and in the course of 1886 Stack had arranged, when relieved at the end of that year of the duties of Secretary by my return to Assam, to put together a complete account of the

* *See* Bibliography, No. 7.

Mikirs and their language, fully illustrated (as his wont was) by ample variety of phrase and idiom, and a collection of stories in Mikir with commentary and vocabulary. But during the latter half of 1886 his health failed. Partly the moist climate of Assam, and partly, perhaps, unsuspected flaws of constitution, told upon his strong and active frame; and, after some months of gradually increasing weakness, he died at sea on the 12th January, 1887, aged 37, just before the vessel reached Adelaide, in South Australia, where he had planned to spend his furlough.

A few months after his death his papers were sent to me at Shillong, and for some time I hoped, with Sārdokā's help, to be able to carry out his purpose. But the steadily increasing pressure of other duties prevented this. I left Shillong on a long tour in November, 1887, and soon after my return in the spring of 1888 I was transferred to the post of Commissioner in the Assam Valley, eventually leaving the province in the autumn of 1889 for engrossing work elsewhere, never to return, except for a brief space as Chief Commissioner in 1894. It had become evident from an examination of the materials that to do what Stack had set before him involved much more labour than I could give. It was necessary to learn the language from the beginning, to construct grammar and dictionary, and to retrace the steps which he had trodden in his progress; and this with an aptitude and power of acquisition far inferior to his. Accordingly, on my departure from Assam, the papers were made over to others, with whom they remained until, on the organization under Dr. G. A. Grierson of the *Linguistic*

Survey of Northern India, they were again inquired for, and utilized, so far as the scope of that work admitted, in preparing an account of the Mikir language for insertion in the Survey.*

In 1904, when Sir Bampfylde Fuller had obtained the sanction of the Government of India to his scheme for the preparation of a series of descriptive monographs on the more important tribes and castes of Assam, he proposed to me to undertake an account of the Mikirs, based on Stack's materials. There were several reasons why I hesitated to accept the task. It was many years since I had left the province, and official work and other studies claimed time and leisure. The materials were themselves in the rough—mere notes and jottings, sufficient for the man who carried the main part of his knowledge in his head, but by no means easy to interpret or set in order for one who had no such knowledge. They dated, too, from twenty years back, and in the interval great changes had occurred in the material development of the tract where the Mikirs live, which is now traversed by the Assam-Bengal Railway. I decided, nevertheless, to make the attempt, and, however imperfectly, to do something to perpetuate the work of a man to whom I was most intimately bound by affection, and whose great powers and attractive personality were the admiration and delight of all who knew him. The present volume is the result.

In addition to Stack's notes, I received from Assam three sets of replies to ethnographical questions which had been circulated to persons acquainted with the

* *See* Bibliography, No. 15.

tribe. These were from Mr. W. C. M. Dundas, Sub-divisional Officer of North Cachar, and the Rev. P. E. Moore and Mr. Allen of the American Baptist Mission.* These replies, which were not very detailed, while quite independent in origin, agreed closely with Stack's data, and showed that the lapse of years had not made the latter inapplicable to the present time. In the following pages any information drawn from these sources has been duly acknowledged.

It was explained in the Introduction to Major Gurdon's Monograph on the Khasis (1907) that the order and arrangement of subjects to be treated in dealing with each tribe had been prescribed by authority; and Stack's notes had to be brought within this framework. As will be seen, under certain heads not much information is forthcoming; and perhaps the more searching standard of inquiry applied by ethnologists in the present day might demand more exhaustive treatment of some points in this presentment of the Mikir people. This, however, must be left for our successors.

Section I has been expanded by adding numerical data from the last Census (1901), and measurements from Lieut.-Colonel L. A. Waddell's *Tribes of the Brahmaputra Valley* (1900). Section II (Domestic Life) is entirely due to Stack. The same is the case with Section III (Laws and Customs), except the Appendix. Section IV (Religion) is wholly Stack's; reading the careful and minute account which it contains of the funeral ceremonies, one is strongly

* I must apologize for the misdescription of these gentlemen at pp. 44 and 70, as of the American *Presbyterian* Mission.

impressed by the thoroughness which he brought to his investigations. Section V (Folk-lore) contains translations of three of the folk-tales written down in Mikir by Stack, of which the original text, with an interlinear rendering, is given in Section VI. These translations, in both Sections, have been made by me. Stack's manuscript supplied the Mikir text, which has been faithfully copied, and a number of explanatory notes, but no connected rendering. I have therefore had to depend upon my study of the language in the linguistic materials collected by him, and those contained in Mr. Neighbor's vocabulary and Sārdokā's dictionary and phrase-book. I had hoped to have the assistance of Sārdokā himself in revising the translations. He served for many years in the Assam Secretariat after Stack's death, and helped in the preparation of the specimens of Mikir for the *Linguistic Survey* in 1902; but in September, 1904, he was transferred as *mauzadār*, or Revenue collector and administrator, to the important *mauza* or territorial division in the Mikir Hills called Duār Bagurī, now divided between the districts of Nowgong and Sibsagar; and on the 8th March, 1905, he most unhappily died there of cholera. Other help was not forthcoming. I must, therefore, ask for the indulgence of those better acquainted than I with Mikir in regard to these renderings. Probably they contain many errors of detail; but at least they seem to hang together as a whole, and to be consistent with what I could ascertain elsewhere of the fashion of Mikir speech. The notes are chiefly from Stack. The sketch of the Grammar in Section VI is reproduced (in a somewhat abridged form) from that which I contributed to the *Linguistic Survey*. Stack himself had drawn up no grammar, though he had put together much illustrative material from which the mechanism of the language could be deduced. The main facts are clear and comparatively simple, though there are not a few idiomatic expressions in the texts of which it is difficult to give a satisfactory account.

For the last Section, that dealing with the probable affinities of the Mikir race, I must take the full responsibility. It is the result of the collation and comparison of materials from many sources, and especially those contained in the three volumes of the *Linguistic Survey* treating of the Tibeto-Burman family of speech. The authorities on which I have relied are indicated in the text.

In the Bibliography I have entered only those works (so far as known to me) which contribute something to our knowledge of the Mikirs. I have not thought it necessary to specify mere casual allusions to the tribe, or to quote imperfect lists of words which have been superseded by more accurate material.

For the coloured illustrations I have to thank Miss Eirene Scott-O'Connor (now Mrs. Philip Rogers), and for the photographs Major Gurdon and Mr. W. C. M. Dundas; the reproductions are by Messrs. W. Griggs and Sons. The map (by Mr. J. G. Bartholomew) showing the localities inhabited by the Mikirs is taken from the new volumes of the *Imperial Gazetteer of India*. An explanation of the system adopted for rendering Mikir words will be found on p. 74.

C. J. LYALL.

April, 1908.

TABLE OF CONTENTS.

SECTION III.

LAWS AND CUSTOMS.

SECTION IV.

RELIGION.

SECTION V.

FOLK-LORE AND FOLK-TALES.

SECTION VI.

LANGUAGE.

SECTION VII.

AFFINITIES.

LIST OF ILLUSTRATIONS.

THE MIKIRS

I.

GENERAL.

Numbers — Habitat — Physical appearance — Traditions as to origin — Affinities—Dress—Tattooing—Ornaments—Weapons.

THE Mikirs are one of the most numerous and homogeneous of the many Tibeto-Burman races inhabiting the Province of Assam. In the tables of the Report on the Census of 1901 the number of Mikirs by race is given as 87,046, and that of speakers of the Mikir language as 82,283; but there are curious discrepancies in the details. In no district are the speakers of Mikir identical in number with those returned as Mikir by race; and it is remarkable that in several, more persons are returned as speaking the language than as belonging to the tribe. On the other hand, in the North Cachar Hills none of the 1446 Mikirs by race are shown as speaking Mikir, which is manifestly absurd. The following are the figures:—

District.	Mikirs by race.	Speaking Mikir.
Cachar Plains	717	728
Sylhet	156	166
Kamrup	10,587	8,026
Darrang	2,646	3,108
Nowgong	35,732	34,273
Sibsagar	22,909	22,803
North Cachar	1,446	*nil.*
Khasi and Jaintia Hills	12,840	13,142
Elsewhere	13	37
Total	87,046	82,283

In Kamrup, Nowgong, and Sibsagar it may reasonably be assumed that the Mikirs returned as speaking some other language (probably Assamese) also spoke the speech of their tribe, being bilingual like other non-Aryan races in Assam; and the 809 persons in Darrang, the Khasi and Jaintia Hills, and elsewhere, returned as speaking Mikir, though not as Mikirs by race, must really have belonged to the tribe. Since 1891, when the number of Mikirs was returned as 94,829, there has been a considerable falling-off, due to the terrible ravages of the disease called *Kălă-ăzăr* * in the Nowgong and Kamrup districts.

The Mikirs inhabit in greatest strength the hills called after them, the isolated mountainous block which fills the triangle between the Brahmaputra on the north, the Dhansiri valley on the east, and the Kopili and Jamuna valleys on the west and south; this tract is now divided between the Nowgong and Sibsagar districts. They are also found in considerable numbers on the northern skirts of the Assam Range, in Nowgong, the Khasi and Jaintia Hills, and Kamrup, and were once numerous, as testified by the local place- and river-names, in North Cachar. They have settled in the plains, and taken to plough cultivation, in Nowgong and Kamrup, and have also established recent settlements of the same kind north of the Brahmaputra in Darrang. The great bulk, however, remain a hill tribe, occupying the forest-clad northern slopes of the central range of Assam, and practising the primitive method of cultivation by axe, fire, and hoe.

In the Mikir Hills there are summits which attain 4,000 feet, but the greater part of the block is of much lower elevation. The rock is chiefly gneiss and granite, with few traces of overlying formations; and the whole is clothed with forest growth, chiefly of bamboo, figs of different species, cinnamon, *Artocarpus, nahor* (*Mesua ferrea*), and a few other trees valuable for their timber. The soil is light, and soon exhausted by cropping; it is naturally most fertile in the valleys, where the deepest deposits are found. The Mikir Hills, in 1886 when Mr. Stack wrote, had been very little explored by Europeans, and their interior was almost unknown. To the north, from Koliabor to Kaziranga, they abut on the Brahmaputra, only a narrow strip of country, traversed by the southern Grand Trunk road,

* This is the official spelling. The real name is *Kalā-jwar*, pronounced *Kŏlā-jŏr* (or *zŏr*), which means "black fever."

intervening between them and the river. This strip has few inhabitants and little cultivation, and is covered with high grass and cotton tree (*semal*) jungle, the haunt of wild buffalo and rhinoceros. To the east is the great Nāmbar forest, a dense area of high trees occupying the Dhansiri valley from Dimapur to within ten miles of Golaghat. To the south-west is the valley of the Jamuna, now traversed by the railway from Gauhati to Lumding, a region of tall grass and sparse tree jungle. The plain which is formed by the alluvial valley of the Kopili (or Kupli) river and its affluents, the Jamuna and the Diyaung (the latter coming from the North Cachar Hills), next intervenes; and to the west the land rises again in the northern skirts of the Jaintia and Khasi Hills. Here the country is of the same character as in the Mikir Hills, but better known. It consists of a series of plateaus or shelves rising from the level of the valley, composed of gneiss and granite, and covered with a red clay soil, the result of the decomposition of the metamorphic sandstones which overlay the igneous rock. The jungle here also is chiefly of bamboo, with a few patches of valuable forest, chiefly *sāl* (*Shorea robusta*), still surviving; but most of the larger timber has been destroyed by the secular practice of axe and fire cultivation.

It is in this hilly country, and in the plains at its base, that the Mikir people are found. The region is continuous, and is distributed, as the figures just given show, between the districts (from east to west) of Sibsagar, Nowgong, North Cachar, the Jaintia and Khasi Hills, and Kamrup. It is malarious and unhealthy for unacclimatized persons, with a very moist climate, and is wanting in the breezy amenities of the higher plateaus of the Khasi and Jaintia Hills; but (save during the recent prevalence of *Kālā-āzār*) the inhabitants appear to have acquired some degree of immunity against the noxious influences of the locality. Side by side with the Mikirs dwell, in the Mikir Hills, the Rengma Nagas (who are recent immigrants from the eastern side of the Dhansiri); in the Jamuna and Diyaung valleys, the Dīmāsā or Kachāris; in the Jaintia Hills, the Kukis and Syntengs; and in the Khasi Hills and along the Nowgong and Kamrup borders, the Lālungs and a few settlements of Khāsis.

The name *Mikir* is that given to the race by the Assamese: its origin is unknown. They call themselves *Ārlèng*, which means *man* in general.* In features the men resemble Assamese of the lower classes more than most of the Tibeto-Burman races. Their colour is light yellowish brown, and the girls are often fair. The men are as tall as the majority of the hill races of Assam, Colonel L. A. Waddell's eighteen specimens averaging 1633 millimetres, or 5·354 feet, in height, the tallest being 5·583 feet, and the shortest 5·108. The average is noticeably higher than that of their neighbours the Khasis. The average head measurements in these specimens were—length, 181 millimetres; breadth, 141; cephalic index, 77·9. The nose is broad at the base, and often flat, giving a nasal index of 85·1, and an orbito-nasal of 107·7. The facial hair is scanty, and only a thin moustache is worn. The front of the head is sometimes, but not generally, shorn. The hair is gathered into a knot behind, which hangs over the nape of the neck. The body is muscular, and the men are capable of prolonged exertion. In frontier expeditions in Assam they have frequently served (like the Khasis) as porters, and carry heavy loads, the burden being borne upon the back and secured by a plaited bamboo (or cane) strap passing round the forehead (Mikir, *sinàm*).

The traditions of the race point to the Eastern portion of the Khasi and Jaintia Hills, bordering on the Kopili (or Kupli) river (where many still remain), as their original abode. They speak of this as *Nihàng,* in contradistinction to *Nilīp,* the Duār Bāguri or Nowgong region which they now inhabit. Being harassed by warfare between Khasi (or Synteng) chiefs,

* It has been asserted that *Ārlèng* means properly only a *Mikir man*, not a man in general, who would be called *monīt* or *munīt*. This, however, is opposed to usage as exemplified in the folk-tales collected by Mr. Stack, and to well-established parallels found elsewhere. Thus, in Assam, *Māndē* (= man) is the national name of the Gāros; *Chingphō* (= man) is the tribal name of the race so called in the Upper Dehing valley; *Boro* (= man) is the proper designation of the Kachāri race. So, in Chutia Nāgpur, the Mundā people of Rānchi call themselves *Horo* (= man). Similar cases are found all over the world. In Europe, for example, the name *Deutsch* for the Germanic race indicates that their ancestors spoke of themselves as "*the* people" (*diot, diota*), ignoring the other members of humankind. *Munīt* is a very recent loan-word from Assamese, and nowhere occurs in the tales.

GROUP OF MIKIRS (NORTH CACHAR).

(1)

p. 5

they resolved to move into Āhom territory, and sent emissaries to claim protection from the Āhom governor of Rahā (Nowgong District). These unfortunate persons, being unable to make themselves understood, were straightway buried alive in the embankment of a tank which the governor was excavating. The hostilities which ensued were concluded by an embassage to the king himself in Sibsagar, and the Mikirs have ever since been living peacefully in the territory assigned to them. They have dim traditions of a king of their own in the good old days, whom they call *Sòt Rĕchō*, and are said by Mr. Stack to expect his return to earth. His seat is said to have been in *Ròng-khàng* (or *Ròng-hàng*), perhaps connected with *Ni-hàng* (*Ròng*, village). They had fights with the Dīmāsā or Hill Kachāris, and were led by Thòng Nòkbē and other captains, who established a fort at Diyaung-mukh (the junction of the Diyaung and Kopili rivers), the ruins of which are still to be seen. Along the northern skirts of the Mikir Hills there are remains of old brick buildings and sculptures, which are now ascribed to the Gods. Old men tell historical legends to the young ones, and there are also legendary songs, sung at festivals; but there is no class specially set apart for the preservation of such traditions, and the memory of the race is short. They are a mild and unwarlike people, and are said to have given up the use of arms when they placed themselves under the protection of the Āhom kings.

They claim kinship with no other tribe in Assam, and are, in fact, difficult to group with other branches of the great Tibeto-Burman stock to which they undoubtedly belong. The conclusions as to their affinities which it seems legitimate to draw from their institutions, culture, and language, will be found stated in Section VII. of this Monograph.

In dress the Mikir man imitates the Khasi, to whom he seems to have lived in subjection in former times. On his head he now wears a turban (*pohu*, *poho*), but formerly the Khasi cap (*phu-tup*), of black or red cloth, was more usually worn. On his loins he wears a *dhoti* (*rikòng*) of cotton cloth, and sometimes, if wealthy, of silk. His coat is a sleeveless striped jacket (*choi*), with a long fringe covering the buttocks and coming round in front (*choi-āprē*). In cold weather he wears a thick wrapper (called in Assamese *boṛ kāpoṛ*) of *ēṛī* silk (*pē-inkī*). The legs are uncovered, and shoes are not worn.

The women wear a petticoat (*pīnī*), secured round the waist by an ornamental girdle (*vànkòk*). The petticoat is of white and red striped *ēṛī* cloth. The upper part of the body is covered with the *jī-sō*, a wrapper passing under the arms and drawn tight over the breasts. The head is uncovered, and the hair is drawn back and tied in a knot behind. In the funeral dances, however, the head is covered with a black scarf (*jī-sō ke-īk*).

The men do not tattoo any part of the body. The women, on attaining puberty, usually tattoo a perpendicular line with indigo down the middle of the forehead, the nose, upper lip, and chin; no other part of the body is tattooed.

A characteristic ornament is a large silver tube inserted into the lobe of the ear, which is much distended thereby; this is called *kadèngchinrō*, and weighs three or four rupees. The ordinary hanging earring (suspended from the outer part of the ear) of gold or silver is called *no-rīk*. Necklaces (*lèk*) are worn, of gold or silver and coral beads, as by the Khasis. Rings (*ārnàn*) and bracelets (*roi*), of gold and silver, are worn. The feathers of the *bhīm-rāj* are worn in the turban on festal occasions, as among the Khasis.

The national weapons are the long knife (*nòk, nòk-jir*), by the English commonly called by the Hindi name *dāo*, the spear (*chir*), and the bow (*thai, bòp-thailī*) made of bamboo, with a string of tough bamboo fibre. In these there is nothing peculiar.

MIKIR GIRL.

p. 6

II.

DOMESTIC LIFE.

Occupations—Houses—Furniture—Implements and utensils—Manufactures—Agriculture—*Rīsōmār*, or lads' clubs—Crops—Hunting—Fishing—Food and Drink.

THE Mikir people have always been agriculturists. Their villages, in the hills which are their proper habitat, are set up in clearings in the forest, and are shifted from place to place when the soil has been exhausted by cropping. Their houses are large and substantial, and are strongly put together. The Mikirs are not now (if they ever were*), as Colonel Dalton relates in his *Ethnology of Bengal*, in the habit of lodging several families, or even the whole village, in one house. The inhabitants of a house are all of one family, but may often be numerous, as married sons frequently live with their parents.

The Mikir house is built on posts, and the floor is raised several feet above the ground. The material of the superstructure is bamboo, slit and flattened out, and the whole is thatched with *san*-grass. A moderate elevation, with a flat top, is preferred for building; a slope will be taken if no better site can be found.

The house is divided lengthwise by a partition called *ārpòng*, or *nòksèk-ārpòng*, into *kàm*, the guests' or servants' chamber, and *kut*, the living-room of the family. *Kàm* is on the right side as you enter, and the only door into the house leads into it. In *kàm* a platform or *chang*, called *tibung*, raised above the floor the diameter of a bamboo, runs along the outside wall; this may be divided off laterally into rooms for sleeping. In *kut*,

* One is tempted to conjecture that this statement is an error based on a confusion between the *Miris* and the *Mikirs* in Colonel Dalton's notebooks. The custom referred to obtains among the Miris.

PLAN OF MIKIR HOUSE.

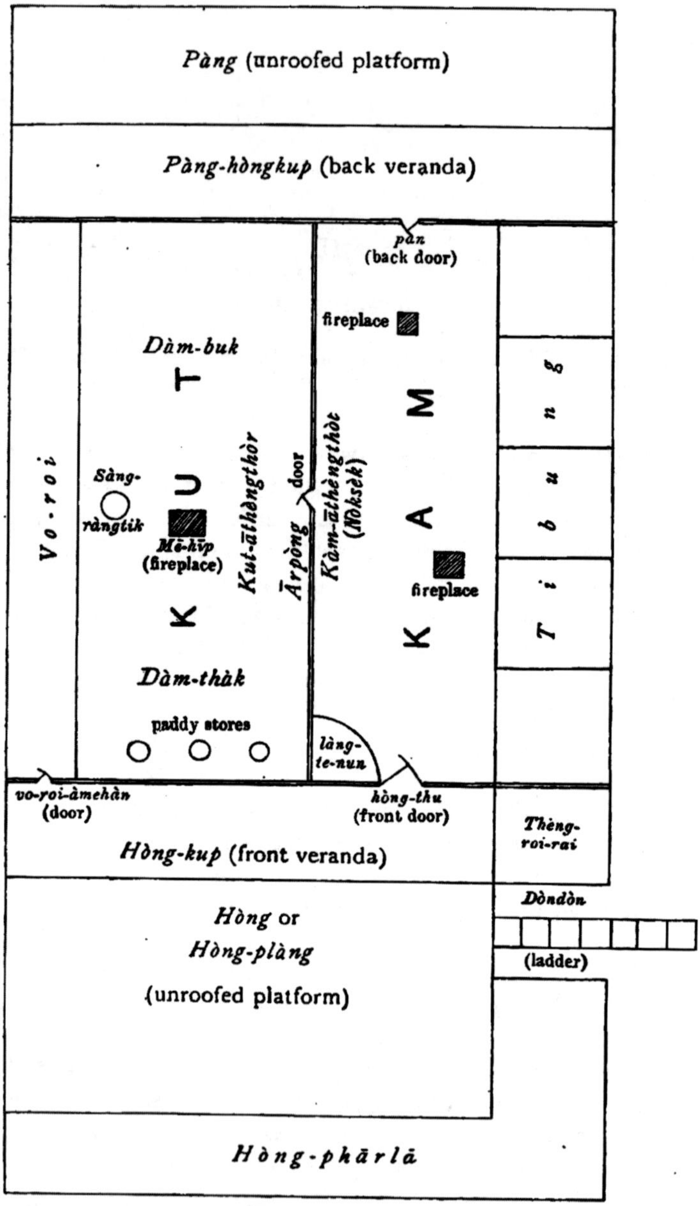

Tikup

(Yard or compound before the house, usually fenced round)

separated off by a partition on the side of the outer wall, is a long, narrow chamber, one bamboo's diameter lower than the floor, called *vō-roi*, in which the fowls and goats are kept at night; it has a separate door, called *vō-roi-āmchàn*. In *kut*, towards the back, is the fireplace (*mēhīp*). The space before it is *dàm-thàk*, where the family sleep, and the bamboo paddy-receptacle stands. Behind the fireplace is *dàm-buk*, a vacant space, where the grown-up daughter or old woman sleeps. Between the fire and the *vō-roi* is the rice-pot (*sàng-ràngtik*), holding the stock of husked rice. Between the fire and the partition (*ārpòng*) is the *kut-āthèngthòr*, a space for miscellaneous articles. Above the *vō-roi* a shelf is raised under the roof. called *vō-hārlīp*, for pots, etc. Opposite the fireplace is a door leading into *kàm*.

In *kàm*, if the house is large, there are two fireplaces. Before the fire the space is called *kàm-āthèngthòt*, or *nòksèk*. In the corner of the front wall and the partition (*ārpòng*) are put the water-*chungas* (*làng-bòng*); it is called *làng-tēnun*. The front door is called *hòngthū*, the back door *pàn*, or *pàn-hòngthū*.

The front veranda is called *hòng-kup*. The *tibung* runs out into it, and the part beyond the front wall of the house is called *thèng-roi-rai*, "the place for bringing (or storing) firewood" (*thèng*). Beyond the *hòng-kup* the platform extends unroofed (*hòng-plàng*). If the house be a large one, a *hòng-phārlā*, roofed over, for strangers to lodge in, is made on the right side of the *hòng-plàng*, but disconnected with the *thèng-roi-rai*; between it and the latter is the ladder to gain access to the platform (*dòndòn*), usually a tree-trunk with notches cut in it for the feet. The *hòng-phārlā* may extend also across the front of the house; it is roofed over, but open towards the house. Similarly, at the back of the house is the *pàng-hòngkup*, or back veranda, and the unroofed *pàng* beyond. No ladder gives access to this.

Under the house are the pigsties, *phàk-roi*, and in front is a yard or compound (*tikup*), usually fenced round.

The furniture of the house is of the simplest description. The floor, or a raised platform of bamboo, serves as a bed. A block of wood (*inghoi*; Ass. *pīrā*) is used as a stool to sit on.

Baskets of bamboo and cane are employed as cupboards in which to store the household goods, the paddy, and the clothes. These baskets are of various shapes and sizes, and bear many different names. Joints of bamboo (Ass. *chungā*; Mikir, *làng-bòng*) are used for holding water, and also as boxes to contain valuables of all kinds.

The Mikirs have few manufactures. Weaving is done by the women of the family on rude wooden looms (*pè-theràng*), the cotton raised in their fields being previously spun on a wheel (*mī-thòngràng*). They also raise *ẹ̄rī* silk (*inkī*), the cocoon of the *Attacus ricini*, fed on the castor-oil plant, and weave it into coarse fabrics, chiefly the *bor-kāpor*, or blanket, used in the cold weather. They dye their thread with indigo (*sibū*), a small patch of which is grown near every house. The indigo is not derived from *Indigofera*, but from a species of *Strobilanthes*, generally identified as *S. flaccidifolius*. Mr. Stack notes that there are two kinds, *bū-thī* and *bū-jīr*; the latter, he says, is trained up poles, and has a longer leaf. The leaves of the plant are bruised in a wooden mortar and mixed with water, and the blue colour develops, as in ordinary indigo, in a few days' time by chemical change. Besides indigo, they use a red dye, the source of which is probably the same as the Khasi red dye (see *Khasi Monograph*, p. 60).

Blacksmiths (*hēmai*) have existed among them from remote times, and they can fashion their own *dāos* and various kinds of knives. They also make needles (for which old umbrella-ribs are in much request), and hooks for fishing.

They also make their own gold and silver ornaments (necklaces, bracelets, rings, ear-ornaments).

Pottery is made *without the wheel*, as among the Khasis (*Monograph*, p. 61). It is thick and durable, and well burnt. There are few potters among them, and the accomplishment is not common.

In all these branches of manufacture the tendency, with the increase of intercourse and the cessation of isolation, is to give up domestic workmanship and rely more upon outside markets.

The main crops are summer rice (*maikum*), sown with the first rains and reaped in November—December, and cotton (*phēlō*), also grown in the rains and gathered in the cold

MIKIR HOUSE: FAMILY GROUP.

(Jaintia Hills).

p. 10

weather. The system of *jhuming*, by which land is prepared for cultivation by cutting down and burning the jungle, is in no respect different from the practice of all hill-tribes in the province. They do not plant out their rice, nor use the plough in cultivating it. There is no irrigation.

Besides these main crops, castor-oil is grown for feeding the *ẹ̄rī* silkworm; maize (*thèngthē*), turmeric (*thārmit*), yams (*hèn*, *Colocasia*), red pepper (*birik*), aubergines (Hindi, *baiṅgan*; Mikir, *hēpī*), and ginger (*hànsō*) are also cultivated in small patches. Another crop is lac, grown on branches of the *arhaṛ* plant (see *Khasi Monograph*, p. 47).

When Mr. Stack wrote, the most important institution from the point of view of agriculture was the association or club of the *dekas* (Ass.), or young men (from twelve to sixteen, eighteen, or twenty years of age) of the village (Mikir, *rī-sō-mār*); but it is reported that this useful form of co-operation is now falling into desuetude. In former days the village youths (as in Naga-land) used to live together in a house by themselves, called in Mikir *māro* or *teràng* (in Assamese, *deka-chang*).* Now there is no *mārō*, and the *rīsōmār* live in the *gaoṅbura's* house, in the *hòng-phārlā*, the place in which strangers are lodged. They send a boy to bring their food from their homes, and all eat together. Each man's share is brought in a leaf-bundle (*àn-bòr*) to keep it warm. The *gaoṅbura* calls the people together, and proposes that, having so many lads in the village, they should start a lads' club. If agreed to, the union of the *rīsōmār* is formed, and the lads take up their quarters in his house. The club is organized under regular officers appointed by themselves. The *gaoṅbura* has general authority over them, but their own chief is the *klèng sārpō*. Next comes the *klèng-dun*, then the *sodār-kethē*, then the *sodār-sō* or *phàndiri*, then the *sànghō-kerai* ("he who fetches the company"), then the *bārlòn* ("carrier of the measuring-rod"). Other officers are the *chèng-brup-pī* and *chèng-brup-sō* (drummers, chief and lieutenant), the *phàn-krī* (the

* In the *Proceedings of the Asiatic Society of Bengal* for 1874, p. 17, there is an illustration and description of a Mikir "bachelors' house," or *teràng*, by Mr. C. Brownlow, a tea-planter in Cachar. The group of Mikirs among whom it was found lived at the head of the Kopili river, looking down on the Cachar valley.

lad who waits on the *klèng sārpō*), the *motàn ār-ē* and *motàn ārvī* ("the right and left outside strips of the field"), the *làngbòng-pō* ("carrier of the water-*chunga*"), *ārphèk-pō* ("carrier of the broom"), and the *chinhàk-pō* ("carrier of the basket of tools"). The *rīsōmār* all work in the fields together, each having his own strip (*ā-mo*) to till. The village fields are allotted each to one house, and the grown men confine their work to their own fields; but the *rīsōmār* go the round of all the fields in the village.

Work is enforced by penalties. They used to *roast* those who shirked their share; now they beat them for failure to work. If the *klèng sārpō* finds a lad refractory, he reports him to the *gaoṅbura*.

Villages like having *deka* clubs. They help greatly in cultivation, practice dancing and singing, and keep alive the village usages and tribal customs. They are in great request at funerals, which are the celebrations in which most spirit is shown.

Hunting, with spears and dogs, is practised. The objects of the chase are deer and wild pig; also the iguana (Ass. *gui*) and tortoise. The dog barks and follows up the track by scent. They also set traps (*ārhàng*) for tigers, with a spear placed so as to be discharged from a spring formed by a bent sapling; twice round the tiger's pug gives the height of his chest, at which the spear is pointed; a rope of creeper stretched across the path releases the spring when the tiger passes that way and comes against it.

Fishing is done with rod and line, but chiefly by means of traps and baskets, as in Assam generally. The trap (*ru*) is a basket of bamboo, constructed so that the fish can get in but cannot get out, and is fixed in an opening in a fence (*ā-ru-pāt*) placed in a stone dam built across a stream.

The staple food is rice, which is husked in the usual way, by being pounded with a long pestle in a wooden mortar, and cooked by the women of the family. The flesh of cows is not eaten; there is said to be a dislike even to keep them, but this prejudice is now dying out. Milk is not drunk. Fowls, goats, and pigs are kept for food, but eaten chiefly at sacrifices; eggs are eaten. A delicacy is the chrysalis of the *ērī* silkworm

(*Attacus ricini*); it is eaten roasted and curried. Children (but not grown folk) cook and eat crabs and rats. In cooking meat, spits (*òk-ākròn*) are used; the meat is either cut up and skewered, or a large lump is placed whole on the embers; it is thoroughly cooked. Fish is cut into slices and put in the sun to dry, or smoked. Meat also is cut into strips and dried on frames in the sun.

The vegetables are those commonly used by the Assamese. Sugar-cane (*nòk*) is not much grown. A favourite seasoning is mint (*lōpòng-brik*).

Men and women eat together, within the house. The right hand is used in eating. Leaf-plates are most used, but platters of pot-metal are also found. No knife is used in eating: the meat is cut up beforehand.

The first meal is cooked and eaten at 7 or 8 a.m., and consists of rice. The evening meal is cooked after the day's field-work is over, unless there be a cook in the house. At each meal a pinch of the food is put aside for the God (*ārnàm*).

The national drink is rice-beer (*hòr, hòrpō*), which is made by each household for itself. The rice is cooked, and well broken up on a mat. It is then mixed with a ferment called *thàp* (Bengali, *bākhar*), made of powdered rice with certain kinds of leaves pounded into it, and the whole dried for use as required. After this has been thoroughly mixed with the boiled rice, the latter is heaped up and covered with plantain leaves, and put aside in the house. In three or four days, in the hot weather, fermentation sets in; in the cold weather a longer time is required. It is then put into an earthern jar or *kalsī* (Beng.) and water added, after which it is emptied into a conical basket, whence it is allowed to strain through a bamboo joint into a pot below. To make *hòr* (Ass. *modh*), rice is taken from the basket and warmed with water, which is strained off, and is the *modh* or *hòrpō*; the rice is thrown to the pigs. The better and stronger beer is that which was drained off the original conical basket, and is called *hòr-ālàng*.

Āràk (Hind.) is the spirit distilled from the fermented rice mixed with water. The still is a rude one of earthern pots connected by a bamboo. A stronger stuff is made by distilling *hòr-ālàng*.

Hòr will keep good for two months if left untouched. It is a common family drink. Gourds are used for keeping it in and carrying it about for use.

Drunkenness is not common in the villages, and the ceremonies and festivities at which beer is drunk are not noisy. The *mē* or general council, however, when large quantities are consumed, is sometimes noisy.

Opium is used to a large extent by the Mikirs as by other Assamese (Mr. Allen states that nearly all male adults indulge in it). Tobacco is smoked, and also chewed with betel. The bowl of the tobacco-pipe is made of burnt clay or of bamboo root. Betel-nut (*kōvē;* Khasi, *kwai*) is largely consumed in the usual way, with lime and *pān*-leaf (*bīthī*); and (as among the Khasis) time and distance are computed by the interval required to chew a nut. (The phrase is *ingtàt ē-òm-tā ēr*, "the time it takes to chew the nut and *pān*-leaf red": *ingtàt*, roll for chewing; *ē*-, one; *òm*, chew; *ēr*, red.)

III.

LAWS AND CUSTOMS.

Internal structure—Sections or divisions—Exogamous groups—Marriage laws—Common names—Marriage ceremony—Female chastity—Polygamy—Divorce—Words for relationship by blood and marriage—Inheritance—Property in land—Decision of disputes—Village council—Relations with neighbouring races—*Appendix:* Lists of exogamous groups given by other authorities compared with those given by Mr. Stack.

THE Mikir people proper—that is, those who continue to live in the hills—are divided into three sections, called Chintòng, Rònghàng, and Āmrī. In the days of the migration eastward from the Kopili region, Āmrī stayed behind, or loitered, and Chintòng and Rònghàng waited for him as they moved from stage to stage. At last, on arriving at the Dhansiri river, Chintòng and Rònghàng resolved to be only two sections in future. The laggard Āmrī afterwards arrived, but was not received back into full fellowship. He has no honour at the general festivals, and in the distribution of rice-beer at feasts he gets no gourd for himself, but has to drink from those of the other two. These are the conditions as they exist in the Mikir Hills and Nowgong (Duār Bāgurī); in Ni-hàng, however (the region of the Kopili), Āmrī is on an equality with the others. The Mikir Hills are chiefly inhabited by the Chintòng section, North Cachar and the hilly parts of Nowgong by the Rònghàng, and the Khasi and Jaintia Hills by Āmrī; but individuals of all three are found dwelling among the others.

These names, however, do not indicate true tribal divisions, supposed to be derived from a common ancestor and united in blood, and are probably in reality local- or place-names. Āmrī, in particular, seems to be a Khasi river-name, and Rònghàng is the legendary site of Sòt Rĕchŏ's capital. The real tribal exogamous divisions run through all three, and are called *kur* (a Khasi word: Assamese, *phoid*). Each of the three sections of the race has within it the same *kurs*, and the individuals belonging to these *kurs*, whether in Chintòng, Ròngbàng, or Āmrī, observe the same rules of exogamy.

The number and names of the *kurs*, or exogamous groups, are differently given by different authorities. The differences appear to be partly explained by the fact that one authority has taken for a principal group-name what another has entered as a sub-group under another larger section. In an appendix will be found the grouping according to several different authorities. Here the data given by Mr. Stack, who appears to have relied chiefly on information obtained in Duār Bāgurī, are reproduced.

He found that the people recognized four *kurs*, called respectively *Ingtī*, *Teràng*,* *Lèkthē*, and *Timung*, under which the smaller groups (also called *kur*) are ranged thus—

I. Ingti.	II. Terang.	III. Lèkthe.	IV. Timung.
(1) Tārō.	(1) Bē.	(1) Hànsē.	(1) Tòkbī.
(2) Kātār.	(2) Krō.	(2) Tutsō.	(2) Sèngnār.
(3) Hènsèk.	(3) Ingjār.	(3) Bòngrun.	(3) Ròngphār.
(4) Inglèng.		(4) Kràmsā.	

As already mentioned, these *kurs* are exogamous: an individual belonging to *kur* Ingtī must go outside that *kur* for his wife; and similarly Teràng, Lèkthē, and Timung cannot marry wives drawn from within the *kur*. The sub-groups are, of course, as parts of the larger groups, also exogamous; and it is easy to perceive how one informant may count as a principal group-division what another may regard as a sub-division. All the *kurs* are now socially on an equality, and have no scruples as to eating together or intermarriage; their traditional rank is, however, as given above. Ingtī is said to have been in former times the priestly clan (Ass. *gōhāiṅ*); Teràng also claims this dignity, but is thought to be of lower rank; but in both cases the office has fallen entirely into desuetude. Lèkthē is said to have been the military clan, while Timung represented the rest of the people.

The Mikirs who settled in the plains of Nowgong and took to plough cultivation are called *Dumrālī* by the Mikirs and

* Other authorities mention a fifth, *Teròn*, which Mr. Stack may have overlooked because of the similarity of its name to *Teràng*.

Tholuā by the Assamese. They are said to have acted as interpreters to the mission which visited the Āhom king at Sibsāgar. They also have the same *kurs* as the other three sections of hill Mikirs.

The children are counted to their father's *kur*, and cannot marry within it. They may, however, marry their first cousins on the mother's side, and indeed this appears to have been formerly the most usual match. This absence of matriarchal institutions strongly marks off the Mikirs from the Khasis, from whom they have in other respects borrowed much.

The following are common personal names among the Mikirs:—

Men.		Women.	
Sārdokā.	Burā.	Karèng.	Karē.
Mòn.	Pātōr.	Kachē.	Kasàng.
Dīlī.	Lòng.	Kabàn.	Kadòm.
Thērē.	Mèn.	Kamàng.	Dīmī.
Kàngthēr.	Bī.	Ka-èt.	Inglē.
Tāmoi.	Sōterā.	Ka-jīr.	
Temèn.		Katū.	

It is said that no meaning is attached to these names; that is, they are not given because of any meaning which they may possess. (It is evident that many of them *have* a meaning: *e.g. Bī* is a goat, *Lòng* a stone, *Pātōr* is a village official among the Khasis, *Burā* is Assamese for "an old man," *Tāmoi* is probably the Assamese for the betel-nut (*tāmol.*) *Sōterā* may be corrupted from *sangtarā*, orange.) The prefix *Ka-* in women's names is manifestly taken from Khasi usage. There are no surnames, but the name of the *kur* is used to distinguish one individual from another, as Mòn Lèkthē, Mòn Timung.

The age for marriage is from fourteen to twenty-five for the man, ten to fifteen for the girl; eighteen or nineteen and fifteen are the most usual ages. Child marriage is unknown. If a young man fancies a girl (from meeting her at dances and the like), he sends one or both parents to her father's house, and if the girl's parents agree, the lad's father leaves a betrothal ring or bracelet with the girl (this is called *ke-roi-dun*); sometimes a gourd of rice beer is taken and accepted, and in that case, if she subsequently marries another, the village council fine her family 25 to 35 rupees; otherwise only the betrothal ring or bracelet is returned. The length of the engagement is uncertain, but the actual marriage does not take place till after puberty. When the marriage day is fixed, both families prepare beer and spirits; if the bridegroom is rich, he provides drink for the whole country-side (*hòr-hàk hòr-tibuk*). The bridegroom's party, giving a gourd of beer to each village they pass through, arrive at the bride's house in the evening. There they sit awhile, and then offer one gourd of beer and one glass bottle of spirits to the bride's father on the *hòng*. A colloquy ensues: the bride's father asks the bridegroom's why they have come, and why these offerings. He answers, "Your sister (*i.e.* the wife of the speaker) is becoming old and cannot work, so we have brought our son to marry your daughter." (The custom formerly was that a boy must marry his first cousin on the mother's side, and if he did not, the maternal uncle could beat the lad as much as he liked; but now they can do as they please.) The reply follows: "My daughter is unworthy, she does not know weaving and other household work." "Never mind, we will teach her ourselves." The bride's father then asks his wife to enquire of the girl if she will take the lad; without her consent the beer and spirits cannot be accepted. If the wife reports consent, the beer and spirits are drunk by the two fathers. Sometimes they sit the whole night before the girl's consent is obtained. If any knowing old men are there, they sing in two parties: "*We* cannot send our daughter to your house!" "*We* cannot leave our boy to stay with you!" When the question of consent is settled, all eat together. Then the bride prepares the bed inside the house for the bridegroom, in the *kàm*; in the *tibung* (see plan *) if there is room: if not, in the *thèngthòr;* but if the lad is ashamed, he sends one of his garments to take his place in the bed.

What follows depends upon the wealth and standing of the parties. If the wedding is *ākejoi*—that is, if no payment is to be made for the bride—the girl goes with her husband next day to her new home. Her parents accompany her, and are entertained with food and drink, returning the following day. If the wedding is *ākemèn* (literally, ripe, *pakkā*), the lad stays in his father-in-law's house. He rests one day, and then works for his

* P. 8.

father-in-law for a year, or two years, or even it may be for life, according to agreement. There is no money payment in any case. If the girl is an heiress or only daughter, the marriage is usually *ākemèn;* but in the great majority of cases it is *ākejoi*. The neighbours of both villages assemble at the marriage, and when the bride goes to her husband's house, the neighbours of the village accompany her and are hospitably entertained.

Before marriage it was reported, when Mr. Stack made his enquiries, that there was little intercourse between the sexes. Seduction rarely occurred, but when it did, the parents of the girl had to give her to the lad in marriage. It was not punished. Old men, however, could remember (1885) when the *teràng* or "bachelors' house" used to be the abode not only of the lads, but also of the maids, and illegitimate births were common. The girls used even to work in the fields with the boys; there was not even a matron to look after them!

After marriage adultery is said to be rare. The case is judged by the *mē*, or village council, who inflict a fine. The guilty pair are tied up and exposed to the scorn of the neighbours until the fine is paid by the man. Adultery was never capitally punished. After the fine is paid, the husband has to take his wife back, unless there are no children, when he might refuse to do so. The fine is not given to the offended husband, but distributed among the elders who compose the *mē*.

The authorities differ on the question whether more than one wife is allowed. When Mr. Stack wrote, in 1883, the chapter on "Castes and Tribes" in the Report on the Assam Census of 1881, he stated that "polygamy is permitted if a man can afford it." His subsequent notes of 1885–86, however, record that monogamy is the rule, and no one is allowed to marry two wives. Mr. W. C. M. Dundas, Subdivisional Officer of North Cachar, writing in 1903, says that an Ārlèng may marry only one wife. On the other hand, the Rev. P. E. Moore, who has a long experience of the Mikirs, writing in 1902, says, "Polygamy is not common. A man sometimes takes a second wife. In one instance which came to my notice recently the two wives were married on the same day. The man is usually fined Rs. 12.8 for this irregularity. The father of a boy who is now in my service had six wives, and was not punished at all." * Perhaps it may be concluded that monogamy is the general rule, and that cases of polygamy have occurred in consequence of the effect of the example of the Assamese, and the weakening of tribal sanctions.

The young couple live in the bridegroom's father's house. The old people often get separate rooms allotted to them as they advance in life, and are supported in idleness.

Widow marriage is allowed. Divorce is rare, but permissible if there is no offspring, or if the girl goes home after marriage and refuses to return to her husband. In that case the husband takes a gourd of beer to her parents and declares himself free. Both parties, after the divorce, can marry again.

[NOTE BY EDITOR.

The following list of Mikir words for family relationship has some points of interest :—

Grandfather, *phu.*	Grandmother, *phi.*
Father, *pŏ.*	Mother, *pēi, pī.*
Husband, *pèng-àn.*	Wife, *pēsō.*

(Wedded pair, *Pèng-àn-sō, Pēngnàn-sō.*)

Wife's father, *hupō, ŏnghai.*	Wife's mother, *nīpī, nihai.*
Husband's father, *lŏk-hai.*	
Father's brother, *punu.*	Father's sister, *pīnu.*
Mother's brother, *ŏng, nihu.*	Father's brother's wife, *ni.*

Child, common gender, without reference to parents, *sō.*

Boy, *osō.*	Girl, *osōpī.*
Son, *sōpō.*	Daughter, *sōpī.*
Grandson, *supō.*	Granddaughter, *supī.*
Brother, in general, *kŏr, kŏrtē.*	Sister, in general, *kŏr, kŏrtē.*
Brother, when speaker is a female, *chèklē.*	
Elder brother } words used by both sexes *īk*; Younger brother } words used by both sexes *mu*	Elder sister { *tē*, when speaker is a female. *ingjīrpī*, when speaker is a male.
	Younger sister, *mu.*
Brother-in-law: wife's brother, *ŏng-sō.*	Brother's wife, for male speaker, *tēpī*; for female speaker, *nèng.*
Sister's husband, *mē, ingjīr-ārlo; kŏrpō.*	Wife's sister, *kŏrpī.*
Son-in-law, *osā.*	
Nephew, generally, *philipō.*	Niece, *philipī.*
Elder brother's son, *īk-āsō.*	
Brother's son, *kŏr-āsō.*	
Sister's son, *osā.*	

* In the story of Harata Kunwar, *post*, p. 57, a second or co-wife is mentioned (Mikir, *pātèng, pāju*).

The remarkable point about these names is that most of them are the same for both sexes, and that the sexes are distinguished only by words indicating gender where this is required. *Pō* is the index for the male, *pī* that for the female.

Again, the same word appears to be used in different senses: *e.g.* *òng* is maternal uncle, but *òng-sō* (*sō* is the syllable indicating a diminutive) is the wife's brother, the "little uncle;" *osā* is both nephew (sister's son) and son-in-law (pointing to the custom of intermarriage of first cousins on the mother's side). *Tē* is sister, but *tēpī* (*pī* indicates greatness) is brother's wife. Similarly, *kòr* is sister (or brother), *kòrpī* is wife's sister, *kòrpō* sister's husband.

It will be observed that brothers and sisters, and brothers-in-law and sisters-in-law, use different forms of address when speaking of their relationship *inter se*.

The whole subject seems to demand further investigation, in the light of comparison with the system of family grouping in other allied tribes, and the history and etymology, so far as it is possible to ascertain them, of the words indicating relationship.]

The sons inherit; if there are none, the brothers; after them the deceased's nearest agnate of his own *kur*. The wife and daughters get nothing. But if the deceased has no sons or brothers, the widow can retain the property by marrying into her husband's *kur*. In any case she retains her personal property, ornaments, clothes, etc. If the widow will not surrender the property, the case has to come before the *mē*.

The eldest son gets somewhat more than the others on the father's death. Generally, however, the property is divided beforehand by the father, who often prefers one son to another. The family usually continues to dwell together, the grown-up sons supporting the widowed mother. Adoption is unknown.

Villages have no fixed or recognized boundaries, but are moved from place to place according to the needs of cultivation. Only house-tax is paid, except by Mikirs cultivating land with the plough in the submontane tracts, who are treated in all respects like other Assamese *raiyats*. In the hills the culturable land, at the first settlement of a village in a new locality, is divided among the householders by the *mē*, or village council, presided over by the *gaoṅbura*, the head of each household choosing his own land for cultivation, and any dispute being referred to the *mē*. Should the dispute not be settled in this manner, the majority prevails, and the dissident households, if they do not acquiesce, may remove elsewhere and set up for themselves as a new community with a *gaoṅbura* of their own.

The following are the Mikir *mauzas*, or territorial divisions including a number of villages, in the Nowgong district:—

Duār Bāguri, Duār Bāmuni, Duār Sālōnā, Ròngkhàng, Duār Āmlā Parbat, Duār Dikhŏru, Duār Kothiatali, Jamunā-pār, Làngphēr, Lumding Mikir. The last two are new *mauzas*, the opening-out of which is due to the Assam-Bengal Railway, which traverses the tract. Each *mauza* has a Mikir *mauzadār* or *bikhoyā*.

The decision of disputes is the business of the village *mē*, or council,* presided over by the *gaoṅbura* (Mikir, *sār-thē*). The *mē* is composed of all the male householders. The *gaoṅbura* is chosen for his personal character by the householders. On election, he repairs, with beer and spirits, to the head *gaoṅbura* or *mauzadar*, bringing with him two or three other *gaoṅburas*. A pig is killed, the company eat and drink together, and the *gaoṅbura* is declared duly elected. The *mē* is summoned by the *gaoṅbura*. It decides all village disputes, and inflicts small fines. It also determines whether the village shall be shifted, and where it shall be removed to. A *mē-pī* ("great council") consists of *gaoṅburas* only, presided over by a *mauzadar* or head *gaoṅbura*. Graver matters, such as charges of adultery, witch-craft aimed at life (*mājā kechòngkoi*), tigers in the *mauza*, questions affecting the *mauza* at large, the arrangements for the *Ròngkēr* or annual village festival, and such like, are referred to the *mē-pī*.

The Mikirs have never been a warlike race, nor are there any traditions of inter-village feuds. Head-hunting has not been practised, but the tribe have often been the victim of raids for this purpose by their neighbours, the Angami Nagas. There are said to have formerly been vendettas between families.

During the Burmese wars in the early part of the last century, the tribe deserted its settlements in the submontane

* This is an Assamese word, *mel*. The Mikirs cannot pronounce a final *l*, and always omit it or change it to *i* or *y* in words adopted from Assamese; *e.g.* *hāl*, plough, becomes *hāy*; *pitol*, brass, *pitoi*; *tāmol*, betel-nut, *tāmoi*.

GROUP OF MIKIRS (NORTH CACHAR).

(2)

p. 23

tract, and fled into the higher hills. Many Assamese are reported to have taken refuge with them during this time, and to have become Mikirs. [Mr. Dundas also mentions that in North Cachar outsiders are admitted into the tribe and are enrolled as members of one of the *kurs*, after purification by one of the Bē-kuru *kur* (Mr. Stack's *Bē* and *Krō*, sub-*kurs* of Teràng). In the group opposite, taken from a photograph supplied by Mr. Dundas, the short man is evidently a Khasi, while the man to his left appears to be an Assamese.]

The Mikirs call their Kachārī neighbours *Pāròk*, the Mikir pronunciation of Bŏrŏ (in the allied dialect of Tipperah *boròk* means "man"); the Assamese are *Āhòm*, the Bengalis *Bòngnai* (*Bòngnai-ādin*, "British rule"), the Nagas *Nākā*. The Khasis generally are called *Chomàng*, the border race of Khasis, adjoining the Kopili or Kupli river, being *Chomàng-Kēchē*. *Kēchē* is, no doubt, equivalent to *Khāsī*, the vowel-change being the same as in *Rēchō* for *Rājā*.

APPENDIX.

1. The *kurs* or exogamous groups of the Mikir race are thus given in the Assam Census Report for 1891 (vol. iii. pp. cii.–ciii) :—

Main Subdivisions.

I. Ingti. II. Terang. III. Teràn. IV. Tumung. V. Inghi or Hengse.

I. Subdivisions of Ingti—

1. Inglē.
2. Ingti-Henchek.
3. Ingti-Kiling.
4. Kāthār.
5. Tārak or Tāro.

II. Subdivisions of Terang—

1. Be-bonghàng (read *Be-Ronghàng*).
2. Be-Jingthong.
3. Injai.
4. Kro.
5. Kro-bonghàng (read *Kro-Ronghàng*.
6. Kro-Jingthong.
7. Kro-ghoria.
8. Lilipo-kro.
9. Rongbijiya.
10. Tarang.
11. Teràng.

III. Subdivisions of Teràn—

1. Ai.
2. Kangkàt.
3. Lànglē.
4. Milik.
5. Tarap.

IV. Subdivisions of Tumung—

1. Benār-pātŏr.
2. Chenār.
3. Derā.
4. Keleng.
5. Rongphār.
6. Rongtar*-Jungthong.
7. Takki.
8. Tumung-pātŏr.

V. Subdivisions of Inghi—

1. Bonrung.
2. Hànchē.
3. Ke-āp.
4. Lekethē.
5. Ronghang-ghoria.
6. Rongpi.
7. Rongchehon.
8. Tuso.
9. Tutab.

An attempt is made in the report to translate some of these names, but it appears very doubtful whether the meanings assigned are correct. So far as they go, the explanations show that some of the names (to which an Assamese form has in some cases been given, as in those ending in *ghoria*) are designations of offices (*e.g.* Pātŏr, Rongchehon = village watchman), while others are local or place-names.

Under I. Ingti, (1) Inglē is evidently Mr. Stack's Inglèng; (4) Kāthār is his Kātār, (2) [Ingti]-Henchek is his Hènsèk, and (5) Tāro his Tāro.

Under II. Terang, (1 and 2) Be is Mr. Stack's Bē, (4, 5, 6, 7) Kro is his Krō, and (3) Injai is probably his Ingjār; the others seem to be either local names (8, Lilipo-kro = Western Krō, Nilīp = west; 9, Rongbijiya = inhabitants of some particular village), or duplicates of the group-name Terang (Nos. 10 and 11).

Mr. Stack had no group named Teràn.

Group IV., Tumung, corresponds to Mr. Stack's Timung; of the subdivisions, 2, Chenar is probably his Sèngnār, 5, Rongphār agrees with his list, and 7, Takki is probably his Tòkbi. Nos. 1 and 8 are explained as office-holders, No. 3 is a place-name, No. 4 is a river (Kiling), and No. 6 seems to be a duplicate of No. 5.

Group V., Inghi, corresponds to Mr. Stack's Lèkthē, which occurs as the name of subdivision 4 in the census list; 1, Bonrung, is Mr. Stack's Bòngrun; 2, Hànchē, is his Hànsē; 8, Tuso, is his Tutsō. His Kràmsā is not found in the census list, but occurs, as will be seen below, in other lists.

2. Mr. Dundas, Subdivisional Officer of North Cachar, writing in March 1903, gives the following groups:—

Main Exogamous Groups.

I. Inghī. II. Timūng. III. Tērŏn. IV. Kāthār. V. Bē. VI. Injāi.

* *Qu.* Rongphār?

I. Inghī has the following subdivisions:—

1. Rongpi, further subdivided into		(*a*) Rongchāichū, (*b*) Rongchēhòn, (*c*) Chinthòng, (*d*) Lindòk.
2. Ronghàng	,, ,,	(*a*) Hèmpi, (*b*) Hèmsō.
3. Inghī	,, ,,	(*a*) Hèmpi, (*b*) Hèmsō.
4. Hànsē	,, ,,	(*a*) Durong, (*b*) Nongkīrlā, (*c*) Chinthòng, (*d*) Kiling.
5. Lèkthē	,, ,,	(*a*) Keāp, (*b*) Tereng.
6. Bòngrung	,, ,,	(*a*) Kràmsā, (*b*) Rongchehòn, (*c*) Hèmsō.
7. Tutsō	,, ,,	(*a*) Mōthō, (*b*) Rongphu, (*c*) Ronghing, (*d*) Rongchitim, (*e*) Rongchaichu, (*f*) Rongchehòn.

(Nos. 4, 6, and 7 agree with Mr. Stack's list under Lèkthē, and Mr. Stack's Kràmsā appears as a further subdivision of Bòngrung. As regards the others, the names beginning with Rong may be local village names; Chinthong and Ronghang are the names of great sections of the Mikir population, not of exogamous groups; Hèmpi and Hèmsō mean merely "great house" and "little house.")

II. Timung (Mr. Stack has the same spelling) comprises—

1. Timung Lindòk,	subdivision	(*a*) Ròngchāichu.
2. Ròngphār	,,	(*a*) Hèmpī, (*b*) Hèmsō.
3. Chinthong	,,	(*a*) Seng-ār, (*b*) Hèmpi, (*c*) Hèmsō.
4. Phàngchu	,,	(*a*) Juiti, (*b*) Rongphàng, (*c*) Hèmpi, (*d*) Hèmsō.
5. Phūrā	,,	(*a*) Dilī.
6. Tòkbī	,,	(*a*) Tòksīkī.
7. Kiling		
8. Mējī		
9. Pātōr		
10. Lòngteroi		
11. Yāchī	,,	(*a*) Hèmpī, (*b*) Hèmsō.
12. Dērā	,,	(*a*) Hémpī, (*b*) Hèmsō.
13. Ròngpi		

(Here Nos. 2 and 6 correspond with Mr. Stack's subdivisions, and No. 3 (*a*), Seng-ār, is his Sengnār; several of the remainder appear to be local names.)

III. Tēròn comprises—

1. Làngnē,	subdivision	(*a*) Ròngchāichu.
2. Kòngkār	,,	(*a*) Dengyā.
3. Mējī		
4. Milik	,,	(*a*) Seràng.
5. Mēlē		
6. Kiling		

(Mr. Stack has none of these names; but Làngnē evidently corresponds to Lànglē in the census list, and Kòngkār to Kangkāt, while Milik is in both.)

IV. Kāthār comprises—

1. Ingti-Kāthār
2. Rīsō
3. Hènsèk
4. Ingti-Kiling
5. Ingling, subdivisions (*a*) Hèmpī, (*b*) Hèmsō.
6. Ingti-Chinthòng
7. Tārō

(These names, except Rīsō, which means "young man," all occur in Mr. Stack's group Ingti. Nos. 4 and 6 are evidently local subdivisions.)

V. Bē comprises—

1. Rònghàng
2. Kiling
3. Lindòk
4. Seng-òt
5. Teràng, subdivisions (*a*) Dili, (*b*) Rongchaichu.
6. Kuru ,, (*a*) Rongchaichu, (*b*) Nihàng, (*c*) Nilīp.

(This group corresponds to Mr. Stack's Teràng; Kuru is his Krō. Subdivisions 1, 2, and 3 are apparently local names.)

VI. Injai comprises—

1. Injai
2. Ing-ār.

(Mr. Stack gives Ingjār as a subdivision of Teràng; the census list also classes Injai under the same main group. Mr. Dundas notes that the Injai may not take a wife from the Bē (*i.e.* Teràng) group, from which it may be concluded that they are really a subdivision of that name, or Teràng.)

3. So far the three lists are in general agreement; but the Rev. Mr. Moore, writing in August 1902, gives what at first sight is an entirely different arrangement. He separates the Mikir people into the following five groups :—

I. E-jàng. II. Tung-ē. III. Kròn-ē. IV. Lo-ē. V. Ni-ē.

I. E-jàng he subdivides into—

1. Ròngpi.
2. Rònghàng.
3. Tutso.
4. Hànsē.
5. Bòngrung.
6. Kràmsā.
7. Keāp.
8. Lèkthē.
9. Ròngchēhòn.

II. Tung-ē comprises—

1. Timung.
2. Tòkbi.
3. Timung-Kiling.
4. Timung-Ròngphār.
5. Timung-Sēnār.
6. Timung-Phàngchu.
7. Timung-Juiti.
8. Tòktiphi.

III. Kròn-ē includes—

1. **Tēròn.**
2. **Tēròn-Kòngkàt.**
3. **Tēròn-Làngnē.**

IV. Lo-ē is divided into—

1. **Bē.**
2. **Krō.**
3. **Tēràng.**
4. **Ingjāi,**
5. **Ingnār.**

V. Ni-ē comprises—

1. **Ingti.**
2. **Inglèng.**
3. **Tārō.**

Comparing the subdivisions with those given by Mr. Stack, we perceive that five of the nine shown under Mr. Moore's I. E-jàng (Nos. 3, 4, 5, 7, and 8) are identical with Mr. Stack's Lèkthē and its subdivisions; the remaining four (Ròngpi, Rònghàng, Ròngchehòn, and Keāp) are all found in the census list of 1891 under Inghi, another name for Lèkthē. Evidently, therefore, E-jàng is the equivalent of Mr. Stack's Lèkthē and the census Inghi.

Under II. Tung-ē all Mr. Stack's names classed under Timung appear; of the remainder, some are found in Mr. Dundas's list, either of subdivisions or smaller sections, under Timung; Tòktiphi is probably Mr. Dundas's Tòksīkī; and Timung-Kiling is the census "Keleng" (a river-name). It is clear, therefore, that Tung-ē is the same as the Timung (Tumung) of the other lists.

III. Kròn-ē is evidently the small group Teròn or Teràn of Mr. Dundas and the census list, not found in Mr. Stack's enumeration.

IV. Lo-ē is also clearly the Teràng of the three other lists, which account for all the names given under it.

V. Ni-ē is the equivalent of Mr. Stack's Ingti, called by the same name in the census list, and Kāthār in Mr. Dundas's list (the omission of the name Kāthār, or Kātār, from Mr. Moore's list is somewhat noticeable).

It thus appears that all the four lists in reality agree in a remarkable manner, quite independent as they are in their origin, and that all observers concur in stating that the Mikir people are divided into five (or four) great exogamous groups, whether situated in the Mikir Hills, in North Cachar, or in the Khasi Hills and the hilly country to the south of Nowgong.

IV.

RELIGION.

General character of popular belief in ghosts and spirits, and a future life—No idols, temples or shrines—Amulets—The Gods and their worship—Divination and magic—Oaths and imprecations—Funeral ceremonies—Festivities—Taboo.

BELIEFS ABOUT THE DEAD.

THE Mikirs have borrowed from the Hindu Assamese the ideas and the names of *Boikuntho* (*Vaikuṇtha,* Vishnu's Paradise) and *Nòròk* (*Naraka,* Hell); but these conceptions do not play much part in their views of a life to come. Better known, and more often mentioned, is *Jòm Rĕchō* (*Jam, Yama Rājā*), the Lord of Spirits, with whom the dead remain below ground. His abode—the abode of the dead—is *Jòm-āròng,** and the elaborate ceremonies of the funeral are the means by which the spirit of the dead gains admittance to Jòm's city. Unless they are duly performed he remains outside.

They speak of having seen the *shade* (image, *ārjàn*) of a dead man (*nē lā ārjàn thèklòk,* "I saw his shade"); a sickly man catches such glimpses in the house, on the road, etc. *Phārlō,* spirit, is used both of living persons and dead. *Tovē nē-phārlō nē lā-ābàng thèk-lòng,* "Last night in my spirit I saw him"; where *phārlō* is the spirit of the sleeping man. When such glimpses are experienced, betel and food are set aside in the house, and after a time thrown away.

On a death occurring, the old women of the village wash and lay out the body. Then one composes a chant, setting forth the parentage and life of the dead: "You will now meet your grand-parents, father, deceased brother, etc., and will stay with

* This name, which means "Jòm or Yama's town," is often incorrectly written Chomarong or Chumarong.

them and eat with them." Then a separate meal of rice and a boiled egg is placed beside the body, and the dead man is invited to eat. This is done twice a day, the meal being cooked separately from the food of the family. After being offered and placed beside the corpse for a time, the food is thrown away. This goes on day by day until the funeral service is held (see below). After that there are no regular offerings, but occasionally a man or woman puts aside from his or her own share of food a portion for the dead, as, for instance, when another funeral reminds them of those who have died before.

There does not appear to be any fear of the dead coming back to trouble the living. Some people, however, it is said, are afraid to pass the burying-place of the dead after dark.

They say that a man called *Thī-rèng Vàng-rèng* (literally, "Dead-alive come-alive") in former times used to travel between this world and Jòm Rechō's abode; he taught them their funeral ceremonies. At last he did not come back. Everything is different in Jòm-āròng. Thīrèng Vàngrèng saw the people there go out to fish, and gather instead pieces of stick. They asked him why he did not gather them too; he answered that they were not fish, but sticks. They waved over them a lighted brand, and he saw them as fish. So, too, there a crab becomes a tiger, or seems to be a tiger. Men do not stay in Jòm Rĕchō's city for ever, but are born again as children, and this goes on indefinitely (here we seem to have a borrowing from Hinduism). "The Mikirs give the names of their dead relations to children born afterwards, and say that the dead have come back; but they believe that the spirit is with Jòm all the same." *

A man with unusually keen and alarming eyes is said to be possessed by a demon (*hī-ī*). The phrase is *ăhī-ī kedo ărlèng,* and, of the eyes, *ămèk ăhī-ī kedo.* But the superstition of the evil eye, as prevalent elsewhere, seems to be unknown, and such a man is not avoided; rather, the *hī-ī* is supposed to give him cleverness. The same phrase is used in familiar abuse to a child: *Ahī-ī kedo osō,* "You devil-possessed brat!"

* Sentences enclosed in quotation marks were so written by Mr. Stack, and are probably the *ipsissima verba* of his informants.

RELIGION—DIVINITIES.

The Mikirs have no idols, temples, or shrines. Some people, however, have fetishes or amulets, called *bòr*. These are pieces of stone or metal, by keeping which they become rich. Sometimes, however, a man unwittingly keeps a *bòr* that brings him ill-luck and loss. A man is said to have got a *bòr*, *bòr kelòng*; *Bòr do-kòklē, plàng-plē-ji mā?* "If you have got a *bòr*, will you not become rich?" *Bòrs* are not common; one gets them by chance in river, field, or jungle. Or a man dreams that he can get a *bòr* in such a place, and finds it there. But these amulets are not objects of worship or propitiation.

The Gods—*Ārnàm-ātum*—are innumerable, and are worshipped in different ways, at different times, and in different places. The names of some of the most important are given below.

Ārnàm Kethē, in spite of his name, which means "The Great God," has no definite authority over the other Gods. He is a house-god, and is sacrificed to once in three years, if no occasion (in consequence of trouble) arises meanwhile. His appropriate offering is a pig. The family obtain *Ārnàm Kethē* by asking him to stay with them, and by castrating a young pig, to be sacrificed three years later. All families have not got *Ārnàm Kethē* to stay with them, nor does he always come when invited. If a man is sick, and the *uchē* (diviner) declares that *Ārnàm Kethē* wishes to join the household, the ceremony is performed, but no offerings are made at the time. After three years—or earlier, if there is any sickness in the family—the pig is killed, and a general feast, with rice, beer, and spirits, given to the village. A booth of leaves is built in the three days before; the first day is devoted to cutting the posts for the booth, and is called *phòng-ròng ketèng;* the second, to garlanding leaves round the posts, called *phòng-ròng ketòm;* and on the third day leaves are laid out for the rice, rice-flour (*pithāguri*, Ass.) is sprinkled about the ground, and plantains and other trees are planted around the booth. All these preparations are done in the early morning before eating. Then follows the ceremony—*Ārnàm Kethē kārаklī*. First, there is the invocation: "To-day has come, and now we will give you your three-years' offering; accept it kindly!" Fowls are killed, and then the pig (all animals killed in sacrifice are beheaded with one stroke of a heavy knife delivered from above). The liver, heart, and lights of both are cooked for the god. Then the hoof, ear, and tail of the pig are offered, then pieces of cooked meat. Afterwards the sacrificers eat *tekār kethī* or *tekār-sō*, then *tekār-pī*. Both are pieces of flesh, the first smaller, the latter larger, eaten with rice-beer. Then all the company set to and eat rice and flesh together. Sometimes three or four pigs and forty different kinds of vegetables are consumed at the sacrificial feast. The women get sixfold or ninefold the shares of the men, and carry them home bound up in leaves (*àn-bòr* and *òk-bòr*).

Pèng is also a household god. His offering is a goat, sacrificed yearly, in the *tikup* or space before the house. Some neighbours are invited to the sacrificial feast. *Pèng* lives *in* the house, *Ārnàm Kethē* in heaven. *Pèng* is also sacrificed to in sickness. Very few houses have not *Pèng*. Maize, rice, and a gourd of rice-beer are placed for him above the veranda of the house, and the firstfruits of the harvest are offered to him. "But these two gods only come to eat, and families avoid taking them if they can."

Hemphū ("head of the house," "householder") owns all the Mikir people. Everybody can sacrifice to him at any time, and pray for deliverance from sickness. *Mukràng* is similar to *Hèmphū*, but slightly lower in dignity. These two gods, the preservers of men, are approached by the sacrifice of a fowl or goat. *Hemphū* must be invoked first in every sacrifice, being the peculiar owner of men.

Rèk-ànglòng ("the mountain of the community") or *Inglòng-pī* ("great mountain") is a house-god, but is worshipped in the field, and only men eat the sacrifice, which is a fowl or a goat once a year. He is the god of the hill they live on, the *Deus loci*, with whom they have to be at peace; but not every family in the village need have him.

Ārnàm pārō ("the hundred god") is the name of a god who takes a hundred shares of rice, *pithāguri*, betel-nut, and the red spathe of the plantain tree cut up. He is worshipped with a white goat or a white fowl as the sacrifice. He and *Rèk-ànglòng* figure particularly in the *Ròngkēr*, or great annual village festival, celebrated in June at the beginning of the year's cultivation. (*Ārnàm-pārō* seems to be a collective name, to include all gods whom it may concern. Kāmākhyā, the Hindu goddess of Nīlāchal above Gauhāti, is mentioned as one of the deities included in *Ārnàm-pārō*.)

The gods named above are all invoked and propitiated to grant prosperity and avert misfortune, both generally and specially. There are, besides, numerous gods who take their names from the special diseases over which they preside or which they are asked to avert; such are—

Chomàng-āsē ("Khasi fever"), a Khasi god, who lives in the house and is propitiated with a goat; he is comparatively rare. This god appears to be identical with *Kēchē-āsē*, which is the rheumatism. (*Chomàng* is the name for the interior Khasis, *Kēchē* for those immediately in contact with the Mikirs.)

Ājō-āsē ("the night fever") is the deity of cholera (*mā-vur* or *pòk-āvur*). The sacrifice to him is two fowls and many eggs, and is offered at night, on the path outside the village. The whole village subscribes to furnish the offering, and with the eatables are combined a load of cotton, a basket of chillies, an offering of yams, and the *image of a gun* (because cholera is thought to be a British disease); also sesamum (*nèmpō*), many bundles consisting of six sticks of a soft wood called *chèknàm* (perhaps the cotton tree, *bombax*) tied together, many bundles of the false cane (*ingsu*), and double wedges of *chèknàm* wood. The god is invoked: "Don't come this way, go that way!" The eatables are eaten, and the other articles thrown away. The houses are then beaten with rods of *chèknàm* and *ingsu*.

Sō-mēmē ("evil pain") is the god to whom barren women have recourse.

Recurring sicknesses and troubles are ascribed to *Thèng-thòn* or *Òk-làngno*, a devil (*hī-ī*); he is propitiated with a goat and a pig, or two or three fowls. A man gasping in sickness is being strangled by Thèng-thòn. If, notwithstanding invocations of the gods, sickness grows worse, a sacrifice is offered to Thèng-thòn without summoning the diviner or *sàng-kelàng-ābàng*.

Mr. Stack gives the following as the names of the chief diseases (besides those already mentioned), the averting of which forms the main object of worship: goitre, *phun-kàng* ("swollen throat"); phthisis, *sī-ī* (also cough); stone, *ingthàk*; diarrhœa, *pòk-kàngsī*; rheumatism, *kĕchē-āsē* ("Khasi fever"); neuralgia, *bàb āsē*; small-pox, *pī-āmīr* ("the Mother's flowers"); black leprosy, *sī-ī*; white leprosy, *āròk*; elephantiasis, *kèng-tòng* (*kèng*, leg; *ingtòng*, funnel-shaped basket); dysentery, *pòk kāpāvī* ("bleeding of belly").

The house-gods come down in the family; no others would be sacrificed to if the family were uniformly prosperous.

All natural objects of a striking or imposing character have their divinity. The sun (*ārnī*) and moon (*chiklo*) are regarded as divine, but are not specially propitiated. But localities of an impressive kind, such as mountains,* waterfalls, deep pools in rivers, great boulders, have each their *ārnàm*, who is concerned in the affairs of men and has to be placated by sacrifice. The expression *ārnàm do*, used of a place, means, generally, to be haunted by something felt as mighty or terrible. All waterfalls (*làngsun*), in particular, have their *ārnàms*. In Bāguri *mauza* there are two great waterfalls in the Diyaung river which are specially venerated as divine; one of these, the *Lànq-kàngtòng* ("Rolling-down water"), can be heard half a day's journey off. Similarly, there are places where a river goes underground (*làng-lut*); these also have their *ārnàm*.† Such local divinities of the jungle are propitiated chiefly to avert mischief from tigers, which are a terrible plague in many parts of the Mikir hills.

There is no worship of trees or animals.

Làm-āphū, "the head or master of words," is a deity probably of recent origin. He is the god sacrificed to by a man

* Sir Joseph Hooker (*Himalayan Journals*, ed. 1855, vol. ii. p. 182) relates that at the Donkia Pass, one of his servants, a Lepcha, being taken ill, "a Lama of our party offered up prayers to Kinchinjhow for his recovery." Perching a saddle on a stone, and burning incense before it, "he scattered rice to the winds, invoking Kinchin, Donkia, and all the neighbouring peaks."

† Such worship of objects and places of an impressive character is, of course, common throughout India. Thus, in the Pachmarhi Hills the writer has seen flowers and red lead (*sindūr*) offered at the brink of a terrible gulf of the kind so common in the plateau. Again, at Balhārpur, in the Chānda district of the Central Provinces, he has seen worship offered to a bastion in a solidly built ruined fort adjoining the village.—(Note by Editor.)

who has a case in court; the sacrifice is one young cock, which should be offered at night, secretly, by the sacrificer alone, in a secret place.

It should be mentioned that, following an ill-sounding idiom of the Assamese, the Mikirs use "*Ārnàm*" as a common (propitiatory) form of address to human beings (Assamese, *dĕutā*). *Pō-ārnàm-pō* ("god-father") to a man, and *pē-ārnàm-pī* ("god-mother") to a woman, are the phrases. In one of the stories given in the next Section, the king is addressed as *Hĕmphū Ārnàm*, "Lord God."

Divination and Magic.

Sickness, if long continued or severe, is frequently attributed to witchcraft (*mājā*). A man suffering from long sickness is said to be *mājā kelòng*—"witchcraft has got hold of him." To discover the author of the spell, or the god or demon who has brought the trouble and must be propitiated, the services of a diviner are necessary. *Uchē*, feminine *uchē-pī* (Hindi, *ōjhā*), is the general name for the cunning in such things. Of these there are two grades—the humbler, whose craft is acquired merely by instruction and practice, and the higher, who works under the inspiration or *afflatus* of divine powers. The former is the *sàng-kelàng ābàng*, "the man who looks at rice," in Assamese, *mangalsuā*; the latter, invariably a woman, is the *lodèt* or *lodèt-pī*. In serious sickness or distress the latter is called in; on ordinary and less important occasions, the former.

The *sàng-kelàng ābàng* picks out of the pot the unbroken grains of rice (*sàng*), and places them, by fives and tens, in pentacle or other fashion. He then counts by couples. If in the groups the odd numbers predominate, the omen is good. If there are no odd grains over, it is very bad. Then all are swept together again, and arranged in three or four heaps. Each heap is counted out, a god being named, and if after the counting, again by couples, three single grains remain, the god named is the one to be propitiated. If three grains do not remain, the process is tried over again. Cowries (*chobai*) are sometimes used instead of rice in the same way. Also, with cowries a handful is taken and spread out, and the number with the slits upwards counted; if they are the majority, the omen is good.*

Another mode of divination used by the *mangalsuā* is to arrange in a circle, equidistant from a point marked on a board (*inghoi*), as many little heaps of clay as there are gods suspected in the case, each heap being called by the name of its god. An egg is then sharply thrown into the middle of the board at the marked point. When it breaks and the yolk is scattered, that clay heap which receives the largest splash of yolk, or towards which the largest and longest splash points, indicates the god responsible for the affliction.†

Another mode is to use the *nòk-jīr*, which is a long-handled iron *dāo* with a cross-piece at the handle and two inclined projecting pieces higher up, before the blade, thus:—

This is held upright in the hand. It shakes of itself when the charm is recited and the *nòk-jīr* invoked to become inspired: *Nàng uchḗ vàng-phlòt!* "Let your spirit (*uchḗ*) come!" The holder asks whether the sick person will recover, and goes over the names of the possibly responsible gods, and the *nòkjīr* shakes at the right answer and name. The charm (the Assamese word *montro* is used) recites the making of the *nòkjīr*, and ends—"if you tell lies, you will be broken up and made into needles" (—the lowest use to which iron can be put, to sew women's petticoats!).‡

The *Lodèt* is an ordinary woman (not belonging to any particular family or *kur*), who feels the divine *afflatus*, and, when it is upon her, yawns continually and calls out the names and the will of the gods. Another *lodètpī* is summoned in to question her, and ascertain if her possession is really divine; a *sàng-kelàng ābàng* may also be consulted. If the report

* So also among the Khasis; see *Khasi Monograph*, p. 119, bottom.

† This also is evidently borrowed from the Khasis. See *Monograph*, p. 221.

‡ Compare the Khasi methods of divination by the lime-case (*shanam*), and the bow (*Monograph*, p. 119).

is favourable, a purificatory offering of a fowl is made to Hèmphū and Mukràng, the preservers of men, and the woman is accepted as a *lodètpī*.

She sits by the bewitched person (*mājā-kelòng*), and the neighbours come in after supper. The *lodètpī* bathes her hands and feet and face in water in which the *tulsi* plant (*Ocymum sanctum*, holy basil) has been steeped, and begins to shake and yawn. A gourd of rice-beer is brought, of which she drinks some, and begins to call out the names of gods, and they descend upon her. She is now inspired, and when questioned indicates, by indirect and riddling answers, the enemy who has bewitched the sufferer, or the gods who must be sacrificed to. When this is ascertained she goes away. The accusation of practising witchcraft is carried before the *mē* or village assembly. The sacrifice to placate the gods proceeds next day, and is usually costly.

To bewitch a person, it is necessary to have some of his hair, or a piece of his clothes; these are buried with one egg, some bones, and some charcoal. A good *lodètpī* can produce these things by the power of her inspiration. A white cloth is tied up into the shape of a bag. She conjures the things into it, and on opening the bag next morning they are found inside. When they are thus recovered, the spirit (*kārjòng*) of the sufferer returns with them, and he gets well.

Charms (*pherèm*) are much used for medicinal purposes, either alone or in combination with other remedies. For an ordinary stomach-ache (*pòk-kesō*), a little mud rubbed on the abdomen, with a muttered charm, is the specific. For rheumatism (*kĕchē-āsē*), a castor-oil leaf is struck on the place, and a charm muttered; if this fails, a sacrifice must be offered to the god *Kĕchē-āsē*. The worker of these remedial measures is called *kàngtòk ābàng*, and the verb is *ingtòk*. Charms are not, as a rule, carried on the person.

The expression *vur kăchethăt*, "to kill for oneself (a fowl) for disease," means to prevent evil by sacrifice after a dream which had previously been followed by mischance.

If a child does not thrive, it is imputed to the sin, or devil (*āhī-ī*) of the maternal uncle (*òng*), or, if there is no maternal uncle, of one of the child's mother's *kur*. The family apply to the person held to be responsible, and he gives a brass ring to be hung round the child's neck, and a rice-ball (*àn ādum*).

There is no entertaining of friends on recovery from sickness. The sick person is tended by his wife and relations.

Tekerē, Thekerē, means a man who knows a spell or *montro*, especially one which protects him against tigers (*tèkē*).

Oaths and Ordeals.

Oaths and imprecations take the place of ordeals. Earth is put on the head, and the man says—"May I be like this dust!" A tiger's tooth is scraped, and the scrapings drunk in water: "May the tiger eat me!" Similarly, an elephant's tusk is scraped, and the scrapings drunk: "May the elephant trample me to death!" (*Ingnār nē pedòng-nàng!*) The copper ring worn by the *uchē* is dipped in water, and the water drunk, the man saying, "May the tiger catch me!" Another form of oath is *Tàmhitni kàngjir āsòntòt nē pàngjir-nàng,* "May I be melted like molten copper (or pot-metal)!" Such oaths are used to confirm promises, and also to attest evidence and proclaim innocence of a charge.

Funeral Ceremonies.

The funeral is the most elaborate, costly, and important of all the ceremonies performed by the Mikirs. Such ceremonies are considered obligatory in all cases except that of a child who has been born dead, or who has died before the after-birth has left the mother; such a child is buried without any ceremony. Victims of small-pox or cholera are buried shortly after death, but the funeral service is performed for them later on, the bones being sometimes dug up and duly cremated. When a person is killed by a tiger, if the body or clothes are found, they are buried at a distance from the village, because the tiger is supposed to visit the burial-place. Such persons cannot gain admittance to *Jòm-āròng* unless there are elaborate funeral ceremonies performed for them. Being killed by a tiger is generally imputed to the victim's sin. His spirit is believed to dwell in the most dreary of the places where dead men's spirits go; there is no notion (such as is found among some races in India) that it animates the tiger who killed him. Except in these cases the dead are disposed of by cremation, the burnt bones being afterwards buried.

The elaborateness of the funeral depends on the means of the family. The description which follows applies to a case where the household is well-to-do. In any case the body is kept in the house for one day after death; if a regular service is held, it may lie as long as from a week to twelve days.

The body lies in the *kut*. The persons occupied with the funeral ceremonies live in the *hòng-phārlā*; the rest of the family cook and eat in the *kàm*, but the officiants, male and female, must go across a stream or creek to cook and eat. As already mentioned, the old women of the family wash and lay out the corpse. Then beer is prepared, rice husked and got ready, and a convenient day fixed for the service. If the house has not a big enough *hòng* (front platform), the neighbours join and build one on to it. From the date of the death, each household in the village gives a man to sleep in the house (in the *hòng-phārlā*). When it is settled that the beer and rice required can be provided in four or five days, the village lads are summoned about 8 o'clock in the evening. They bring their drum (*chèng*), and drum up to the *tikup* (front yard); they drum there awhile, and then, while one keeps time with the drum, dance by pairs, holding in their left hands shields (*chòng-kechèngnàn*), and in their right hands sticks. They go round twice in a circle; then they all dance round, holding each the other's hands (this is called *chomàng-kàn*, "Khasi dance"). After an hour spent in this way they go back to the *gaonbura's* house to sleep. Early next morning they come without beat of drum, and dance the *chomàng-kàn* to the drum; they then dance the shield-dance as before (*chòng-kechèngnàn*) to the drum, and go home. Next night they come as before, but a little later, and go through the same ceremonies. Next morning they proceed as before, and in the usual course they kill a fowl and roast it in pieces on spits in the *tikup*, and eat it there. The third and last night is that of the *kàn-pī* ("great dance").

Meantime, during the day, the *rīsōmār* have to work at getting ready the *tèlē*—the stout bamboo to which the corpse is to be slung: the *bànjār*—a bamboo ornamented with curled shavings (*bū*) hung in tufts to projecting arms; and the *serōsō*—shorter bamboo sticks similarly ornamented and tipped with leaves. The men have to go to the *therī* (village burning-place) and prepare there a *chang* or platform, with logs for burning the body arranged under it; this *chang* is built in a peculiar manner, known only to adepts. The *uchēpī* (a skilled old woman) is summoned to prepare the *viaticum* for the dead, and the *duhuidī*, with an assistant, who beat the two drums which have now been hung up in the *kàm-āthèngthòt:* the *duhuidī* is one skilled in tolling on these drums. Then comes the girl called *obòkpī* (not necessarily a maid), that is, the "carrier" of the dead man; but in place of the dead she carries on her back a gourd for holding beer; she must belong to his mother's *kur*. Also the *nihu*, the maternal uncle or other male representative of the mother's *kur*, and the *ingjīr-ārlo*, sister's husband, or father's sister's husband, of the deceased; it is his office to kill the goat for the dead, if they can afford one.

About midnight the villagers, with torches, drums, and the attendant *rīsōmār*, assemble in the *tikup*. The neighbouring villages, if so minded, may come too (*āròng ārī* is the phrase for the contingents as they arrive). Each contingent is welcomed with the drum, and joins in the drumming concert; the lads and girls are dressed in their best, and provided with betel. The chief of the village lads (*klèng-sārpo*) then calls the other *rīsōmār* to *touch* (not taste) the beer, *hòr kāchemē.** Then follows the shield-dance, first by the *rīsōmār* of the village, then by the outside contingents in order of arrival or merit. Then all together take hands and dance in a circle. The young women join in the line, taking hold of the lads' coats, while the lads take hold of them by the belt (*vànkòk*); the girls cover their heads and faces with a black scarf (*jīsō ke-īk*): the petticoat is a red-striped Mikir *ēṛī* cloth. Near the first cock-crow, seven young men go up on the *hòng* or house-platform from the dancing, with the *duhuidī* and his assistant; one lad

* Mr. Stack notes that there was some reluctance on the part of his informant to explain what was meant.

goes in and dances in the inside of *kàm*, in the space by the partition-wall (*nòksèk*), while the six others stand at the door (*hòngthū*, or *inghàp ànghō* = "door's mouth"), and dance there. The six whoop three times together as they dance. After a quarter of an hour they return to the circle of dancers in the *tikup*. At dawn they go up again, and dance till sunrise. The circle breaks up at daylight, and then follows the shield-dance. Then all the drums go round the circle where they dance ten to twenty times, playing a different tune each time. Then, while they all drum standing, a pig is brought forth, tied up for killing. The *rīsōmār* in successive parties recount over the tied-up pig the history of the funeral service; this is called *phàk āphū kācholàng*. Then the pig is killed and cut up for the *rīsōmār*, and for the men engaged in the funeral service. The latter have to cook and eat their shares of the meat, which is given in leaf-bundles (*òk-bòr*) or on spits (*òk-kròn*), beyond the river. The *rīsōmār* also get their shares in the same way, and cook them in the dancing-ring. A small piece of flesh is cooked by the *uchēpī* for the dead man, and this is put in the plate of the dead and carried by the *ingjīr-ārlo* up to the body in the *kut*, the *duhuidī* tolling the drum as he goes in; this ceremony is called *kāsolē*. Meantime the old experienced men, braving the horrid stench, have been performing certain rites * about the body. The remainder of the cooked flesh, with rice, is distributed to the young girls. The *rīsōmār* then, provided with rice, beer, salt, chillies, and greens from the dead man's house, disperse to houses in the village to eat, and the officiants go off beyond the river to prepare and eat their food. This part of the ceremony is called *rīsō kāchirū*, "the lads' entertainment."

Then two or three of the *rīsōmār* take a cock on the road to the burning-place, and kill, cook, and eat it there. A small pig is killed by the other lads where they dance, and the head and one leg are sent to the road-side *rīsōmār*. The blood is caught in a bamboo-joint, and smeared on the *bànjār*, which is set up in the road like a maypole; it is a thick bamboo about seven feet long, with sticks projecting on three sides, from which hang tassels of curled bamboo shavings (*bànjār ābū*)

* Not further explained.

These shavings also are smeared with the blood, so as to look like flowers. Six shorter pieces of bamboo, three feet long, also ornamented with tufts of shavings, are called *serōsōs*, and these too are smeared with blood: likewise the *tèlē* for carrying the corpse to the pyre. Six young men, each taking a *serōsō*, dance round the *bànjăr*.

The *uchēpī* has now prepared all the food. The *obòkpī* takes the beer-gourd on her back, and one egg in her hand, and the *uchēpī* a beer-gourd, and they break the egg and the gourd against the *tèlē* as it lies upon the house-ladder (*dòndòn*). The *duhuidī* tolls the drum, and dancing as before takes place on the *hòng* and in the *kàm*, but not with the *serōsōs*. The *uchēpī* and the *obòkpī* then go on to the burning-place. The *tèlē* is now taken up by the old men into the house, and the corpse tied to it and brought down; all the dead man's clothes are hung over the bamboo. Then a pair of ducks and another of pigeons are killed by the *nihu*, and a goat by the *ingjīr-ārlo*, each previously going thrice round the dancing circle with the sun. The goat is called *hòngvàt-ābī;* the heads are thrown to the *rīsōmār*, the rest of the meat kept and cooked later on by those who remain. Preceded by the *duhuidī* and his assistant tolling the drums, they all march in procession, carrying the *bànjăr* and *serōsōs*, to the burning-place. The body is untied from the *tèlē* and placed on the pyre, which is lighted. While the pyre is burning, knowing women sing the *kāchārhē*—a chant describing the dead man's life, whither he is going on leaving this earth, how he will see his dead relations, and the messages he has to carry to them. A few of the lads dance while the cremation is proceeding.

The body is thoroughly burnt, and the bones that remain are tied up in a cloth and buried. The *tèlē* is either laid down whole or cut into three pieces, which are split again into six, and placed in the little house which is then erected over the grave. This is built with the *bànjăr* and the *serōsōs*, the former being in the middle and the latter used as props for the roof. The food prepared by the *uchēpī* is now placed on a flat stone over the grave, and the ceremony is at an end.

The company, returning, clean and wash the house, and cook and eat and drink on the *hòng*. On coming back from the cremation, the *nihu* gets some money, clothes, salt, and a knife He shares the salt with his own *kur*, if any are present. The *ingjīr-ārlo* next morning has to clean up the dancing ring (*ròng-rū kàngrū*, or *tikup kārkòk*).

The ceremonies of the funeral are performed by the neighbours and cunning men and women of the village, and the old people of the family. The wife, children, parents, brothers and sisters of the dead sit beside him and mourn, in spite of corruption, or even sleep beside the decomposing corpse. "It is genuine grief, a national characteristic. Even after the funeral service, they remember and mourn; and the death of another renews their grief." The mourners continue their lamentation, heedless of the dancing.

If a great man, such as a *mauzadar* (*bikhōyā*) or leading *gaonbura* (*sārlār, sārthē*), dies, in addition to the ceremonial described above, there is another, called *Làngtuk* ("the well"). A well or pit is dug outside the village, four-square, with sides ten to fifteen feet: it need not be carried down to the water; stairs are made to the bottom. At the corners are planted various trees. A tall upright stone (*lòng-chòng*) and a broad flat stone (*lòng-pàk*), supported on short uprights, are brought and set up, as in the Khasi hills. The *rīsōmār* come and dance there the whole day, with manifold apparatus. The *uchēpī* sings and places food of different kinds on the flat stone for the dead man; his clothes and umbrella are put upon the tall stone, with flowers. A fowl is killed for the well at the bottom of the pit, and a goat, two ducks, and two pigeons are killed at the top, and their heads thrown to the *rīsōmār*. Then the people of thirty to forty villages assemble. The *uchēpī* sings extemporaneously before the memorial stone, and the people dance and eat there until dark. After dark the company go to the house and perform the usual service already described. The *làngtuk* is very costly, for people have to be fed at two places, and double the quantity of food for an ordinary funeral has to be provided.

FESTIVITIES.

The *Ròngkēr* is the annual compulsory village festival, held at the time of the beginning of cultivation (June), or in some villages during the cold season. Goats and fowls are sacrificed. *Ārnàm-pārō* gets a goat, and so do the local gods of hills and rivers. A small village will sacrifice two or three goats, a large village ten or twelve. The flesh of the victims is eaten, with rice and rice-beer, but only men can partake of the sacrifice. They must sleep on the *hòng* apart from their wives that night. The gods are invoked in the following terms: "We live in your district: save us and help us! send no tigers or sickness, prosper our crops and keep us in good health, and year by year we will sacrifice like this. We depend wholly upon you!" There is no music or dancing at the *Ròngkēr*.

At harvest-home there is no sacrifice, but the whole village help mutually in getting the crops in, and feast together on rice and beer, and dried fish and dried flesh saved up against this celebration, or fresh fish if procurable. No animals are killed, except in some houses a fowl, lest the paddy brought home should decrease; this fowl is eaten. On this occasion there is a little dancing on the *hòng*, but with this exception music and dancing take place *only at funerals.*

Occasionally there is a *Ròngkēr-pī* ("*great Ròngkēr*") for the whole *mauza,* as, for instance, to expel man-eating tigers. Each village, headed by its *gaonbura,* brings its contribution to the great sacrifice, and repairs to the *mauzadar's* or *bor-gaonbura's* house, where the feast is celebrated.

Mr. Stack's notes do not mention the observance by the Mikirs of general *tabus,* called in Assamese *genna,* such as are common among the Naga tribes; * but personal *tabus* of various kinds, entailing separate eating of food and abstinence from commerce of the sexes, have already been indicated. Women during menstruation are said to be unclean and unable to touch the cooking-pots.

* See, however, what is said above as to the *Ròngkēr,* which agrees with the observances elsewhere known as *gennas.*

V.

FOLK-LORE AND FOLK-TALES.

Three Mikir stories—Legend of creation (Mr. Allen).

THE Mikirs are fond of telling stories, but the historical material which they contain does not appear to be of very ancient date. Reference has already been made to the deliverance of the Arlengs from slavery to the Khasis, and their contests with the Kacharis under the leadership of Thòng-Nòkbē; also to their early relations with the Ahoms. They have also myths dealing with the creation of the earth and man, one of which has been related by Mr. Allen, of the American Presbyterian Mission, and will be found in the Appendix to this Section; it seems doubtful, however, whether it is a genuine legend, or due to imagination stimulated by questions: the concluding episode strongly resembles the Biblical story of the Tower of Babel. These legends have not been handled by Mr. Stack, and are therefore not reproduced here. The Rev. Mr. Moore notes that "Mikir stories in general do not agree very minutely," and this appears to be particularly the case in respect of tales of the intervention of the gods in human affairs.

Mr. Stack wrote down, chiefly from the dictation of a Mikir named Sārdokā, who had become a Christian, a number of excellent stories, which well deserve separate publication. Three specimens of these are given here. They correspond in every respect, as will be seen, with the general characteristics of folk-literature all over the world. Folk-tales containing the same incidents, as is well known, are found from Iceland to Japan, from Alaska to Patagonia. The original source of such a tale is now incapable of identification. The same sequence of events and general form recur everywhere; what is distinctive and characteristic is not the progress of incident, but the local dressing, the narrator's point of view, the colour of his daily life which he lends to the details of the story.

The first of the three specimens is the favourite Indian form of a sequence, well known in Sanskrit literature, but quite as popular in Europe and in general folk-lore. It is given here, because another version of the same narrative has been included by Dr. Grierson in his *Linguistic Survey*, vol. iii. Part III. p. 223, as found among the Aimol Kukis, a race of Tibeto-Burmans dwelling, far away from the Mikir country, in the hills bordering the valley of Manipur on the east.

The second specimen tells of the adventures of an orphan, the son of a widow, a stock figure in Mikir folk-tales, and abounds in local colour. Here too the incidents in part coincide with those of a folk-tale belonging to a very distant country, the part of Kumaon bordering on Tibet, which will be found in vol. iii., Part I. of the *Linguistic Survey*, pp. 483, 495, 510, 522.

The third is a remarkably complete and interesting version of the wide-spread folk-tale of the Swan-maidens. It was most probably derived from some Indian source, though, so far as known, no version of the tale in its entirety, as told by Hindus, has yet been published. The name of the hero, *Hārātā-Kuṅwar*, may be the Indian *Sarat-Kumār*, and is evidently not Mikir. But all the setting—the colloquies of the six brothers and their father, the attempt on Harata-Kuṅwar's life, his methods in defeating his treacherous kinsmen, his device for winning his fairy wife, and many other features of the story—seems genuinely local. The narrative is an excellent specimen of Mikir diction, and shows no little skill in composition. In vol. iii. Part II. of the *Linguistic Survey*, there will be found, at pp. 218–220, a short story, entitled, "How Jesu got a goddess for his wife," which is identical in motive with this tale of Harata-Kuṅwar. It is current among the Angāmi Nagas, a race much less influenced by Hindu culture than the Mikirs.

The original Mikir text of these tales will be found in the next Section; the English translation here given is as literal as it was possible to make it. In the *Linguistic Survey*, vol. iii.

Part II. pp. 395–403, two other short stories of the same character, both text and translation, have been printed. The second of these, the story of the clever swindler Tèntòn, evidently belongs to the cycle of tales called *Tenton-Charit*, mentioned, in its Assamese version, as existing in manuscript by Mr. E. A. Gait, at page 68 of his *Report on the Progress of Historical Research in Assam*, 1897.

1. Story of a Frog.

One day a big black ant went to carry a meal of rice to his uncle. A frog sat down in the road and blocked it. The ant said, "Please make way for me, frog; I want to carry this rice to my uncle." The frog answered, "You can get by if you creep under me. Every one has to pass under me who goes this way." The ant said, "My uncle's rice is tied up in a bundle of leaves; how can I possibly creep under you?" But the frog would not give way, so the ant would not go. In this manner things went on till noon. Then the ant said, "Oh, my uncle will be hungry for his rice and angry with me because he does not get it!" And he crept under the frog. Then the frog sat down flat on the top of the ant. Thereupon the ant gave the frog a sharp bite in the loins. Then the frog, becoming angry, jumped on the ladder of a big old squirrel, and broke it. The old squirrel, becoming angry, cut in two the stem of a gourd.* The gourd, becoming angry, fell plump on the back of a wild boar. The wild boar, becoming angry, rooted up a plantain-tree. The plantain-tree, becoming angry, fell upon a sparrow's † nest and broke it. The sparrow, becoming angry, flew into the ear of a deaf elephant. The deaf elephant,

* "Gourd": the word *hànthār* in the original is explained by Mr. Stack as the name of "a creeper, with a fruit as big as a small pumpkin, with a hard kernel in soft rind; the kernel is the size of a mango-stone; the marrow inside is in two slices; when washed, it loses its bitter taste, and can be fried, oil exuding. It is a favourite dish with the Mikirs." It is, therefore, not really a gourd, but I am unable to identify the species.

† "Sparrow": *vo-ār-bipi*, explained as a small bird, the size of a sparrow. In the Aimol version the corresponding word is rendered "bat"; but a bat in Mikir is *vo-ārplàk*, and a bat has no nest (*tār*) as the bird has here.

becoming angry, rooted up a rock. The rock, becoming angry, rolled down and killed the Raja's son.

Then the Raja held a court to try the case. "Who is it that killed my son?" "Oh, the rock rolled down and killed him," they said. So they summoned the rock. "O rock, rock! why did you roll down and slay my son?" The rock answered, "Oh, Lord God King! how was I to help rolling down and killing him? The deaf elephant uprooted me on a sudden from my place, and then gave me a push. As for me, I have no hands or legs; how then could I withstand him? Your son being in the way where I was rolling down, I rolled upon him and killed him."

Then the Raja said, "Oh, then that deaf elephant was the cause of all this trouble," and summoned the elephant. "O elephant, elephant! what did you root up the rock for?" The elephant answered, "Oh! how could I help uprooting it, Lord God? The sparrow flew into my ear, and I lost all control of myself, and so I tore up the rock."

Then the Raja said, "Oh, then that sparrow was the cause of it all," and summoned the sparrow. "O sparrow, sparrow! why did you fly into the elephant's ear?" The sparrow answered, "Oh, Lord, how could I help it? The plantain-stalk fell upon my nest and smashed it, and being very disturbed in mind, I flew into the elephant's ear."

Then the Raja said, "Oh! then that plantain-tree was the cause of the trouble," and called the plantain. "O plantain, plantain! what did you tumble on the sparrow's nest and smash it for?" The plantain answered, "Oh, how could I help it, Lord God? The wild boar tore me up out of the ground, and I had no root left at all. How was I to go on standing in my place? I have neither hands nor feet."

"Oh! then that pig was the cause of it all," the Raja said, and summoned the pig. "O pig, pig! what did you tear up the plantain for?" The pig answered, "How could I help it? As I was feeding quietly by myself, the gourd fell plump on my back. I was in great pain, and therefore tore up the plantain tree."

Then the king said, "Oh, the gourd caused all this trouble," and summoned the gourd. "O gourd, gourd! what did you tumble on the wild boar's back for?" "How was I to help it, Lord God? The squirrel cut through my stem. I have neither hands nor feet, nothing but a stalk; if that is cut through, I cannot but fall. So I was obliged to tumble on the wild boar's back."

Then the Raja said, "Oh, that squirrel caused all the mischief," and summoned the squirrel. "O squirrel, squirrel! what did you cut through the stem of the gourd for?" The squirrel answered, "Oh, how could I help it, Lord God? The frog jumped on my ladder and broke it. Then I had no road to get out, and I had to cut the stalk of the gourd."

The Raja said, "Oh, then that frog caused the mischief," and summoned the frog. "O frog, frog! what did you jump on the squirrel's ladder and break it for?" The frog answered, "How was I to help it? A big black ant bit me sharply in the loins, and with the pain of the bite, not knowing what I was doing, I jumped on the squirrel's ladder and broke it."

Again the Raja said, "Oh, it was the ant that caused all the trouble," and summoned the ant. "O ant, ant! what did you bite the frog in the loins for?" The ant said, "How could I help biting him? In the morning I was carrying my uncle's rice along the road. The frog sat down and blocked the way. I said, 'Please make room for me to pass.' 'Creep under me,' said he. I crept under him, and he sat down tight on the top of me. That was why I bit his loins."

Then said the king, "You are both of you guilty." They tied the ant fast with a hair from a man's head; so now his waist is very small. The frog they beat severely with a stinging-nettle,* so now he is spotty all over.

2. Story of an Orphan and his Uncles.

Once upon a time a widow woman had an only son. His mother had six brothers. One day at evening his uncles said to the orphan, "Nephew, let us go and set up a fish-trap." † So

* "Stinging-nettle": *tārmē-làngbòng;* this is probably not a nettle (*urtica*), but some other kind of blistering plant found in the Assam jungles; *tārmē* means a creeper, *làngbòng* a vessel made of bamboo to hold water.

† Fish-trap, *rū:* a bamboo cage placed in an opening in a weir or dam

the orphan went with them. Then the six brothers, his uncles, having built a good weir up-stream, set the trap. The orphan, having put together a few stones down-stream, below his uncle's trap-weir, set his own trap carelessly in the middle of them. and returned home. The next morning they all came to look at their traps. The uncles' trap, though very well put together, had not caught so much as a cray-fish; as for the orphan's trap, it was quite full of fish. Then the uncles said, "Nephew, we will set up our trap here; do you go down-stream and set up your trap again." Then, after the uncles had set up their trap in the orphan's trap-weir, the orphan again set up his trap down-stream. But again the fish entered it just in the same way; while not one fish had got into the uncles' trap, the orphan's trap was quite full of fish. Every morning the uncles continued to take for themselves the place where the orphan's trap had been. At last the orphan, becoming very tired of continually setting up his trap in a different place, one morning, instead of fixing the trap in the stream, placed it on a clump of grass and left it there. Next morning his uncles came and called to the orphan: "Nephew, let us go and look at the traps." The orphan answered, "For my part, I have not set up my trap at all; nevertheless I will go with you as your companion." So saying, he went with them. Then he went to look at his trap, and found that a wood-pigeon had got inside it. He tied this wood-pigeon with a noose and brought it home.

That orphan had one calf; you could not imagine how fat and sleek it was. His uncles, being unable through envy to look at that calf, killed it. Then the orphan, having taken off the calf's skin, took one leg and secretly hid it in the house of a rich brahman who lived at a distance. Then the orphan said, "Oh! how strongly the house smells of cow's flesh!" The brahman, becoming angry, said, "May a tiger eat you, you wicked boy!* How should there be any cow's flesh here? I

built of stones or constructed of wattled boughs, so that the fish entering cannot get out. The same word is used later (see note p. 53) for the iron cage (*ingchin āru*) in which the orphan is confined.

* "May a tiger eat you, you wicked boy!" *Tekē nàng kòrdutpī ā-osṓ*, literally, "You tiger-bitten boy!" *pī* is a syllable used in abuse, as *pō* ("father") is used in the opposite sense, *e.g.* *pō-ārnàm-pō*, "My good sir!" literally, "father-god-father;" lower down, addressing a girl, *pē* ("mother") is similarly used: "*pē-ārnàm-pī*," "dear girl!"

am a brahman—produce it, if you can: if you cannot, I will take your life." The orphan said, "Very well, I will make a search." He began to search in a careless, lounging way; but coming to the place where he had hidden the calf's leg, he suddenly pulled it out. "See, this is cow's flesh," said he; "I told you so." Then the brahman, fearing lest, if other people came in and saw this, his caste would be destroyed, said to the orphan, "Orphan, my good sir! don't tell any one. I will give you a cloth-full of money." * So saying, he gave him a cloth-full of silver, which the orphan took with him to his home. When he arrived there, he said to his mother: "Go and ask my uncles for their basket." His mother went and called out: "Brothers! your nephew says he wants a basket." Then the widow's brothers, having given her a basket, said among themselves, "What does he want to do with the basket? Go and watch." So they sent the youngest of them, and he went and watched, and saw the orphan measuring the money with the basket. Then the one who had watched returned home and told his brothers: "Where did that nephew of ours get all this money? He is actually measuring the rupees with a basket!" After they had finished measuring the money, the orphan's mother went and returned the basket. Her brothers said to her, "Send our nephew here." When the widow reached her house she said to her son, "Your uncles bid me ask you to go and see them; they want to speak to you." So the orphan went, and his uncles asked him, "Where did you get all that money?" He answered, "It is the price of cow's flesh; I went a-selling the flesh of my cow which you killed. The people said, 'There is not enough of it for us,' and they all bade me to bring more." His uncles asked him again, "Then if we go selling cow's flesh, they will take more of it?" The orphan replied, "Certainly they will take more; you have many cows, and if you kill them all and go and sell their flesh, how much money will you bring back!" Then each one of his six uncles killed a cow, and having made the flesh into loads went to sell it. The orphan explained to them, "When you arrive at the village of that rich brahman, offer your meat for

* Cloth-full, *mànthung:* a cloth or wrapper (*pĕ*) folded cylindrically into a bag, and tied at the top and bottom with slit bamboo (*jìngtàk*).

sale. Call out in the village as soon as you reach it, 'Who will take more cow's flesh?'" So these six brothers, taking up their beef, went on their way, and, arriving at the brahman's village, they cried, "Who will take more cow's flesh?" The people answered, "We will take more; bring it here," and called them in. So when they arrived at the brahman's house, all the inhabitants of the village, having gathered together, seized those six brothers who had come to sell cow's flesh, and having tied their hands, beat them soundly, and said, "We are brahmans; do you dare to come here and traffic, offering cow's flesh for sale?" So saying, they let them go. Then those men who had brought the beef returned homewards, and on the way took counsel together: "Oh, how that orphan has cheated us! Not only has he caused us to kill our cattle; over and above that, he has got us skins that smart all over. As soon as we get home, let us set fire to his house!" So when they reached home, they set fire to the orphan's house. Then the orphan, having woven two baskets, collected the ashes of his burnt house, and made them into a load, and went to a distant village where the people suffered from sore eyes. In that village there was not a man who had not a pain in his eyes. When they saw the orphan coming with his load of ashes, they asked him "Why have you come hither?" The orphan answered, "Oh! when I heard that your whole village was suffering severely from sore eyes, I came to sell medicine to cure the complaint." "Oh, that is very good indeed, dear sir," said they, and all the people of the village collected a load of money, and gave it to the orphan. Then the orphan said, "Do not apply this medicine to your eyes just yet; after I have gone a bit of the way I will call out to you, 'Apply it'; then rub it in." So the orphan, having got a load of money in exchange for his ashes, started for home; and when he had got a little bit of the way, the people with sore eyes called out to him, "Shall we not apply the medicine yet?" He answered "Wait a bit!"; and he continued telling them to wait so long as he was near the village. But when he arrived at a distance where he thought they could not catch him, he called out, "Now apply the medicine!" Then the sore-eyed people applied to their eyes the ashes they had bought from the orphan. As soon as the medicine touched them, their eyes began to smart as you cannot imagine! The pain in their eyes became much worse than ever before. They said among themselves, "Oh! how that fellow has cheated us, and gone away! if he comes again, let us bind his hands fast and beat him!"

When the orphan reached home, he sent his mother again to fetch his uncles' basket. The widow went to her brothers' house, and, having lent her the basket, those six brothers said among themselves, "Go, young one, watch again; what is he going to do with the basket?" So the youngest went again secretly to watch. Again he saw the orphan measuring money; and again he went back and carried the news to his brothers: "Our nephew has returned, bringing with him much more money than the last time." Then the six brothers went to the orphan, and asked him, "Where did you get so much more money?" The orphan answered, "It is the price of the ashes of my house that you set fire to. The people in the place where I sold the ashes were crying, 'It is not enough, bring us as much more again!' Now, my house was but a little one, and so the ashes were not much. But your houses are big, and if you set fire to them and sell the ashes, how much money will you get for them! It will be more than you can possibly carry." Then the six brothers, his uncles, said one to another, "Let us too set fire to our houses." So, having burned down their houses, they gathered together the ashes, and each brother took as heavy a load as he could carry. Then the orphan explained to them: "Take the loads to the village of sore-eyed people, and, when you arrive near it, say, 'Will any one take ashes?'" So these six brothers went their way, and, when they came near the village of sore eyes, they called out, "Will any one take ashes?" Then the sore-eyed folk called out, "Bring them here." So they went into the village. As soon as they got inside, all the people bound them fast with ropes, and rubbed into their eyes the ashes which they themselves had brought, and thrashed them soundly. When the thrashing was over, the six brothers started to return home. On the way they took counsel again together: "Oh, how that villain has deceived us! Not only has he got us smarting skins; he has, over and above that, caused us to burn down our houses and our harvests. Now, immediately we get home, let us make him fast in an iron cage,* and throw him into the river."

So when they got home they seized the orphan, and having shut him up in an iron cage they took him to the bank of a great pool in a river in the jungle. Then they said, "In a little while we will drown him; now there is no chance for him to escape us, so let us go and eat our rice." So saying, they went to eat their food. When they had gone away, a certain king's son, who was hunting deer, came by. When he arrived where the orphan was, he asked him, "What is the reason why you are tied up in that iron cage?" The orphan answered, "My uncles have a daughter, so lovely! You cannot imagine how fair she is. They tell me to marry her, but I always answer that I will not. So my uncles, becoming angry, have shut me up in this cage." Then the king's son said, "Oh! then can I get her to wife?" "If you get into this cage and stay there, you will be able to get her," the orphan answered; "after a while my uncles will come, and will say, 'Have you nothing more to say?' If they ask you this, then answer them, 'All I have to say is that I will take her, uncles.'" "Very good then," said the prince. Then the orphan said to the king's son, "If you go into the cage wearing your own fine clothes, they will recognize you at once. So let me out. I will give you my clothes, and then you can enter the cage." So the king's son opened the cage and let out the orphan, and the orphan gave his clothes to the prince, while the prince gave his coat, *dhoti*, necklace, and bracelets in exchange to the orphan, and entered into the cage. Then the orphan made fast the door of the cage, and having dressed himself in the prince's clothes, necklace, and bracelets, went away to his home. Then the orphan's uncles returned from eating their rice, and coming up to the cage asked, "Have you anything more to say, nephew?" "All right, uncles, I agree to take her," answered the king's son, as the orphan had told him to say. Then they threw him in the iron cage into the deep pool. Thereupon the six brothers, the orphan's uncles, said one to another, "How much trouble that

* "Iron cage": see note on p. 48 above.

fellow caused us all! Now, however, he is dead and done with!" Then they returned home.

When they got there, lo! they saw the orphan again, not dead at all, wearing the king's son's clothes, necklace, and bracelets, splendidly adorned and decked out as you could not imagine! They said one to another, "The orphan is not dead after all! There he is, decked out and strutting in his finery!" They went up to him and asked, "Nephew, how is it that you arrived here so soon?" The orphan answered, "Oh, uncles, my grandmothers and grandfathers sent me back here in a *pālki* very quickly. Immediately I arrived there, my grandparents gave me these fine clothes, this necklace, and these bracelets. Only look at them! They sent word, too, that they wanted you also to be told to come to them; as a token, they sent this gold knife—see!" So saying, he showed it to them. Then his uncles said, "How shall we manage to get there?" "Let each one of you take an iron cage with him to the river bank, and get into it there," answered the orphan. So each man took a cage to the river bank and got inside. Then the orphan tied each tightly up in his iron cage, and threw the eldest brother in his cage into the deep pool. As he fell, quantities of bubbles came up on the surface of the water. The orphan cried, "Look, uncles! My eldest uncle has drunk so much of the rice-beer which my grandparents have given him, that he is vomiting." Then he brought the next brother and threw him into the water; and so having cast all his six uncles, one after another, into the stream, the orphan returned to his home. Then his aunts, his uncles' wives, asked him, "When will your uncles come back again?" "They will not come very soon; have they not just met their parents, after being separated from them for so long a time?" replied the orphan. So after waiting three or four nights his aunts asked the orphan again, "Why have your uncles not come back by this time?" He answered, "They will come very soon." Then after waiting two or three nights more they asked again, "Why have not your uncles come yet?" Then the orphan spoke clearly, "Put each man's share of rice in the *nòksèk*." * So his aunts cried, "Ah! they are

* The *nòksèk*: the part of the house (in *kàm*: see plan, p. 8) between

dead and gone!" And understanding this at last, they wept and made lamentation.

So the orphan became rich, and there was no one left to envy him. And having become a great king, he lived a happy life.

NOTE.—Two incidents in this story, viz. the profit made by the orphan by disposing of the flesh of his slaughtered calf, and his gain by selling the ashes of his burnt house, and the disappointment of his uncles when they endeavoured to imitate him, much resemble the incidents of a folk-tale given as an illustration of the Tibeto-Burman dialects of Rangkas, Dārmā, Chaudāngs, and Byāngs in vol. iii. Part I., of the *Linguistic Survey*. These dialects are spoken in the northern portion of Kumaon, on the borders of Tibet. In this version the animals slaughtered are goats and sheep, and the profit is made out of their skins, while the ashes of the burnt house are by an accident exchanged for a load of flour. Still, the *motif* is the same, and the great distance of the country where this tale is current from that of the Mikirs, and the impossibility of intercommunication, make the coincidences interesting.

3. STORY OF HARATA KUNWAR

Harata Kunwar was one of six brothers, the youngest of them. From his very birth he spent his time in shooting deer and wild pig, and never laboured in the fields. His elder brothers, the five, did the field work. Then they, the five brothers, took counsel together with their father, saying, "This Harata Kunwar does no field work, but spends his time in hunting. Let us talk the matter over at night." So that night they talked it over. The father said to his eldest son, "How will you supply me with rice?" He answered, "As for me, I will become a head man of a village, and sit in assembly night and day; from the rice-beer which people will bring me as the head man's perquisites, I will supply you with good white rice and beer." "And you, the second son, how will you supply me with rice?" "As for me, I will become a blacksmith; night and day will I spend in forging knives and *dāos*; with the money produced by these I will furnish you with beer, betel, *pān*, good white rice, and all kinds of spirit." "And you, the third son, how will you supply me with rice?" "As for me, I will labour in the fields, and having filled granaries and

the fireplace and the middle partition, where the offerings of food for the spirits of the dead are placed.

barns with produce I will give you good beer and good white rice." "And you, the fourth, how will you provide for me?" "As for me, I will go as a companion to some one, and what that person gives me of rice and beer I will give you." "And you, the fifth, how will you provide for me?" "As for me, I will become some one's slave, and will support you with the rice and beer he gives me." "And you, Harata Kunwar, in what way will you furnish me with rice?" "As for me, I will marry a daughter of the Sun-god, and having become a great king, I will seat you on a throne, on a fine couch, I will cause slaves, male and female, to bathe your arms and legs, and I will give you beer, rice, and spirits." So they finished their talk. Next day, in the place where they worked at their field, Harata Kunwar not being with them, those five brothers consulted again together with their father. "This Harata Kunwar says he will take to wife the daughter of the Sun-god and become a king, forsooth! Where will he get his kingship? Let us kill him, and let us talk about it again to-night." That night, after they had eaten and drunk, they consulted together about the way in which the killing was to be done. "Let us build a field-watcher's hut* for Harata Kunwar, on the border of the jungle let us build it, and make him watch there; then at night let us go and thrust him through with a spear." Harata Kunwar's sister-in-law overheard them as they were conspiring together. Next morning, after they had eaten and drunk and gone away to their work in the fields, Harata Kunwar came home from his hunting. His sister-in-law gave him his rice, and after he had eaten and drunk she said, "Let me kill that insect on you, Harata Kunwar." Then she killed a louse, and as she killed it a tear fell upon Harata Kunwar's leg. He asked her, "Sister-in-law, are you crying?" And his sister-in-law said, "I am not crying, a raindrop fell upon you." Again, as she killed a louse, a tear fell the second time. Harata Kunwar asked her again, "You really are crying, sister-in-law; tell me why you are weeping." So she told

* "A field-watcher's hut," *hèm-thàp*: a small hut, raised high upon posts and thatched over, built in a clearing for cultivation, in which the cultivator passes the night for the purpose of scaring wild pigs and deer away from the crop.

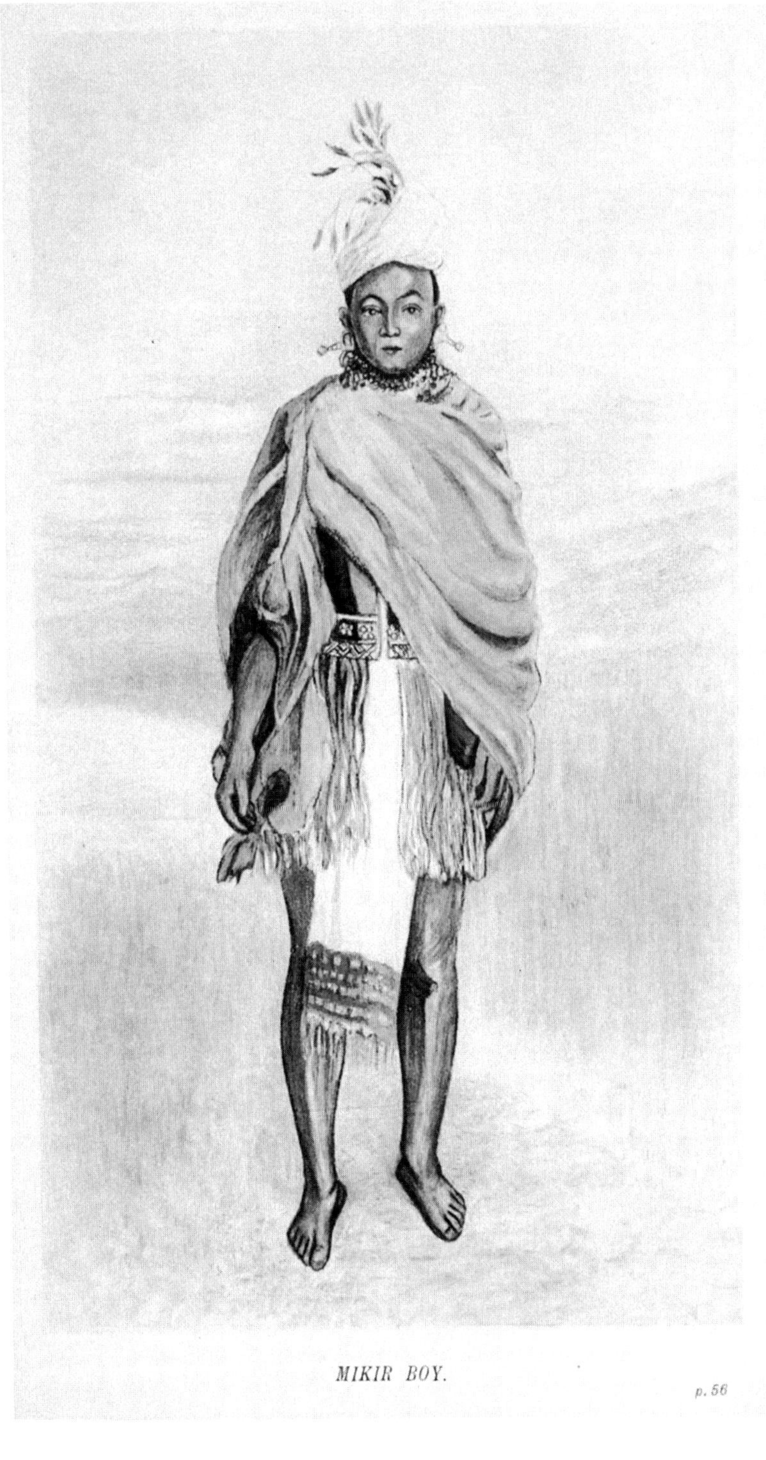

MIKIR BOY.

p. 56

him: "My father-in-law and your elder brothers have plotted together to make you watch by night in a jungle hut, and then they will thrust you through there with a spear, they say; that is why I am weeping." Harata Kunwar said, "You need not be afraid; you have told me: it is well. To-morrow morning you will see what happens. If I am not dead, I will come home to you after they have gone, and I will throw six clods, taken from the worm-castings, on the roof of this house. If you don't hear the noise of them on the roof, you will know that I am dead." So in the evening his brothers came home from the field, and his father said, "This night Harata Kunwar must go and watch for us in the jungle hut. Wild pigs are eating up our paddy. There, by the side of the jungle-clearing, we have built for you a watcher's hut." So, having eaten and drunk, Harata Kunwar took with him his bow and went. Then having gathered the fruit of the *pūroi-sāk*,* he put the juice of it into the sheath of a plantain-stalk, and having made it like the form of a sleeping man he put some clothes on it and laid it as though sleeping in the hut. He himself hid quietly under the shelter of the rice plants. Then, after their first sleep, his father and brothers awoke one another: "Come! let us go and kill Harata Kunwar." Then, each one taking with him a spear, they went to Harata Kunwar's jungle hut. Then the father said, "Go thou, eldest, climb up and thrust him through." The eldest said, "How should I dare to put my spear through him? he is our brother, our youngest brother, we have one mother and father, and besides, we have sucked both of us at the same breast, the same nipple. Since we are brothers, how should I dare to kill him? I dare not." "Go, then, you, the second." The second answered, "Oh! he is not the son of a second wife, own brother he is, our younger brother; how then should I dare to kill him? I dare not." "Go, then, you, the third." He answered, "Our thigh is one, our foot is one, our arm is one, our hand is one; we have grown up together, he is our brother. How could I possibly kill him? I cannot." "Go, then, thou, the fourth." He said, "We sucked together at one nipple, own brothers are we, no sister has he,

* A species of potherb, so-called in Assamese: Bengali *pūtikā*, *Basella lucida*. It has red juicy fruit.

how could I venture to kill him? I dare not." "Go, then, you, the youngest." "Oh! why do you send me on such an errand? I am the next to him. From childhood it was I who grew up with him together. We ate our rice together from one platter; we drank our beer from the same mug. How should I dare to kill such a one? I dare not!" Then their father became angry. "Then why did you dare to say, 'We must kill Harata Kunwar'? If you cannot bring yourselves to do it, you will never become men." So saying, he climbed up the posts of the hut, and thrust his spear through that plantain-sheath, and the juice of the *pūroi sāk* came dropping out from it. Then he called out, "Harata Kunwar, strong though he be, has got his deserts now at last! Let him marry the Sun-god's daughter and make himself a king now!" Harata Kunwar overheard all this. "What, what are you saying, my brothers?" he called out. Then, saying "Harata Kunwar has his bow with him!" they ran away in fear, stumbling and falling as they ran. When they got to their own jungle hut, they vomited, and on the night clearing away, with great difficulty in the morning they reached home. Then Harata Kunwar, after they had come, himself came up, and took six clods from the worm-casts and threw them on the roof. So after they had eaten and drunk, his brothers went away to their field. Then Harata Kunwar came in, and his sister-in-law gave him his rice. After eating and drinking, he said, "Sister! I cannot remain here with you; my own brothers, nay, even my own father, aim at my life, and are plotting to kill me. I must therefore go a-wandering. Get ready and give me a store of rice to take with me, bread, and parched grain." So his sister-in-law prepared food for him, bread and parched rice. And he said to her when he parted: "If I do not come by my death, then when I come here again I will throw six clods from the worm-castings on the roof; then, when you hear them, wash and make ready the stools and benches!" So they wept together, and parted. Then Harata Kunwar, taking his bow with him, went on his way. At last he arrived at his grandmother's house. "Oh, granny! are you there?" The old woman answered, "Who is there? as for this place, I have neither kin nor helper. Who is come?" Harata Kunwar answered, "It is I, granny." Then the old

OLD MIKIR WOMAN.

p. 59

woman said, "Why are you come, my dear? I am a poor widow. I have neither house nor field. I live only by begging my food. Why have you come?" Harata Kunwar answered, "I will stay here with you and be your companion." The old woman said, "You, who are fit to be a king; a great man, how will you be able to live with me here?" Harata Kunwar answered, "Very good, granny; here I will stay." So he became her companion there. Then his granny the widow said, "Harata Kunwar, spread the paddy out in the sun to dry. I will go and beg paddy in the king's village. After you have spread out the paddy, if you want to bathe in the river, don't go up-stream; bathe on the shore close by this house of ours." So having spread out the paddy, his granny the widow went to the king's village. Harata Kunwar took charge of the paddy; frequently turning it over, in a very short time he dried it. Then he collected the paddy together and went to bathe in the river. He thought in his own mind, "for what reason did my granny, when she went away, tell me not to go up-stream to bathe? I will go up-stream and see for myself." So saying, he went up-stream. There he saw shards of broken water-vessels of gold and silver lying. "Oh! that is why granny told me when she went away not to go up-stream. At night I will ask her whose *ghāt* (watering-place) this is." So he returned home. Then his granny the widow in the evening also came home again from the king's village. So at night, after they had eaten and drunk, Harata Kunwar asked her, "Whose *ghāt* is that up-stream? There are broken pieces of gold and silver water-vessels strewn all about it." Then the widow said, "I told you when I went away not to go up-stream. You have been disobeying me and have gone up there, I know?" Harata Kunwar answered, "Yes, I did go, granny; now tell me whose *ghāt* it is." So his granny the widow told him: "It is the *ghāt* of the King of the Great Palace. His daughters, six sisters, come to that place to bathe; don't go there any more." Then Harata Kunwar considered again by himself: "My granny tells me not to go again, but go I will and see for myself." So up-stream he went again, and hid himself quietly under the river bank. At midday the six daughters of the King of the Great Palace came to bathe there in the river.

Descending beautifully, each one laid aside her clothes and jumped into the water. This did one after the other, and fair it was to see—like the brightness of the moon and sun; there they bathed and frolicked in the water. Then when the day became cool, the eldest sister admonished the rest:* "O my dears, it is cooking time! time to serve up the food: time to house for the night our fowls and our pigs. Our mother will scold us, our father will scold us, if we stay any longer. Let us go." So they ended their bathing and playing in the water. One after another they shook out their clothes in the breeze and put them on, and beautifully flew away; but the youngest of them flew away last of all, lovely like the brightness of the moon or the sun. Until they were lost to sight in the heaven Harata Kunwar continued gazing after them till his neck got a crook in it. So they entered heaven, and he saw them no more. And he returned to his house, thinking to himself, "How fair, how lovely! (I will not rest) until I get one of them to be my wife! To-night I will ask granny about it." So home he came, and after supper Harata Kunwar asked his granny: "Oh, granny! such beautiful, such lovely ones I never saw; how shall I get one to wife? Tell me a plan." His granny said, "Oh, Harata Kunwar, these are children of the Sun-god, children of a great king; how should you, who are a man's son, succeed in getting one to wife?" Harata Kunwar said, "Not so, granny: get one to wife I must and will. Show me a plan!" Since he continued to press her with questions, at last she said to him, "If you must and will get one for your wife, then clear a field on the river bank." "Very good, granny," said Harata Kunwar, "to-morrow, this very next day, I will go and clear it." So he remained watching for the dawn to break, until the sun fully rose. Then, taking with him a *dāo,* he went. From the moment he reached the place he rested not, but cut and hacked down the jungle there, till in a single day he had finished the clearing. Then, having heaped the fallen trees together, he set fire to them, and the fire devoured them there, till there was not a single piece or stock left that was not burnt. Then he dibbled in maize, small millet, sugar cane, plantains; besides

* Notice the simplicity of life indicated by the occupations the fairy princesses have to attend to on their return to their celestial home.

these he planted flowers—marvel of Peru, white lilies, marigolds,* many kinds of flowers. Then the daughters of the King of the Great Palace came down to bathe in the river; beautifully they descended, fair as never was seen; like the moon, like the sun in splendour, they came right down there. So, having finished bathing and splashing about in the water, they spied Harata Kunwar's garden plot. They said, "Oh, whose field is this? It is very pretty indeed!" The eldest answered, "It must be our brother-in-law Harata Kunwar's field." So they flew away beautifully again to heaven together. Harata Kunwar there pondered in his mind: "Shall I ever succeed in getting her to wife?" And again he asked his grandmother, "Granny, when shall I succeed in getting one to wife?" His granny answered, "Not in that way, grandson. Build for yourself a jungle hut." So next morning a jungle hut he went to build. In a single day he finished building one, great and big, and came home again. "The jungle-hut is finished, granny," he said. "Then cut for yourself a flute," advised his granny. So he cut several flutes for himself, and bored holes in them. Then the time for maize and millet to ripen came. And his granny advised him: "Go and watch in your jungle hut, and play the flute." As for his field, in a very short time flowers blossomed there as you never saw! Then the daughters of the King of the Great Palace arrived to bathe in the river; flying down beautifully one after another they laid aside their clothes and jumped into the water, and bathed and frolicked. Then the eldest admonished them: "Come, my dears, let us go." Thereupon Harata Kunwar began to play on his flute so beautifully that you never heard the like. "Oh! this flute-playing is very pretty to hear! Surely it is the man (called) Harata Kunwar. Come, dears, let us go and ask for a few flowers." So they went. "Harata Kunwar, we would like to pluck for ourselves a few flowers. May we pluck and take some, sir?" "Yes," said Harata Kunwar, "you can pluck as many as you like." Then each one plucked some flowers and went away. Gracefully they flew away with the flowers. Until they disappeared in the sky, Harata Kunwar gazed after them, until his eyes became

* The exact species of these flowers is not vouched for; those named are common in the house-gardens of Assamese cultivators.

quite sore with gazing. So they returned into heaven. When he could see them no more, Harata Kunwar also returned home. And his granny the widow asked him, "Did you have any talk to-day with the daughters of the King of the Great Palace?" "Yes, we had some talk; they even asked to be allowed to gather some of my flowers." Then his granny explained a plan: "To-morrow is a lucky day. Go, you, before the Great King's daughters come down to bathe, and hide yourself as I tell you, and watch by the river. The elder sisters, all five, have got husbands already. As for the youngest, the King of the Winds is asking for her to marry her to his son; already the gourds and *chungas* of beer (for the wedding-feast) have arrived. Nevertheless, having singled out her petticoat from among the others, while they are all bathing, bring it here to me. I will weave a petticoat just like it in exchange for it; take that one back there and put it down again in the same place where her real petticoat was; her own petticoat let us hide away. Then she will not be able to fly away. If she asks for her petticoat back again, say 'One or other of you must marry me.'" "Yes, very good indeed, granny," said Harata Kunwar. From the time that his granny imparted to him that plan, Harata Kunwar's mind was so cheerful as you could not imagine. All night long he could not close his eyes, but went on thinking continually. So morning dawned. Then, having breakfasted, he went to his field. "Oh, when will it be midday?" he said, as he went on waiting. Then he hid himself quietly under the sand. Then at midday the daughters of the King of the Great Palace came. Gracefully they flew down there, and one after another removed her garments and plunged into the stream. So when they were all in the water, Harata Kunwar rose stealthily and seized the petticoat and striped cloth of that youngest one, and carried them off straightway to his granny the widow. And his granny wove in place of them another petticoat and striped cloth just like them. In a very short time she had done them, and Harata Kunwar ran back again there, and having put the new petticoat and striped cloth in the same place, himself went into his jungle hut and played the flute. Wonderfully he played it there; never was heard such playing.

So when they had had enough of bathing and sporting in the

water, the eldest admonished her sisters: * "O my sisters, let us go! it is time to pound the rice, time to clean it after pounding: time to cook, time to serve up: time to heat the beer, time to squeeze it from the rice-grains." So having put on her clothes she said again, "Come, let us go and ask for a few flowers." Then, having plucked some flowers, first the eldest flew up, then the younger sisters also flew up to her gracefully, and last of all the youngest also tried to fly, but found she could not. If she flew she fell back again there; if she got up and tried to fly again, she fell back a second time. Then the eldest said, "Oh! what in the world is the matter?" So the elder sisters also came down again there, and went and said to Harata Kunwar, "O Harata Kunwar, without doubt it is you who have changed our youngest sister's petticoat; therefore, bring it back!" So they called out, and Harata Kunwar answered, "One or other of you must be my wife." The daughters of the King of the Great Palace said, "How is it possible that any of us should stay here and be your wife? We have each of us got husbands already." Harata Kunwar said, "Then I cannot give you the petticoat; one of you must positively marry me." Then the daughters of the King of the Great Palace said to one another, "Sister! do you marry him." The eldest answered, "How should I marry him? I have a number of children already." "Then you, the next, you marry him." "How can I marry him? I also have four children already." "You, the third, you marry him, then." "How can I, when I also have three children already?" "Then you, the fourth, you marry him." "I also have two children already; how should I marry him?" "You, the fifth, you marry him." "I cannot marry him; don't you know that I also have one child already?" "Then you, the youngest, you marry him." The youngest answered, "As for me, the King of the Winds is asking for me to marry me to his son, the gourds and *chungas* of beer (for the wedding feast) have arrived already. How can I possibly marry him?" Her eldest sisters said, "Well, but you are not married yet. You must marry him, dear. It is getting dark; we must go. There at home our fowls and our pigs will be calling out for us; besides, our mother and father will be looking

* See the note on p. 60.

out for us. And we will come and visit you from time to time." Then the youngest one said, "What is to be done, sisters? Well, I will marry him; you go. Our mother and father will be angry." Then the eldest one said: "Harata Kunwar, you would not listen to our instructions, therefore we are leaving our youngest sister here with you; but be careful not to grieve or trouble her. Do not make her cook or serve up; moreover, touch not her hand or her foot." So, after giving parting instructions to their youngest sister, they flew away gracefully to heaven again together. The pair who were left behind continued gazing after them till they were lost in the heaven and they could see them no more. Then Harata Kunwar said: "It is getting dark, let us two also go home." So Harata Kunwar was happy and joyful. Night and day he shot deer and wild pig, and his platform and drying stand * (for drying flesh on) were never dry (*i. e.* without flesh exposed on them to dry).

So one year came to an end. "O Granny, I say to myself, 'I will go home'; what am I to do?" said Harata Kunwar. "Sure, you have your own house, you have your own field; you can go if you like; nevertheless your wife is not yet entirely at one with you here." "Nay, but," said Harata Kunwar, "is it not a whole year (since we were married), granny?" "Nevertheless, you have not come to perfect agreement yet." "Oh, then," said Harata Kunwar, "I cannot go yet." So Harata Kunwar stayed there, working in the field and labouring, and getting barns and granaries stored with the produce to such an extent that the widow's house was filled up with baskets and barrels full of grain. And God gave Harata Kunwar a child, one son only. Then he asked his grandmother again: "Granny! I keep saying to myself, 'we will go home to my mother and father.'" The widow answered, "Your wife has not yet thoroughly accommodated herself to you, grandson." "Not so, granny; she has indeed. Has she not already borne me a son?" "Go, then. You would not listen to the warnings I gave you from time to time. Go

* The flesh of animals killed by hunters is cut into strips and dried in the sun on frames of bamboo, for future use. The frames are called in Mikir *ur* and *ràp*.

together. But your wife has not yet made up her mind to stay with you, I assure you." So Harata Kunwar said to his wife, "My dear! let us two go together to our home." His wife answered, "Go. Wherever you take me (I will go too)." Then the morning dawned, and they took their breakfast and started. They went a bit of the way. Now, his child and his wife Harata Kunwar bound firmly to his waist with his turban, and so carried them. And so as they went on they saw a jungle-cock * scratching the ground in a wonderful way on the mountain side. Harata Kunwar said, "Oh, jungle-cock, what are you doing there? I am in a hurry to get home; leave the road open to me." The jungle-cock answered, "I will not leave the road open to you. I say to myself, 'Harata Kunwar to-day will bring along his wife and child,' and I am watching the way he is coming." Harata Kunwar rejoined, "What jest is this? Be careful, lest in a little you have to say, 'when Harata Kunwar brought his wife and child to his home and field, my life was lost.'" The jungle-cock said, "I don't say so; to-day (we will see whether) you or I will prevail." Harata Kunwar said, "Is that true?" "True." "Do you swear it?" "I swear it." Then Harata Kunwar, setting an arrow to his bow, shot him.

Then as he went on a little further (he came upon) a cock-pheasant † blocking the road, and scratching in a wonderful way on the mountain side. And Harata Kunwar said again, "Oh, cock-pheasant, what are you doing there? I am in a hurry to get home; leave the road free to me." The cock-pheasant answered, "I won't leave the road free to you. I say to myself, 'To-day Harata Kunwar will bring along his wife and child,' and I am watching here the way he is coming." Harata Kunwar said, "Oh, don't be silly, lest you have to say in a little while, 'when Harata Kunwar brought along his wife and child, I lost my life.'" The cock-pheasant said, "I don't say so." Harata Kunwar said again, "Are you in earnest?" "In earnest." "Do you swear it?" "I swear it." Then Harata Kunwar set his bow and shot him.

* "Jungle-cock": *Gallus ferrugineus*, the wild fowl of Assam jungles.
† "Cock-pheasant": *vorĕk ālōpō*, the *dorīk* (Ass.) or "derrick," *Gennœus Horsfieldi*, the black-breasted *kalij* pheasant of north-east India.

Then, as they went on still further, a wild boar, so big as you never saw or imagined, with his tusks overlapping his mouth, was straddling across the road, and rooting up the earth there on the mountain side in an extraordinary way. And Harata Kunwar said, "Oh, wild boar, what are you doing there? leave me the road open, I want to get home quickly." The wild boar answered, "I will by no means leave you the road; saying to myself, 'To-day Harata Kunwar will bring along his wife and child,' I am watching the road he is coming." Harata Kunwar said, "Oh, don't joke! is it true or not?" The wild boar answered, "It is true." Harata Kunwar said, "Be careful, lest in a little while you have to say, 'when Harata Kunwar brought along his wife and child, my life was lost.'" The wild boar said, "I don't say so." "Are you in earnest?" "Yes." "Do you swear it?" "I swear it." "Oh, then——" So saying, Harata Kunwar set his bow and shot him.

Then, when he had nearly arrived at his house, he collected six clods from the worm-casts, and threw them on the roof. Then his sister-in-law said, "Harata Kunwar has come home! Wash the stools and the benches!" Then they washed all the stools and seats and planks and benches. And Harata Kunwar, bringing along with him that wild boar, put it down beside the hedge, and entered the house. And as soon as he arrived, his sister-in-law gave him there beer, bread, and parched rice. His wife was so very beautiful that no one could look her in the face, as one cannot look straight at the brightness of the sun. Then his brothers were perplexed, saying, "What in the world has happened to us this night?" And Harata Kunwar said, "A short time ago I shot a little pig on the road. I just put it down there beside the hedge. Go and get it and scorch it (for cooking)." So his five brothers went, but the boar was so very big that they could not even move it; they could do nothing with it at all. So Harata Kunwar went with them. With one hand he easily lifted it and brought it away; and they scorched it and cut it up. So home they brought it and cooked it and served it up, and joyful, noisy, laughing and jesting, they ate and drank.

Then next morning dawned. Hearing that Harata Kunwar had brought his wife home, all the people of the whole country-side kept coming and going to gaze upon her, in such crowds as you never saw. And Harata Kunwar put away carefully in a bamboo chunga his wife's own petticoat and striped cloth, with her gold ornaments, her necklace, and her gold drum (Ass. *mādolī*) worn on the breast, and tied them up in the pitch of the roof. So Harata Kunwar went to pay visits to the people of the village, and the ryots of the country-side camė to visit him; and then they went on to gaze upon his wife. And all the women—aunts on mother's and father's side, sisters-in-law, elder brothers' wives—each one said, "Oh! is she not lovely, sister!" Thus they wondered at her. Then Harata Kunwar's wife answered, "Not so lovely yet as I might be. If I were to put on again my own petticoat, my striped cloth, my necklace and my bracelets, then, indeed, there would be something to see!" Then some old woman said, "Oh, then, give them to her." And Harata Kunwar's old father said, "Where in the world did that idiot of a boy put them away? Why did he not give her her own petticoat and striped cloth?" Then Harata Kunwar's wife explained: "They are there in the roof-pitch where he has tied them up." So his father untied the bundle and gave it to her. Then she put the things on and arrayed herself. Thereupon she became inconceivably beautiful. "Oh!" they cried, "lovely! beautiful indeed! It is not for nothing that she is called child of the Sun-god!" Thereupon Harata Kunwar's wife rose up to her full height, and flapped her clothes, and gracefully flew away back to her own place. Then Harata Kunwar, happening to see her from where he was on a distant road, kept continually bending his bow. And his wife said, as she left him: "Wait, wait! hereafter we shall meet again." So Harata Kunwar, weeping bitterly, sick and sorry at heart, came to his house. Immediately he got there, without eating or drinking, he took his child on his back, and straightway set out for the house of his grandmother the widow woman. Thus he went on till he arrived, and at once on arrival began to weep and wail as you could not imagine. Then his grandmother said: "I told you from the first that your wife was not yet reconciled to her lot with you. How will you get to see her now? How will you be able to reach her in heaven?" This only aggravated his weeping; refusing meat and drink, he followed his grandmother wherever she went, continually dogging her steps, and was like to die of grief. At last his grandmother said, "Harata Kunwar, take a little food, and then I will tell you of a plan." So he took something to eat, bread and parched rice, and then his grandmother told him her scheme. "To-morrow," she said, "the son of the King of the Winds will come there to marry your wife. Before that, your father-in-law's elephant will come here to bathe. Do you go and hide yourself there under the sand. When the elephant (after its bath) is just about to go, hold on tight to its tail, and bind your child firmly to your waist with your turban. If the elephant asks you anything, say that you also are going to the place where your wife is. Then to-morrow, in the evening, you will arrive there. Remain concealed on the river bank. Then male and female slaves will come to draw water there in order to bathe your wife. Call out to them, 'Give me one draught of water for the child.' Then, if they give you the water, drop into the water-pot a gold ring. Then she (*i.e.* your wife) will call for you. Go to her, and when you arrive, put down your child on the ground; then the child will go of itself towards its mother."

The morning dawned, and Harata Kunwar, after eating and drinking, went to the river bank and hid himself quietly under the sand. Then the elephant came down to bathe in the river, and having bathed, was just about to go away, when Harata Kunwar grasped firmly hold of its tail, and with his turban tied his child securely to his waist. Then the elephant flew up with him to heaven, and put him down on the river bank there. And all the people of the King of the Winds had come to the house of the King of the Great Palace in order to celebrate the marriage of the son of the King of the Winds with Harata Kunwar's wife. And the King's slaves, male and female, came to draw water in order to bathe Harata Kunwar's wife. And Harata Kunwar called out to them for water for his child: "Give me just one draught of water for my son, good mothers!" One after another paid no attention to his request, till at last an old woman came up. So Harata Kunwar called out again: "Give me water, one draught only, good madam, for my child." So the old woman gave him some water. Making as though he

VI.

LANGUAGE.

Outline of Mikir grammar—The original text of the three stories translated in Section V., analysed and elucidated.

THE language spoken by the Mikirs belongs to the great family of Indo-Chinese speech called Tibeto-Burman, the general characteristics of which have been fully set forth in *The Linguistic Survey of India*, vol. iii. Mikir itself is treated on pp. 380 *ff.* of Part II. of that volume, and is described by Dr. Grierson as a member of the Nāgā-Boḍo sub-group, in which it is classed together with Ēmpēo or Kachchā Nāgā, Kabui, and Khoirāo. It is unnecessary here to occupy space with any demonstration of the fact that Mikir is a Tibeto-Burman language, or to cite lists of words in it agreeing with those of other languages of the same great class. In the next section an attempt will be made to examine its affinities with other varieties of Tibeto-Burman speech, and to define more clearly its place in the family; in this the language will be dealt with in its internal structure only, and, as specimens, the original text of the three stories translated in Section V. will be given, with an interlinear rendering and a running commentary.

A grammatical sketch of Mikir was printed at pp. 381–391 of Part II. vol. iii. of the *Linguistic Survey*. What follows is mainly borrowed from that source, which was the first published attempt to explain systematically the facts and mechanism of the language.

SOUNDS.

Mikir has no written character of its own. The first publication printed in it, a short catechism issued by a missionary press at Sibsagar in 1875, used the Assamese character; since then, so far as is known, the Roman alphabet has always been employed to express the sounds of the language. Mr. Stack, from whose materials this monograph has been compiled, distinguished the following vowel sounds:—

ā, long *a* as in *father* (chiefly in open syllables);

à, the same shortened and pronounced abruptly, as in the German *Mann*, always in closed syllables;

(N.B. The language does not possess the short Hindī *a*, representing the *u* in *but.*)

ē, the long *e* in the French *scène*;

e, the same sound shortened, as in *belief*;

è, the sharp *e* in the English *men* (always in closed syllables);

ī, the long *i* in *machine*;

i, the short *i* in *it*;

ō, the long *o* in *bone*;

o, the same shortened, as in *obey*;

ò, the sharp abrupt sound in *pot* (always in closed syllables);

ū, the long *u* in *June*;

u, the short *u* in *full*.

The diphthongs are—

ai, as in *aisle*;

ei, almost as in *feign*, with the *i* audible;

oi, as in *boil*;

ui, long *ū* with *i* added: no English equivalent.

The consonants used in Mikir are *b, ch, d, h, j, k, l, m, n, ng, p, r, s, t, v* (all with their value as in English), and the aspirates *kh, ph, th* (pronounced as in *cookhouse, haphazard, anthill*). *Bh, dh,* and *g* occur only in a few borrowed words, and *bh* and *dh* are commonly resolved, as *bahār* (for Hindī *bhār*), "a load," and *dohòn* (for Ass. *dhon*), "money." *F, sh, w, y,* and *z* are not used. *Ng* is never initial, and the *g* is not separately heard (always as in *singer*, never as in *younger*).

Monosyllabic Roots.

The root words of the language, whether nouns, adjectives, pronouns, verbs, or adverbs, are generally monosyllabic; where simple roots have more than one syllable, the additions are formative *prefixes*, once probably separate words, which have become incorporated. Such are the prefix *ke-*, *ki-*, *kā-*, used to form adjectives, present participles, and verbal nouns; and the prefixes *ār-* (in *ārnī*, "sun," *ārlòng*, "stone," *ārlèng*, "man," etc.), *ing-* (in *inglòng*, "mountain"; *inghòn*, "pity," etc.), and *te-*, *ti-*, *to-* (in *teràm*, "call," *tekàng*, "abandon," *tikup*, "house-yard," *tovār*, "road," etc.), of which the precise significance is not now traceable. In compound roots, formed by combining monosyllabic elements, the force of each individual syllable is still fully felt; such compounds are exceedingly common.

Words are not inflected, but are located in sense by their position in the sentence or by the addition of particles. These particles may often be omitted where ambiguity is not likely to occur; such omission is particularly frequent as regards the postpositions indicating case, and the tense-affixes of the verb.

Gender.

Gender is not distinguished except for animated beings, and in them either (1) by added words indicating sex (as *sō-pō*, "boy," *sō-pī*, "girl"; *āsō-pinsō*, "male child"; *āsō-pī*, "daughter"; *chainòng-ālō*, "bull"; *chainòng-āpī*, "cow"), or (2) by the use of different terms (*pō*, "father," *pē* or *pei*, "mother," *phū*, "grandfather," *phī*, "grandmother," etc.).

Number.

The ordinary suffix for the plural is *-tum* (which is originally a separate word meaning "company," "followers"); but other words are occasionally employed, as *mār*, a "mass, quantity, or company"; *òng*, "many"; and *lī*, a respectful form used in addressing a number of persons. When *-tum* is suffixed to a noun, it takes the prefixed *ā-* of relation, as *ārlèng-ātum*, "men"; when added to a personal pronoun it does not require this adjunct, as will be explained below (*nē*, "I," *nē-tum*, "we"; *nàng*, "thou," *nàng-tum*, "ye"; *lā*, "he, she, it," *lā-tum*, "they").

Case.

Case is indicated by position, or by postpositions. The nominative, and, generally speaking, the accusative, have no postpositions, but are ascertained by their position in the sentence, the nominative at the beginning, the accusative following it before the verb. Both, when necessary, can be emphasised by the addition of the particles *-kē* and *-sī*, which in some sort play the part of the definite article; but these are not case-postpositions. There is no device (as in Tibetan) for distinguishing the case of the agent with transitive verbs.

The genitive always precedes the noun on which it is dependent. When the word in the genitive is a pronoun of the first or second person, nothing intervenes between them: *nē-mèn*, "my name"; *nàng-pē*, "thy clothes." But when the pronoun is in the third person, or a noun is in the genitive case, the following noun has *ā-* prefixed: *e.g. lā ā-pō*, "his father"; *Ārnàm ā-hèm*, "God's house"; *hijai-ātum ā-kàm*, "the jackals' work"; *ārnī-kàngsàm ā-pòr*, "day-becoming-cool time." This prefixed *ā-* is really the pronoun of the third person, and means *his, her, its, their;* the full meaning of the combinations given above is therefore "he, his father": "God, his house": "the jackals, their work": "day becoming cool, its time." As in many other languages of the Tibeto-Burman family, nouns (especially those denoting personal relations, parts of the body, etc.) are seldom conceived as abstract and self-contained; they most often occur in relation to some other noun, and thus the syllable *ā-* is more often prefixed to them than not. Especially is this the case with adjectives; these ordinarily follow the noun which they qualify, and almost always have *ā-* prefixed; *e.g. Ārnàm ā-kethē*, "God Almighty": *lā ā-kibī ā-bàng*, "that younger one." Sometimes this prefixed *ā-* is thinned down to *ē-*, as in *hèm-ē-pī, hèm-ē-pō*, "widow, widower," literally "female or male owner of the house": *hijai ē-hur*, "a pack of jackals." Most postpositions (originally nouns joined to the genitive of the qualified word) similarly require *ā-* before them; and the suffix *-tum* of the plural, since it means "a company," also in this manner assumes the form *ă-tum.* Before *ing-* the prefix *ă-* is absorbed, and the result is *àng.*

The other cases are formed by postpositions. The *instrumental* is generally indicated by *pèn* (sometimes with prefixed *ă-* or *ē-*, as *ăpèn*, *ēpèn*, but more often without), or *pèn-sī.* The *dative* takes *ă-phàn*, "to or for," which is also occasionally used for the *accusative.* The sign of the dative of purpose is *ăpòt: pī-ăpòt*, "what for, why?" *kopī-ăpòtsī*, id. The *ablative* is formed with *pèn* or *pènsī: nòn-pèn*, "from now"; *dàk-pèn*, "from here"; *ăpără* (Ass. *pară*) is also used, generally with *pèn* as well. The *locative* has a number of postpositions, according to the position required: *-sī* is used for "in," as *hèm-sī*, "in the house," *ădèt-sī*, "in his country"; *ărlō* is also used for "in, inside." *Lē* (properly the conjunctive participle of a verb meaning "arrive, reach to a place") is often used as a postposition for "at, in." Other common locative postpositions are *ă-thàk*, "upon, on," *àngsòng*, "above, upon," *ărum*, "below," *ăbēr*, "below," *ălòng* "together with" (*lòng* means "place"), *ădun, ădung*, "beside, next to" (*dun* is a verb meaning "to be with, accompany"), *ădàk*, "between," *àngbòng*, "in the middle of," *ăphī*, "after."

ADJECTIVES.

Adjectives are regularly formed by prefixing *ke-*, *ki-*, or *kă-* to the root, and do not change for gender, number, or case. Thus, from the root *mē*, "to be good," we have *kemē*, "good"; *hēlō*, "distance," *kăhēlō*, "far off"; *dòk*, "to have savour," *kedòk*, "savoury"; *hō*, "to be bitter," *kehō*, "bitter"; *lòk*, "to be white," *kelòk*, "white"; *rī*, "to be rich," *kirī*, "rich." *Ke-* and *ki-* are generally used with monosyllables, *kă-* with longer words; *kă-* with *ing-* forms *kàng.*

The form of the adjective is precisely the same as that of the present participle of the verbal root, used to form the present tense, and also as that of the infinitive or abstract of that root, and the collocation of the sentence alone determines the meaning of the word used. When particles of comparison or other modifying elements are added to the adjective, the prefix *kē-* etc. is often dropped as unnecessary; thus—

kelòk, "white"; *lòk-hik*, "whitish."
kemē, "good"; *mē-mū*, "better"; *mē-nē*, "best."
keding, "tall"; *ding-mū*, "taller."
But *kàngtui*, "high"; *kàngtui-mū*, "higher"; *kàngtui-nē*, "highest."

Comparison is effected by means of the postpositions *āpār* and *āphàn*; "his brother is taller than his sister," *ā-tē āpār* (or *āphàn*) *ā-kòr ding-mū*.

Adjectives commonly follow the noun qualified; when they precede, the construction corresponds to what in Aryan languages would be indicated by the relative pronoun (see below, p. 80).

NUMERALS.

The cardinal numerals are *isī*, one; *hinī*, two; *kethòm*, three; *philī*, four; *phòngō*, five; *theròk*, six; *theròk-sī*, seven; *nērkèp*, eight; *sirkèp*, nine; *kèp*, ten. It will be seen that seven is six *plus* one, eight ten *minus* two, nine ten *minus* one. From eleven to nineteen *krē* takes the place of *kèp*: *krē-isī*, eleven; *krē-hinī*, twelve; *krē-kethòm*, thirteen, etc. A score is *ingkoi*, and from this point onwards the syllable *rā* is inserted between the multiple of ten and the added units: *ingkoi-rā-isī*, twenty-one; *ingkoi-rā-hinī*, twenty-two, etc. Thirty, forty, etc. are formed by adding *kèp* to the multiplier unit: *thòm-kèp*, *philī-kēp*, etc. Eighty is *theròk-nērkèp*, ninety *theròk-sērkèp*. A hundred is *phārō* or *pārō*, a thousand *surī*.

The numeral follows the noun. In composition *hinī* (except with *bàng*, "person") is reduced to *nī*, and *kethòm* to *thòm*, as *jō-nī jō-thòm*, "two or three nights." *Philī* and *theròk* are often contracted to *phlī* and *thròk*.

Generic determinatives, as in many other Tibeto-Burman languages, are commonly used with numbers:—

with persons, *bàng*, as *ā-òng-mār kòrtē bàng-theròk*, "his uncles, the six brothers";

with animals, *jòn* (perhaps an Assamese loan-word), as *chelòng jòn-philī*, "four buffaloes";

with trees and things standing up, *ròng*: *thèngpī ròng-theròk* "six trees";

with houses, *hum*, as *hèm hum-theròk-kèp*, "sixty houses";

with flat things, as a mat, a leaf, a knife, *pàk:* as *tār pàk-phòngō*, "five mats"; *lō pàk-philī*, "four leaves"; *nōkē pàk-thòm*, "three knives";

with globular things, as an egg, a gourd, a vessel, *pum:* as *vo-tī pum-nī*, "two eggs"; *bòng pum-theròksī*, "seven gourds";

with parts of the body, and also with rings, bracelets, and other ornaments, *hòng:* as *kèng ē-hòng*, "one leg"; *roi hòng-nī*, "two bracelets."

One of anything is not formed with *īsī*, but, if a person is spoken of, *īnut* (a Khasi loan-word) is used: if anything else, *ē-* is prefixed to the generic determinative; "one cow," *chainòng ē-jòn;* "one tree," *thèngpī ē-ròng*; "one book," *puthī ē-pàk;* "one egg," *vo-tī ē-pum.* This *ē-* appears to be borrowed from Assamese, where it is shortened from *èk.*

Ordinals are formed by prefixing *bātai* to the cardinal, as *bātai-kethòm*, "third," *bātai philī*, "fourth." They seem to be little used: in the story of Harata Kuñwar it will be seen that clumsy periphrases are employed to designate the second, third, fourth, and fifth brother of the family to which the hero belonged. Distributive numeral adverbs are formed by prefixing *pur* or *phòng* to the cardinal: *pur-thòm* or *phòng-thòm*, "thrice."

PRONOUNS.

The following are the *personal pronouns :—*

1st Person: *nē*, I; *nē-tum, nē-lī, nē-lī-tum*, we, excluding the person addressed: *ī-tum, ī-lī*, we, including the person addressed;

2nd Person: *nàng*, thou; *nàng-tum, nàng-lī, nàng-lī-tum*, ye;

3rd Person { *lā*, he, she, it; *lā-tum*, they; *ālàng*, he, she; *ālàng-lī, ālàng-ātum, ālàng-lī-tum*, they.

(The pronoun *lā* is really a demonstrative, = this, that: it is probable that the original pronoun of the third person was *ā.*)

These pronouns take the postpositions like nouns. The possessive or genitive prefixes are *nē*, my, our, excluding the person addressed; *ē-* or *ī-*, our, including the person addressed; *nàng-*, thy, your; *ā-*, his, her, its, their.

The *demonstrative pronouns* are—*lā, lābàngsō, bàngsō*, this; pl. *lābàngsō-ātum*, these: *hālā, hālābàngsō*, that; pl. *hālā-tum, hālābàngsō-ātum*, those. The syllable *hā-* connotes distance, as *dàksī, lādàk*, here; *hā-dàk*, there; *hā āhèm che-voi-lo*, "he returned home from a distance."

(There appears once to have been another demonstrative pronoun, *pi, pe, pā*, still preserved in the compound words *pi-nī*, "to-day," *penàp*, "to-morrow," *pedàp*, this morning," *pā-ningvē*, "to-night." Instead of *pi* and *pe* we also find *mi, me*, as *mi-nī, me-nàp*. This survival is important for the purpose of comparison with other Tibeto-Burman languages.)

As in other Tibeto-Burman languages, there is *no relative pronoun*; its place is taken by descriptive adjectival phrases. Thus "those six brothers who had gone to sell cow's flesh" is—

lā chainòng ā-òk kejòr-dàm-ā-tum kòrtē bàng-theròk.
Those cow 's flesh to sell going (plural) brothers persons-six;

"The man whom Tenton had tied with an iron chain" is—

Tentòn ingchin ā-nī-pèn ke-kòk ārlèng.
Tenton iron chain-with tied-up man.

In these constructions, it will be seen, the adjective or qualifying participle *precedes* the noun.

The interrogative syllable, used to form *interrogative pronouns*, is *ko-*: *komàt, komàt-sī*, who? *kopī, pī*, what? *ko-pu, ko-pu-sī, kolopu, kolopu-sòn*, how? *ko-àn, ko-ànsī*, how many? *konàt, konàthu*, where? *konàm-tu, nàm-tu, nàm-tu-sī*, when? Always when the sentence does not contain an interrogative pronoun, and sometimes when it does, the syllable *mā* at the end marks a question: "Are you afraid," *nàng pherē-dèt mā?* *Nē* (probably an Assamese loan-word) is also used instead of *mā*: "Will you marry him or not?" *do-jī-nē do-dē-nē?*

The *reflexive pronoun* is *āmethàng*, self; *binòng*, own; but the most usual way of indicating that the action affects oneself is to prefix the particle *che-* (*chi-, ching-, chēng-*, and rarely *cho-*) to the verbal root: *lā hèm che-voi-lo*, "he returned home," *i.e.* to his own house; *ā-òng-mār-ātum che-pu-lo*, "his uncles said to one another"; *che-hàng-jō*, "they asked for themselves." With initial *ing-*, *che-* coalesces to *ching*: with *ār-* it unites to form *chēr*.

Verbs.

The Mikir verb indicates time, past, present, or future, by means of particles prefixed or suffixed to the root. It does not vary for number,* gender, or person. There is no separate verb-substantive, though there are several ways of expressing existence, as *do*, "stay, abide," used also for "have, possess"; *plàng*, "become"; *làng*, "exist, continue (with a sense of incompleteness)"; *lē*, "arrive, happen," etc. Great use is made of adjectival or participial forms, and, in narrative, of the conjunctive participle. Compound roots are very extensively used, the principal verb being put first, then the modifying supplements, and last the time-index.

The *simple*, or *indeterminate present* is expressed by the participle with *ke-*, *kā-*, without any suffix: *konàtsī nàng kedo*, "where do you live?"; *vo kàngjār*, "the bird flies"; *sārbūrā thī-lòt-sī nē kā-chirū*, "the old man having died, I am weeping"; *nē-phū ke-sō-kòn*, "my head is aching badly." This tense, as in other languages, is often used historically for the past.

The *definite* or *determinate present* is expressed by the same participle with *-lo* added: *lā kopī kànghoi-lo?* "What is he doing (now)?"

The *habitual present* is expressed by the verbal root with *-lo*: as *vo-ātum-kē nē-phū-āthàk ingjār-lo*, "the birds fly above our heads."

The *simple* or *narrative past* is formed by the verbal root with *-lo* or *-dèt* added: *lā pu-lo* or *pu-dèt*, "he said"; *nē-phū sō-dèt*, "my head was aching"; *lā kerī-āphī-sī lòng-lo*, "he, after searching, found it." Sometimes *dèt* and *lo* are used together: *lā nē ingtòn-dèt-lo*, "he abused me." *Dèt* may also be used for the present when the state indicated by the verb is one that began in the past and still continues: *e.g.* "Why are you afraid?" may be rendered *kopī āpòtsī nàng pherē-dèt*, or *kopī āpòtsī nàng kāpherē?*

The *complete past* is indicated by the root with *tànglo* added: *lā-āpòtsī nē dām-tànglo*, "I went, or had gone, on his account";

* There are certain particles, *jō*, *jùm*, *hur*, *hòr*, and *krei*, used to indicate plurality when this is necessary; but they are inserted between the root and the tense-suffix, which is invariable.

telòng lònglē phō-tànglo, "the boat has touched ground." *Tang* is a verb meaning "to finish." There are besides a great number of other particles indicating past time used with particular verbs. Thus, with verbs meaning "to fall," *bup* and *buk* are common: *hālā che-koi-bup,* "he fell down"; *hèm ru-bup,* "the house collapsed"; *lòng-chòng klī-bup,* "the upright memorial stone fell down"; *lòng-pàk klō-buk,* "the flat memorial stone fell down"; *thèngpī àngsòng-pèn nàng-klō-buk,* "he fell down from the top of the tree." Such particles generally indicate not only past time but abruptness.

A periphrastic past, with the root followed by *inghoi-lo,* "did," frequently occurs; this is probably an imitation of Assamese idiom.

Here may be noticed the prefix *nàng,* used, as the specimens show, with great frequency in narrative. It has the effect of fixing the occurrence to a known place, and may generally be rendered "there." It is probable that this particle is originally the pronoun of the second person, and that it refers to the knowledge of the person addressed: "as you know," "as you see."

The *future* is represented in two ways: (1) by *-po* added to the root, to indicate an action beginning now and continuing in the future; as *ītum nònkē lābàngsō ākàm āpòtsī pu-po,* "we will talk about this affair now;" and (2) by *-jī* added, for an action which commences later on; as *bādu ārlèng-tā thī-jī,* "all men will die" (*i.e.* at some future time). As *-po* includes the present in the case of continuing action, it may be, and often is, used in a present sense; *-jī* is restricted to future time.

A *compound future* may be formed by adding to the root with *-jī* the words *dòkdòk-lo: lā thī-jī dòkdòk-lo,* "he is just about to die"; *àn chō-jī dòkdòk-lo,* "it is near breakfast-time" (rice-eating); *àn īk-jī dòkdòk-lo,* "the rice is nearly all done." A *doubtful future* may be expressed by *-jī* added to the present participle: *konàt chainòng ā-òk-sī dàk-sī kedo-jī,* "where should cow's flesh be here?"

From the above it will be seen that there is much indefiniteness in the indications of time afforded by the Mikir verb: except *tàng* for the past complete, and *-jī* for the future, the other suffixes may, according to circumstances, be rendered by the past, present, or future; they may also on occasion be omitted altogether. But the context generally removes all ambiguity.

Conditional phrases are formed by putting *-tē* or *-lē*, "if," at the end of the first member, and the second generally in the future with *-jī* or *-po*. Of the *conditional future* an example is *nàng dàm-tē, nàng lā thèk-dàm-jī*, "if you go, you will see him." The *conditional past* inserts *āsòn* ("like, supposing that,") before *-tē*: *dohòn do-āsòn-tē, nē lā nàm-jī*, "if I had money, I would buy it." The *conditional pluperfect* modifies the second member thus: *nàng dàm āsòn-tē, nàng lā lòng-lòk āpòtlo*, "if you had gone, you would have got it"; *nàng nē thàn āsòn-tē, nē lā klèm tàng-lo*, "if you had explained to me, I would have done it."

The *imperative* is, for the second person, the bare root, or more usually the root strengthened by the addition of *nòn* or *thā*, and dialectically of *noi*; *nòn* (= "now") is the strongest form. The other persons are formed by the addition of *nàng* (a verb meaning "to be necessary") to the future in *-po* or present in *-lo*: "let us go" is *ī-tum dàm-po-nàng;* "let us go to the field and plough," *rīt hai-bai dàm-lo-nàng*. We may, for the third person, use the causative form of the verb: *lā-kē pedàm-nòn*, "let him go."

Participles. The *present participle* has the form of the adjective, with the prefixed *ke-* (*ki-*) or *kā-*; as *kedàm*, "going," *kā-chirū*, "weeping." The past participle is the root or the present participle with *tàng* added: *dàm-tàng*, "gone," *thèk-tàng*, "having seen," *kā pàngtu-tàng*, "fattened."

Perhaps the most used form of the verb, especially in narrative, is the *conjunctive participle*, which is either the bare root, or the root with *-sī*; *hèm che-voi-sī thèk-lo*, "having returned home, he saw." When the past is indicated, *dèt* is used, either with or without *-sī*, as *chō-dèt jun-dèt, sārburā, tòn-ārlo kaibòng pātu-joi-sī, ī-lo*, "having finished eating and drinking, the old man, having quietly hidden his club in a basket, lay down"; *Tentòn, dohòn-ālàngbòng lòng-sī, rīt dàm-dē-dèt-sī, kàt-jui-lo*, "Tenton, having got the bamboo-joint with the money, without returning to the field, ran away."

When the phrase in which the conjunctive participle occurs

is terminated by an imperative, the suffix is not *-sī* but *-rā*: "having eaten your rice, go," is *àn chō-rā dàm-nòn;* but "having eaten his rice, he went," is *ān chōdet-sī dàm-lo.* While *-sī* links together parts of a narrative, *-rā* links together a string of imperatives.

The *infinitive* or verbal noun is identical in form with the present participle; *kum-kiròt tàngtē kekàn ārkī nàng ārju-lònglo,* "he heard (got to hear) there (*nàng*) the sound (*ārkī*) of fiddle (*kum*) scraping (*ki-ròt*) and dancing (*ke-kàn*)." All words beginning with *ke-*, *ki-*, and *kā-* may therefore be regarded as (1) adjectives, (2) participles forming tenses of the verb, or (3) verbal nouns; and it will be seen from the analysis of the specimens how clearly this at first sight strange allocation of forms can be made to express the required sense.

In all Tibeto-Burman languages the passive voice is either non-existent or little used; a sentence which in English would be stated passively is turned the other way, and appears in an active form. Thus—"Four trees were uprooted by the wind" would be rendered *tomòn thèngpī ròng-philī pi-pur-koi-lo,* "the wind uprooted four trees"; "this house has been thrown down by an earthquake" is *chiklī-sī lābàngsō āhèm pi-ru-hup-lo,* "an earthquake has thrown down this house." Sometimes a passive may be expressed by a periphrasis, as "I was beaten," *nē kechòk èn-tàng,* lit. "I received a beating." The only unquestionable example of a passive is in the case of past participles, and here the passive is expressed by the simple expedient of putting the participle before instead of after the noun: *bàng kevàn āhòr,* "the drink brought by people"; *mājā kelòng ārlèng,* "a man bewitched"; *nē ke-pī ā-àn āhòr,* "the to-me-given rice and beer." This construction is exactly parallel to the method (explained above) of expressing the relative phrase by putting the adjective first, instead of after the noun, and is in fact another case of the same idiom. The participle, which may also (as just explained) be regarded as a verbal noun, comes *before* the subject of the sentence, because the action passes on to the subject, instead of emanating from it, as in an active construction. We are tempted to think that languages which lack what seems to European modes of thought such essential elements as a relative pronoun and a passive voice cannot be capable of any subtlety of expression; yet this phenomenon is common to forms of speech like Tibetan, Burmese, and Chinese, which possess vast literatures dealing with all kinds of subjects, and in which it is possible to render ideas of the greatest complexity and variety. Even in Europe, the clearest and most logical of languages, French, prefers to use the active form of phrase (with *on*) rather than the passive.

The *negative verb* is a very interesting and remarkable feature of the language. A separate negative root, formed by prefixing or suffixing a negative particle, and conjugated in the same way as the positive, is indeed a common property of Tibeto-Burman speech; but in Mikir this secondary root is formed in a peculiar manner. The negating syllable *-ē* is added to the primitive, as *un*, "can," *un-ē*, "cannot"; *òng*, "be much," *òng-ē*, "be not much"; *ī*, "lie down," *ī-ē*, "not lie down." But when the root begins with a consonant or a *nexus* of consonants, and is monosyllabic, the consonant or *nexus* is repeated before the added vowel: *thèk*, "see, be able"; *thèk-thē*, "not see, be unable"; *dàm*, "go," *dàm-dē*, "not go"; *kroi*, "believe, obey," *kroi-krē*, "disbelieve, disobey"; *mèk-pràng*, "eye-open, awake," *mèk-pràng-prē*, "not awake." When the verb is of two or more syllables, the last is chosen for reduplication: *inghoi*, "do," *inghoi-hē*, "not do"; *ingjinsō*, "show mercy," *ingjinsō-sē*, "not show mercy"; *chini* (Ass. loan-word), "recognise," *chini-nē*, "not recognise."

The secondary root thus obtained is treated in construction just like the positive root, and takes the tense-suffixes: *pàk-tā pī-vàng-vē-dèt-lo*, "anybody to give him (anything) came not." The time-index is, however, with negative verbs more often dropped as unnecessary, owing to the context showing what the time-relation is.

In the imperative the reduplication is not used; the particle *-rī* is added to the positive root, with or without *nòn* as well: *thèk-nòn*, "see!"; *thèk-rī*, or *thèk-rī-nòn*, "see not!"

It may be added that this method of forming the negative by reduplication is also applied to verbal adjectives in *ke-*, *ki-*, *kā-*, which thereupon usually drop the prefix: *kesō*, "in pain, sick"; *sō-sē*, "not sick, well"; but *kàngjinsō*, "merciful"; *kàng-jinsō-sē*, "merciless."

Besides this organic negative, there is a periphrastic negative formed by adding the word *ăvē*, "is not": *Ărnàm ăbàng ăvē, kechèng ăvē, kăpetàng ăvē*, "God has no body, no beginning, no end" (lit. "God his body is not, beginning is not, end is not"). The *ă* in *ăvē* is the usual *ă* of relation, and may be dropped: *ălàm-ăvē* "without a word"; *làm-vē*, "word-less, dumb." *Kă-* may be prefixed, forming *kăvē*, used as an adjectival negative: *kopai* (Ass. *kopăl*), "fortune," *kopai-kăvē*, "unfortunate." Another negative used separately, in emphatic assertions, is *kălī*: *tovăr nàng kepèk-jī kălī*, "the way I will by no means yield to you"; *nē-thibuk kălī*, "it is not my water-jar."

The *causal verb* is formed by prefixing the syllable *pe-*, *pĭ-*, *pă-** to the root: this is probably the verb *pī*, meaning "to give"; *e.g.* *chō*, "eat," *pechō*, "feed"; *tàng*, "finish," *petàng*, "cause to finish, end"; *ingrum*, "be gathered together," *pàng-rum*, "collect"; *vīrdèt*, "be lost," *pī-vīrdèt*, "destroy." This syllable takes precedure of *che-* in reflexive verbs: *ē-chainòng ē-pă-chi-thū-koi-làng*, "he has caused us to slaughter all our cows": here *ē-* is the pronoun of the first person plural inclusive of the addressee; *pă-*, the causal prefix; *chi-*, the reflexive particle, indicating that the cattle slaughtered were their own; *thū*, a verb, "to kill by cutting"; *koi*, a particle indicating completeness; *làng*, the tense-suffix.

Compound verbs meet us at every step in Mikir. Roots are heaped together, and the compound is closed by the tense-suffix. Ordinarily the first root determines the general meaning of the compound, the rest being adverbial supplements of modifying force:—*chirū-pī-lèm-lo*, "he pretended to weep" (*chirū*, "weep," *lèm*, "seem, appear," *pī-lèm*, "cause to seem, pretend"); *ke-phlòng-dàm ăbàng*, "somebody who will go and set fire (to the funeral pile) ("*phlòng*, "kindle," *dàm*, "go"); *kroi-dun-lo*, "she consented" (*kroi*, "agree, obey," *dun*, "go or be with another"); *nē do-dun-jī-mă*, "will you stay with me?" (*do*, "stay," *dun*, as above). The texts which follow supply a multitude of other examples.

These adverbial supplements to verbs, inserted between the principal verb and the tense-suffixes, are a very characteristic

* *Pe-* and *pi-* are used with monosyllables, *pă-* with most polysyllables; *pă* + *ing* = *pàng*.

feature of the language, and their proper use is one of the most difficult things for a learner to master. Certain roots take constant supplements of this kind, and are scarcely ever found without them; thus the verbs *thī*, "die," *ī*, "lie down to sleep," and *jàng*, "close the eyes," are almost invariably followed by *lòt; rèng*, "to live," takes *èt* before verbal suffixes; *lòng*, "to get," takes *lòk*; *chingbār*, "to be equal (in size, weight, height)," and *chingdòn*, "to be equal in length," take *chit*; *inghòn*, "to love," and *ingjinsō*, "to pity," both take *duk*; *jòk* and *thèt*, both meaning "to escape, get loose," take *phlòt*. The complements for verbs meaning "to fall" have been mentioned above (p. 82). These supplements frequently cause the tense-endings to be dispensed with, in which case the action is understood to be in the narrative past or historic present. No doubt most of them were originally separate verbal roots, but are not now capable of being used separately.

The brief outline given above will, it is hoped, enable the reader to apprehend the general construction of the narratives which follow, and display the language in action; for further analysis reference should be made to the notes appended to the texts.

I.

CHÒNGHŌLOSŌ ĀTOMŌ.
FROG STORY.

Ārnī-sī mīsō-ròngpō ā-òng àn che-thòn-dàmlo.
Day-one a big black ant (to) his uncle rice to carry went.
Chònghōlosō tovār ingnī-thīp. Ànsī mīsō
a frog the way sat down and blocked. Then the ant
pulo: "Tovār nē pèk-thā, chònghōlosō; nē nē-òng
said: "The way for me leave free, frog; I my-uncle
àn chethòn-dàm-jī." Chònghōlosō pudèt: "Nē-rum
rice carry-go-will." The frog answered: "Under me
nē-lut-thòt-rā dàm-tē: pàktā nē-rum-sī dàm-
entering (creeping) go your way: every one under me
hòr-lē." Mīsō pudèt: "Nē-òng ā-àn bòr do-
passes." The ant said: "My uncle's rice leaf-bundle being
kòk-lē, pusī nàng-rum-lē nàng-kelut-thèk-jī?"
tied up, how you-underneath enter, creep, shall I be able?"
Ànsī chònghō-tā pèk-pē, mīsō-tā dàm-dē.
So the frog would not give way, the ant could not go.
Ànsī nērlo chitīm-lo. Ànsī mīsō—"Ai, nē-òng
So day became middle. So the ant—"Oh, my uncle
àn-ingchīr-sī āning-nē-thī-po" pulo; chònghōlosō-ārum
rice-hunger-in angry with me will be" said; the frog-under
lut-thòt-lo. Àn-lo chònghōlosō mīsō-āthàk ingnī-dun-
he entered, crept. Then the frog the ant-upon sat-down-
chèt-lo. Lāsī mīsō-ròngpō chònghōlosō ā-mī kòr-ràk.
flat. Thereupon the big black ant the frog's loins bit-severely.
Ànsī chònghō āning-thī-ning-thī kārlē-sārpō-ā-dòn
Then the frog becoming very angry squirrel-big-old's ladder

chòn-rai. Kārlē-sārpō āningthī-ningthī
(on) jumped and broke. The big old squirrel becoming very angry

hànthār-ā-kòk ròt-pèt. Hànthār āningthī-ningthī
gourd's stem cut in two. The gourd becoming very angry

phàk-belèngpī ā-moi klō-dup. Phàk-belèngpī āningthī-
a wild boar's back (on) fell plump. The wild boar becoming

ningthī lō-bòng thīmur-phàk. Lōbòng
very angry a plantain-tree rooted up. The plantain-tree

āningthī-ningthī vo-ārbīpī ā-tār sàp-rai.
becoming very angry a sparrow 's nest struck and broke.

Vo-ārbīpī āningthī-ningthī ingnār nō-thòng-pō ā-nō
The sparrow becoming very angry an elephant deaf-big 's ear

lut-thòt. Ingnār nō-thòng-pō āningthī-ningthī ārlòng
entered. The elephant deaf-big becoming very angry a rock

hēlàng-phlut. Ārlòng āningthī-ningthī Rēchō- ā-sō
tore up suddenly. The rock becoming very angry the King 's son

kònglòng-pī-bup. Ànsī Rēchō nàng-bisār-lo: "Màt-sī
rolling-down killed. Then the King made an enquiry: "Who

nē-pō pithī-lòtlo?" "Ai, ārlòng-sī kònglòng-bup,"
my son has killed?" "Oh, the rock rolled down on him,"

pulo. Ànsī ārlòng ārju-dàmlo: "O ārlòng,
they said. Then the rock he summoned to answer: "O rock,

ārlòng! pī-āpòt nàng nē-sō kònglòng-bup?"
rock! for what reason you my son did roll down upon?"

Ārlòng pudèt: "Chē! Hèmphū-ārnàm-rēchō, pī nē kònglòng-
The rock said: "Oh! Lord- God- King, how I to roll

bup-bē-jī? Ingnār nō-thòngpō-sī nē hēlàng-
down-not was I? The elephant big-deaf me torn up

phlut-lē nē doi-phit-lo; nē-kē nē-rī āvē,
suddenly having, me pushed out; as for me, (to) me hands are not,

nē-kèng āvē, kolo-pu-sī chēr-chàk-thèk-jī? Nàng-
(to) me legs are not, how then withstand could I? Your

sōpō nē kekònglòng ā-tovār dokòksī, nē kònglòng-
honourable son my rolling down-path being-in, I rolled down

bup-lo-tē."
upon him accordingly."

Ànsī Rēchō pulo: "Mai! lā ingnār nō-thòng-pō
Then the king said: "Oh! that elephant deaf-big

lā-ànsèt bòn-hē"— pusi, ingnār nō-thòng-pō
that so much (trouble) caused"—saying, elephant deaf-big

ārju-dàm-lo. "O ingnār ingnār! kopi-āpòt nàng
summoned. "O elephant, elephant! for what reason you

ārlòng hēlàng-phlut?" Ingnār pudèt: "Chē!
the rock tore up suddenly?" The elephant answered: "Oh,

pī nē hēlàng-phlut-phlē-jī, Hèmphū ārnàm? Vo-ārbīpī
how I was to help tearing it up, Lord God? The sparrow

nē-nō nē-kelut-thòt-sī, nē ā-bīdī thèk-thē-dèt-lo-lē,
my ear having entered into, my wits having lost control of me,

lā-hēlo nē ārlòng hēlàng-phlut."
therefore I the rock tore up suddenly.

Ànsī Rēchō pudèt—"Mai! lā vo-ārbīpī lā-ànpin
Then the King said— "Oh! that sparrow that so much

bòn-hē" pu, ārju-dàmlo. "O vo-ārbīpī voārbīpī!
(trouble) caused" saying, summoned. "O sparrow, sparrow!

ingnār ā-nō kopi-āpòt nàng lut-thòt?" Voārbīpī
elephant's ear for what reason did you enter?" The sparrow

thàkdèt—"Chē! Hèmphū! pī nē lut-lē-jī?
answered— "Oh! Lord! how I was I not to enter?

lōbòng nē-tār kesàp-rai-lē, lā-hēlo
the plantain-stalk my nest falling on having broken, therefore

nē-ning oi-òng, nē ingnār ā-nō lut-thòt."
my mind being very disturbed, I elephant's ear entered."

Ànsī Rēchō pu—"Mai! lā lōbòng lāpu
Then the King said— "Oh! that plantain-stalk, it seems;

ànpin bòn-hē"— pusi ārju-dàm-lo. "O lōbòng
so much (trouble) caused"—saying he summoned. "O plantain,

lōbòng! nàng kopi-āpòt vo-ārbīpī ā-tār sàp-
plantain! you for what reason the sparrow's nest fell upon

rai?" Lōbòng pudèt—"Chē! pī nē sàp-rai-
and broke?" The plantain said— "Oh! how I was not to

rē-jī, Hèmphū ārnàm? Phàk-belèng-pī-sī nē
fall and break, Lord God? The wild boar me

kāthīmur-phàk-le : nē thīmur-phàk-lo-tē nē ingkur
rooted me up suddenly : I having been rooted up, I root
kāvē-dèt-lo-lē : kopu-si nē kārjàp thèk-jī-làng ?
none had at all : how I standing-up was to be able to continue ?
Thàngbàk nē-rī nē-kèng lē-kedo kālī-dèt-lē."
Any to me-hand to me-leg being, existing, not-at-all there is."

"Mai ! lā phàk pu àn-pin bon-hē," pu
"Oh ! that pig, it seems, all the (trouble) caused," saying
Rēchō pulo. Ànsī phāk-āphàn ārju-dàm-lo. "O phàk phàk !
the King said. So the pig (accus.) *he summoned. "O pig, pig !*
pī-āpòt nàng lōbòng thīmur-phàk" ? Phàk pudèt
for what reason you the plantain rooted up" ? The pig answered

"Pī nē thīmur-phàk-phē-jī ? Nē chōpàn-vèk,
"How I could help rooting it up ? (as) I was feeding, grazing,
mamàtsī hànthār nē-moi keklō-dàp-lē : lā-hēlo
suddenly, the gourd my back (on) came tumbling down : therefore
kesō-òng nē lōbòng thīmur-phàk."
being in great pain I the plantain rooted up."

Ànsī Rēchō—"Mai ! hànthār pu àn-pin bòn-hē"
So the king—"Oh ! the gourd, then, all this (trouble) caused,"
pusi hànthār ārju-dàm-lo. "O hànthār hànthār ! pī-āpòt
saying the gourd summoned. "O gourd, gourd ! for what
phàk-belèng-pī ā-moi nàng klō-dup ?" "Pī nē
reason the wild boar 's back (on) you fell-plump ?" "How I
klō-dup-dē-jī, Hèmphū Ārnàm ? Kārlē-sī nē-kòk
could help falling ? Lord God ? The squirrel my stem (to me)
nē-keròt-pèt-lē, nē-kē thàngbàk nē-rī, nē-kèng
having cut through, I at all to me hand, to me foot
lē-kedo kālī-dèt, nē-kòk īsī-pèt àn-hēlo, lā-lē
there-not-existing, my stem, one-only, so much having, that if
nē ròt-pèt-lo-tē, nē klō-nàng-po. Phàk-belèng-pī
to me is cut through, I must necessarily fall. The wild boar
ā-moi keklō-nàng-dup."
's back (on) falling became necessary."

Ànsī Rēchō pu-lē-lo—"Mai ! lā kārlē pu àn-pin
So the King said again—"Oh ! that squirrel then so much

bònhē" pusi kārlē ārju-dàm-lo. "O kārlē
(trouble) caused" saying the squirrel summoned. "O squirrel,
kārlē! kopī-āpòt nàng hànthār ā-kòk ròt-pèt?"
squirrel! for what reason did you the gourd 's stem cut through?"
Kārlē pudèt—"Chē! pī nē ròt-rē-jī, Hèmphū
The squirrel said—"Oh, how I was not to cut it, Lord
Ārnàm? Chònghōlosō-sī nē-dòn chòn-rai-lē. Lā-
God? The frog my ladder (on) jumping broke: There-
sī nē tovār āvē-dèt-lo: nē hànthār ā-kòk ròt-
fore to me a road did not remain: I the gourd 's stem had
pèt."
to cut."

Rēchō pudèt—"Mai! lā chònghō lā-pu àn-pin
The King said—"Oh! that frog, it seems, so much (trouble)
bòn-hē" pusi ārju-dàm-lo. "O chònghōlosō chònghōlosō!
caused" saying he summoned. "O frog, frog!
kopī-āpòt nàng kārlē ā-dòn chòn-rai?"
for what reason you the squirrel's ladder jumping on broke?"
Chònghō thàkdèt—"Pī nē chòn-rai-rē-jī?
The frog answered—"How I was to help jumping on and breaking?
Mīsō-ròng-pō-sī nē-mī nē-kē kòr-ràk-lē: lā kesō-òng-
The big black ant my loins, even me, bit hard: that pain-great-
sī nē kārlē-ādòn-bō-pō nē chini-nē-dèt-si chòn-
from I squirrel's ladder (honorific) *I not knowingly jumped upon*
rai-tē."
and broke."

Rēchō pu-lē-lo—"Mai! mīsō pu àn-pin
The King said again—"Oh! the ant, then, caused all the
bòn-hē" pusi ārju-dàm-lo. "O mīsō mīsō! pī-āpòt nàng
trouble" saying summoned. "O ant, ant! what-for did you
chònghōlosō-ā-mī kòr-ràk?" Mīsō pudèt—"Pī nē kòr-
the frog's loins bite severely?" The ant said—"How I was to
ràk-rē-jī? Ādàp nē-òng àn che-thòn-
help biting him? In the morning to my uncle rice I was going
dàm-lo: Chònghō tovār ingnī-thīp. Lā-lo
along carrying: the frog the road sitting down blocked. Thereupon

nē 'tovār nē pèk-thā' pulo: 'nē-rum-lē lut-nòn' pu.
I 'road to me free-leave' said: 'me underneath creep' he said.

Nē lut-thòt-lo: chònghō nē-thàk nē ingnī-thīp;
I crept under him: the frog on the top of me sat down tight;

lāsī nē ā-mī kòr-ràk."
therefore I his loins bit-severely."

Ànsī Rēchō pulo—"Nàng bàng-hīnī kelèt-dèt." Mīsō-kē
Then the King said—"You persons-two guilty-are." The ant

chujèng-pèn kòk-chèk-lo: nòn ā-vàm chèng-jàn.
hair of head-with they tied-firmly: now his-waist is very slender.

Chònghō-kē tārmē-làng-bòng-pèn sàp-phràt-phràt;
The frog a blistering creeper-with they soundly thrashed;

lāsī nòn phròk-se-nòk-tòk.
therefore now he is speckled all over.

NOTES.

This simple and direct narrative, easy of analysis, affords an excellent illustration of the mechanism of Mikir speech. First, we observe that the indication of time is put at the beginning of the sentence: *ārnī-sī*, "one day"; *ādàp*, "in the morning." Then follows the subject, then the object, and last the verb, with all its qualifications. The most frequent conjunction is *ànsī*, "and, so," which appears to be made up of *àn*, the particle indicating quantity, and *sī*, the particle indicating locality, used also for the conjunctive participle; the meaning would then be—"so much having passed (what follows comes next)." *Àn-kē*, *àn-lē* and *àn-lo* have the same force.

For the tenses we find the usual suffixes, *-lo*, *-dèt*, for the narrative past, *-po* for the present-future, and *-jī* for the future. In the narrative a much-used auxiliary is *-lē*, which means "having arrived." The passage is remarkable for the number of cases in which, no ambiguity being possible, the tense-particle is omitted, and the past is expressed by the bare root, without, or more commonly with, an adverbial supplement. Thus, we have *pulo*, *pudèt*, and *pu* for "said"; *ingnī-thīp*, "he sat down and blocked," *kòr-ràk*, "bit severely," *chòn-rai*, "jumped upon and broke," *ròt-pèt*, "cut in two," *klō-dup*, "fell plump," *thīmur-phàk*, "rooted up," *sàp-rai*, "struck and broke," *lut-thòt*, "entered," *hēlàng-phlut*, "tore up suddenly," *pī-bup*, "killed by tumbling on him," *chò-pàn-vèk*, "was feeding, grazing," *sàp-phràt-phràt*, "beat soundly." Then, we notice that the great majority of these cases are examples of roots qualified by the addition of a particle which, while not used separately by itself, gives energy and definiteness to the verbal root; this method of heightening the force of verbs is a great characteristic of Mikir diction, and is at once the chief beauty and the chief difficulty (to a foreigner) of the language. The adverbial particles so used are very numerous, but they are appropriated to particular verbal roots, and if they were wrongly applied the result would be nonsense. Thus, the particle *lòt* is used with three verbs only, *thī*, "die," *ī*, "lie down," and *jàng* "close the eyes," and always precedes the verbal suffixes with these roots: it cannot be used with any other. *Thòt*, again, always occurs with *lut*, "to enter," *jòk* and *vār*, "to throw." *Bup* conveys the idea of a sudden blow or fall, and is used with verbs of falling or striking. *Dàp* and *dup* seem to have much the same force. *Pèt, koi, klip* are particles used to indicate completeness; *lut-pèt-lo*, "all have gone in," *ròt-pèt-lo*, "he cut through," *chō-koi-lo*, "he ate up," *thū-koi-lo*, "he killed them all," *chō-klip-lo*, "he devoured them." Several of these auxiliary particles seem to be onomatopoetic.

Much resembling the use of these particles are the cases in which verbal roots are combined together to form a single expression. Thus, in our story, *thòn-dàm-lo* "he carrying went"; *do-kòk-lē* "remaining tied-up"; *ingnī-dun-chèt-lo* "he sat down suddenly (*chèt*) when the ant was passing (*dun*)" (*dun* means "to be with," and is constantly used as an auxiliary, but can also be employed alone in the sense "to go with"); *ārju-dàm-lo* "he summoned to answer"; *nē klō-nàng-po* "I must necessarily fall" (*nàng*, verb of necessity).

The story gives a number of examples of the remarkable Mikir negative verb: *pèk-pē*, "did not give way (*pèk*)"; *dàm-dē*, "did not go"; *pī nē kònglòng-bup-bē-jī*, "how was I not to roll down upon him and smash him?" where the negative syllable *bē* borrows the initial consonant of the qualifying particle *bup;* similarly, *hēlàng-phlut-phlē* "not suddenly root up"; *sàp-raī-rē* "not strike and break"; *chòn-rai-rē* "not jump upon and break"; *chini-nē-dèt-sī* "not knowing" (where *chini* is a loan-word from Assamese).

As regards vocabulary, *thā* in *nē-pèk-thā* is the imperative particle: another such particle (rarely occurring) is *tē* in *nē lut-thòt-rā dàm-tē; rā* is used as the suffix of the conjunctive participle in a string of imperatives. *Hòr* in *dàm-hòr-lē* indicates plurality: "*every one* has to pass under me"; other such particles are *jō* and *jàm*. *Tā* in *chònghō-tā* and *misō-tā* gives definiteness and emphasis; so also *kē* in *nē-kē*, &c. *Sārpō* in *kārlē sārpō* means "big chief": *pō* is a syllable added to give honour and dignity. Notice intensiveness indicated by reduplication in *āningthī-ningthī*, "*very* angry"; *ning-thī*, angry, is made up of *ning*, mind, and *thī* to be vexed (also to die). *Hànthār*: see note on p. 46. *Ròt-pèt* means to cut down a slender stem or twig by drawing a knife across it: *pī-pèt* to cut down a thick trunk of a tree; *ròt* is used for drawing a bow across a fiddle in *kum-kiròt* "fiddle-scraping." *Belèng* means a shovel or tray for winnowing rice; *phàk-belèng-pī* is a wild pig, because he roots about in the earth with his snout like a shovel; *-pī* is a syllable used to form augmentatives, as *-sō* indicates a diminutive. *Bisār*, to hold a judicial inquiry, is Assamese. *Hèmphū*, "owner," the God Mikirs belong to. *Vo-ārbīpī*, "a small bird, the size of a sparrow" (not the sparrow itself, which in Mikir is *vo-puru*). *Nē chōpàn-vèk*, "I was grazing"; *chōpàn* is used of feeding for animals only; *vèk* (or *vèk-vèk*) is a particle indicating continuance. *Mamàtsī* is used of some sudden and unpleasant interruption: *klèm-vèk-vèk mamàtsī thī-lo*, "he died suddenly as he was working"; *nē àn chō-vèk mamàtsī nē chòk-dèt*, "he beat me while I was eating." Notice, finally, *nòn*, the particle most often used to indicate a strong imperative, here in its original sense of "now"; in this meaning it is usually emphasised by adding *kē* or *lē*, *nònkē*, *nònlē*.

II.

JÀNGRĒSŌ PÈN Ā-ÒNG-ĀTUM ATOMŌ.

THE ORPHAN AND HIS UNCLES ' STORY.

Hākō inut āhèm-ēpī āsōpō inut-pèt do; lā
Once on a time one widow a son only one had; she

āchèklē-mār kòrtē bàng-theròk do. Ànsī
(woman's) brothers (plural) *brothers persons-six had. Now*

ārnī-sī ārnī-kàngsàm ā-òngmār-ātum
one day in the cool of the day (*evening*) *his maternal uncles*

NOTES.

Here we have a narrative of a more complex character than that of the first story, with a richer vocabulary, and abounding in the descriptive adverbial particles which are the main feature of the language.

Jàngrē, orphan: *sō* is a diminutive particle. *Jàngrē* indicates that one parent is dead; *jàngrèng* is used when neither survives.

Inut, a loan-word from the Khasi *ngut*, used for the enumeration of persons: in Mikir initial *ng* is inadmissible.

Hèm-ēpī, widow, literally, "sole mistress of the house" (*hèm*); the syllable *ē* is perhaps a thinning down of *ā*; *pī* is the feminine affix, here of dignity.

Āchèklē, brother, used only by a woman speaking of her brothers; *ik* is used by both sexes; *mār*, collective particle, used to form plurals: often *ātum* is added; *kòrtē*, brother; both *kòr* and *tē* separately may be used for either brother or sister; *bàng*, the class-word used for human beings before numerals.

Do, a verb meaning to stay, dwell, exist; specially, it has the meaning "to live with as a wife," and is the correlative of *èn*, "to take (to wife)."

Ārnī-kàngsàm, "day-becoming-cool-time," the late afternoon. As is natural where there are no clocks, the divisions of the day are marked by other means than the count of hours. *Ārnī* is a day (or sun), regarded without reference to the lapse of time = French *jour; ānērlo* is a day's space = *journée.* Similarly, *ājō* is a night, *jīrlo* a night's space. The first indication of coming day is *vo-khu ē-thē*, "first cock-crow"; then follows *vo-khu thē-nī*, "second cock-crow," and *vo-khu thē-thòm*, "third cock-crow"; then *thē-àng prinprē-lē*, "just before dawn"; then *ādàp kàng-thàng*, dawn (*ādàp*, general word for morning); then *nērlo-chitim*, "day-middle," noon; then *ārnī thē-lēlo*, "the sun at its height"; then *ārnī-kàngsàm*, "the sun becoming cool," afternoon; then *ingting lim-rim*, or *ingting-rim*, dusk. Then begins *ājō*, night, when the evening meal is

vàng-sī jàngrēsō-āphàn nàng-hànglo— "Osā́!
having come the orphan (accus.) *called-to— "Nephew!*

rū cho-dū-dàm-nàng." Ànsī jàngrēsō-tā dun-lo.
fish-trap set up-go-let-us." So the orphan went with them.

Ànsī āòng-mār kòrtē bàng-theròk-kē làng-thàk-sī pàt
Then his uncles, the brothers persons-six, up-stream a dam

mē-sèn-sī rū dū-lo. Jàngrēsō-kē ā-òngmār-ātum
having well built the trap set up. The orphan his uncles

ā-rū-pàt ā-bēr-sī ārlòng dū-ī phàng-ō-phàng-ā-sī
'trap-dam below stones having set up carelessly, disorderly,

rū dū-lo, ànsī hèm nàng-che-voi-lo. Ànsī lātum ādàp
trap set up, and home returned Then they in the morning

rū che-vàt-dàm-lo. Ā-òngmār-ātum ā-rū-pàt
the trap-their went to inspect. His uncles 'trap-dam

àn kepàt-pemē-tā, chikung-chikàng-tā che-vār-
so very well-built though, one cray-fish even had not thrown

thòt-thē; jàngrēsō ā-rū pukē, òk kejàng
itself into it; the orphan's trap as for, fish holding, entering

ā-rū tèngsèt. Ànsī ā-òngmār-ātum pulo—"Osā́!
his trap was quite full. Then his uncles said "Nephew!

taken, after which soon comes the first sleep, *àn-chō mèk-bur*, "rice-having-eaten eye-close"; then *jīrlo chitīm*, midnight.

Nàng-, a particle used, prefixed to verbs, to give vividness, is really the pronoun of the 2nd person singular, emphasis being given by referring the verb to the person addressed. *Nàng* at the end of the phrase is the verb of necessity = must; it often means "let us do this or that."

Pàt, as a noun, is a stone dam or fence, put across a stream with an opening in the middle in which the bamboo cage or fish-trap, *rū*, is placed; as a verb, it means to build such a dam or fence; *dū* means to place a thing so that it will catch or intercept something else.

Làng, water, stream: *làng-thàk* up-stream, *lāng-bēr* down-stream.

Che- prefixed to verbs gives them a reflexive meaning, and indicates that the action relates to the subject; *hèm che-voi-lo*, "he went home, to *his own* house"; *che-pu-lo*, "they said *to one another*"; *rū che-vàt-dàm-lo*, "they went to inspect *their own* fish-trap."

Chikung, a cray-fish; *chikàng* is an imitative sequent; similarly *phàng-ō*, carelessly, is followed by *phàng-ā*.

Jàng, as a verb, means to fill up, or, of the containing vessel, to hold —*òk-kejàng ā-rū*, "fish-to-hold-trap." Notice that *òk* means both fish and flesh; alone, it has usually the former meaning, or that of game, animals hunted; when joined to the name of an animal, the latter: *chainòng-ā-òk*, beef; *phàk-ā-òk*, pork; *bī-ā-òk*, goat's flesh.

Tèng and *plèng* both mean to be full: *sèt* is a particle added to strengthen the verb, taking the place of the tense-affix.

nētum dàk rū pàt-po, nàngli-kē làng-bēr-lē pàt-dàm-
we here trap will build, do you down-stream go and set

thu-nòn." Ànsī jàngrēsō ā-rū-pàt ā-òng-
your dam again." So the orphan's trap-dam (in) his

mār-ātum ā-rū dū-sī, jàngrēsō-kē làngbērsī
uncles their trap having set up, the orphan down stream

pàt-dàm-thu-lo; bòntā òk kejàng lāpu-thàk-thàk,
again built his dam; but the fish holding just that same way,

ā-òngmār-ātum ā-rū-kē òk-ējòn-nàt-tā jàng-thòt-thē,
the uncles 'trap one single fish even did not hold,

jàngrēsō ā-rū-kē òk kejàng plèngsèt-plèngsèt. Ànsī
the orphan's trap fish holding was quite full. So

ādàp-vàng-tā jàngrēsō ā-rū-pàt ā-òng-ātum che-
morning-every the orphan's trap-dam his uncles took for

rai-vēr-lo. Lāsī ādàp-vàng ālòng
themselves continually. Therefore every morning a place

kāprèk rū-pàt selèt-òng-sī, ādàp-īsī-kē
different (in) trap-set-up becoming very weary, morning one

rū dū-tekàng-kē-dètsī, bàp ā-phàng-āthàk bī
the trap not setting up at all, grass clump upon placing

tekàng-kòk. Ànsī ādàp lē-lō, ā-òngmār-ātum vàng-sī
he left it. So morning arrived, his uncles having come

jàngrēsō-āphàn nàng-hàng-lo: "Osā́, rū chevàt-dàm-
to the orphan called out: "Nephew! our traps let us go

lē-lo-nàng." Ànsī jàngrēsō pulo: "Nēlī-kē rū-tā
again and visit." Then the orphan said: "As for me, a trap

dū-tekàng-kē; dā bòntā, nànglītum-ārī
I have not even set up; come, nevertheless, (as) your companion

nàng-dun-jī," pusī dun-lo. Ànsī ā-rū
I will go with you," so saying he went with them. Then his trap

Ādàp-vàng, "every morning"; literally, "as (each) morning came." *Che-rai-vēr-lo*: here *che-* is the reflexive particle, *rai* a verb, to occupy, take up, *vēr* a particle indicating continuance, *lo* the tense-affix; the whole therefore means "they kept on taking up for themselves."

Dū-tekàng-kē-dèt-sī; *dū*, verb, to place, set; *tekàng*, a verb, to leave, depart; *kē*, negative syllable, reduplicated from last syllable of *tekàng*, *dèt*, particle of past time, *sī* affix of conjunctive participle; the whole therefore means "not having placed and left," "without setting up at all."

che-làng-dàmlo. Vo-thung lut-thòt thèk-dàm-lo.
he went to look at. A wood-pigeon having entered he found.

Ànsī lābàngsō ā-vo-thung ārī chekòksī hèm
So that wood pigeon his cord (with) having tied up home

che-vàn-lo.
he bought.

Lābàngsō ā-jàngrēsō chainòng-āsō-tā ē-jòn do, lā
That orphan a cow's child (a calf) also one had, it

kàngtu pukē māthā-thèk-thē jādi-thèk-thē, nei-bòt àn-
fat so very, as could not be imagined (doublet) *very sleek so*

pin. Ànkē ā-òngmār-ātum làng-un-ē-sī
greatly. Now his uncles to look at-being unable (through envy)

lābàngsō ā-chainòng-āsō thū-pèt-lo. Ànsī jàngrēsō
that calf killed (entirely). Then the orphan

lābàngsō ā-chainòng-āsō ā-rèng lumsī ākèng-ēhòng
that calf's skin having taken off, leg one

hā bāmòn kirī-pō ā-hèm pòn-sī pātu-dàm-
to a distance a brahman rich-big's house (to) taking, hid it

joi-lo. Ànsī jàngrēsō: "Mai! hèm-tā chainòng-
quietly. Then the orphan (said): "Oh! the house cow's

ā-òk āngnim-hai-òng-hē!" Ànkē bāmòn-pō
flesh (of) smells strongly!" Then the big brahman,

āningthī-sī pulo: "Tèkē nàng-kòrdut-pī ā-osō! konàt
becoming angry, said: "Tiger-bitten boy! where

Ējòn: jòn is the class-word for animals, as *bàng* is for persons, used with numerals; *ē-* is the prefix for "one"; the other numerals follow—*phàk jòn-nī, jòn-thòm*, two, three pigs.

Māthā thèk-thē; māthā, verb, to think, imagine; *thèk*, verb, to be able (also to see); *thē* negative affix: the whole therefore means "as could not be imagined"; *jādi-thèk-thē* is a doublet of the same meaning. *Àn-pin: àn*, particle of quantity; *pin* up to; also *tik; àn-pin* or *àn-tik* therefore means "to such a degree.'

Ākèng ē-hòng: ā its (the calf's), *kèng*, leg, *ē-*, one (as before), *hòng* class-word for enumerating parts of the body; *hā*, particle indicating distance; *Lā*, this, *hā-lā* that: *lā-dàk*, here, *hā-dàk*, there.

Tèkē-nàng-kòrdut-pī ā-osō: tèkē, "tiger"; *nàng*, particle of vividness, or, possibly, "you"; *kòr*, verb, to bite, *dut*, particle strengthening the verb and dispensing with tense-affix, *pī* syllable used in abuse, *ā-* syllable of relation, *osō* boy: the substantive being put last indicates that the verb is to be taken passively: "you tiger-bitten scoundrel of a boy!" As the Mikirs consider that to be eaten by a tiger is conclusive evidence of

āchainòng-ā-òksī dàk-lē ke-do-jī? Nē-kē bāmòn-lē.
cow's flesh here should be? I am a brahman.

Nàng peklàng thèk-sēr-mā-sī: thèkthē-lē nàng-pràn
You produce, show, must be able to: you cannot-if, your life

nàng-èn-jī." Ànsī jàngrēsō pulo— "Dei, tàngtē nē
I will take here." Then the orphan said—"Very well, then I

ri-po," pu-sī ri-lo. Ri-phàng-ō-phàng-ā-sī, ālàng
will search," saying he searched: searching carelessly, he

kāpātu-ālòng dàm-sī chainòng-āsō ā-kèng vung-dàm-phlut
hiding-place (to) going the calf's leg pull out suddenly

inghoi-lo: "Làng-nòn, chainòng ā-òk do," pu—
did: See-now, cow's flesh there is," saying—

"nē nàng pu-lo-hē!" Ànsī bāmòn pō— "Bàng-kāprèk-
"I told you so!" Then the big brahman— "people other

ātum vàng-thèk-dun-tē, nē-jàt vīrdèt-jī" pu,
(plur.) *come-see-together-if, my-caste will be destroyed" saying,*

pherē-sī jàngrēsō-āphàn pulo: "Jàngrēsō, pō-ārnàm-pō! pàk-tà
fearing the orphan-to said: "Orphan, my good sir! any one

thàn-ri-nòn! dohòn màntung-īsī nàng pī-po"— pusī
do not tell! money a cloth-full-one you I will give," saying

dohòn màntung-īsī pīlo. Ànsī jàngrēsō lābàngsō ādohòn
money a cloth-full gave. Then the orphan that money

the wickedness of the victim, the phrase is equivalent to "you wicked wretch of a boy!"

Nàng peklàng thèk-sēr mā-sī; *nàng*, "you," *klàng*, verb, "to see, observe"; *pe-*, causative particle, so that *peklàng* means "to show, to produce"; *thèk*, verb, to be able, *sēr* strengthening particle, "fully": *mā*, syllable used for direct or indirect questions: *dojī-mā?* "will you marry me?" *Nàng pēsō èn-tàng-mā?* "have you taken a wife?"; then, for alternatives, *do-jī-mā do-dē-mā?* "will you marry him or not?"; and lastly, as here, "*if* you are not able to produce—then," etc.; *sī*, affix of conjunctive participle, properly a locative particle.

Dei, "very good," a loan-word from Khasi. *Tàng-tē*, "then,"—properly "not having finished"; *tàng* is the verb meaning to be ended, completed, *tē* the negative syllable.

Vung-dàm-phlut inghoi-lo. This periphrastic construction, in which *inghoi*, to do, is used to strengthen the verb, seems to be borrowed from Assamese; many examples occur further on.

Pō-ārnàm-pō! a honorific form of address; *pō*, literally, "father," but used also of a son (*cf.* the Hindustani *bābā*) *ārnàm*, God (Ass. *dēutā*), *pō*, big, honourable. For a girl the corresponding phrase is *pē-ārnàm-pī*. *Dohòn*, Assamese *dhòn* (*dhan*), wealth, money; notice that the *dh* is resolved by the insertion of a vowel; similarly, further on, *bahār* occurs for *bhār* (Ass.), a load; neither *dh* nor *bh* is used in purely Mikir words.

pòn-sī hèm che-voi-lo. Hèm che-lē-lo, ànsī
taking with him home returned. House his he arrived, and

ā-pei che-pu-lo: "nē-òng-ātum ā-tòn hàng-dàm-thā."
his mother (to) said: my uncles' basket go-ask-for."

Ànsī āpei dàm-sī hàng-dàm-lo: "Īk-mār-lī! nànglī
So his mother going asked for it: "Brothers! your

osā́ kipu, 'tòn tànghō.'" Ànsī tòn nàng-lō-lo. Ànsī
nephew says, 'a basket I want.'" So a basket they sent. Then

hèm-ēpī ā-īk-mār-ātum tòn pīsī che-
the widow's brothers the basket having given said among

pu-lo—"Tòn pī kànghoi-ī-jī-nē? làng-dun-tòn-
themselves—"The basket what is to do with? go and peep

thā"— pusi ākibī-ābàng toi-dun-lo; ànsī lā nàng-
(imper.)*—saying their youngest one they sent and he there*

làng-dun-tòn-lo, ànkē hotòn-pèn dohòn ketèng
went and watched, and the basket-with money measuring

nàng-thèk-dun-lo. Ansī nàng-kelàng-dun-tòn-ābàng
there he saw. Then there-the-one-who-had-watched-person

hèm che-voi-sī, ā-īk-mār thàn-dàm-lo—"Lā
house his having returned to, his brothers informed—"That

ē-osā́ konàt-tòng kelòng-dàm-lo-nē? hotòn-pèn
our-nephew wherever get-did he (all this money)? with a basket

dohòn ketèng chinàm sai-sē." Ànsī dohòn
money measure really he has to." So the money

tèng-tàng-dèt jàngrēsō ā-pei-tā tòn
measuring-finished-having the orphan's mother the basket

thòn-dàm-lo, ànkē āchèklē-mār nàng-pu-dun-lo "Osā́
returned, and her brothers there said to her "Nephew

Tòn, hotòn, one of the numerous words for basket. *Tàng-hō,* a word used by a messenger to express the wish of him who sent him to ask for something: not used in other phrases. *Tòn pī kànghoi-ī-jī nē* "the basket for the purpose of doing what is?" *Pī,* what, *kànghoi,* infinitive, to do, *-ī* syllable added to indicate purpose, *jī* affix of future, *nē,* particle of enquiry, an Assamese loan-word. *Làng-dun-tòn-thā: làng,* verb, to look, *dun,* verb, to go with, to be with, *tòn,* verb, to peep, pry, *thā,* imperative particle. *Tèng,* to measure, with a vessel of known contents; originally, to fill (see above, *tèngsèt = plèngsèt*). *Konàt-tòng kelòng-dàm-lo-nē: konàt,* where: *tòng,* a particle expressing uncertainty: "where on earth did he get it"? *Sai-sē* "in order to"; "he really (*chinàm*) has to use a basket *in order to* measure this mass of money!" *Thòn,* to return

nàng-toi-thā." Ànsī hèm-ēpī hèm nàng-che-lē-sī āsōpō-
here send." So the widow home having arrived her son

āphàn che-pulo—"Nàng òng-ātum kipu 'Vàng-thā-tu tànghō
to said— "Your uncles say 'Come here, we want you,

pō.'" Ànsī jàngrēsō-tā dàmlo. Ànkē ā-òng-ātum nàng
father.'" So the orphan went. And his uncles there

ārju-lo—"Konàt ādohòn-sī nànglī kelòng-dàm?" Ànsī
asked—"Where all this money you obtained?" And

jàngrēsō pulo: "Chainòng-ā-òk ā-nàm: nànglī-tum-nē-
the orphan said: "Cow's flesh (of) price (it is): (by) you my

kithū-pī-pèt ā-chainòng ā-òk-sī nēlī kejòr-dàm;
killed-entirely cow's flesh I went a-selling;

chetàngtē chehàng-jō 'àn-pin làng?'"
it not being sufficient, together they asked 'is there only so much?'"

Ànsī āòng-mār ārju-thu-lē-lo: "Tàngtē chainòng-ā-òk jòr-
Then his uncles asked again: "Then cow's flesh go

dàm-tē lā-tum ènjī-làng-mā?" Ànsī jàngrēsō
a-selling if (we), they will taking-go on?" And the orphan

pulo— "En-jī làng-tē; nànglī-tum-kē
said—"They will go on taking certainly; you

chainòng-do-ō-pārā lālē thū-koi-rā ā-òk
cows having many because, therefore killing them all their flesh

a thing borrowed. *Vàng-thā-tu tàng-hō-pō:* notice the use of *pō*, father, as a respectful address, by the mother to her son; so also the uncles address their nephew respectfully with *nàng-lī*. *Nànglī-tum-nē-kithū-pī-pèt āchainòng:* notice the string of descriptive words prefixed adjectivally to the noun: this is an excellent example of the manner in which Mikir deals with what in English would be a relative sentence—"the cow of mine which you put to death by cutting her up"; literally, "by-you-my-killed-and-cut-up cow." *Thū*, to kill by cutting: *pī*, here a verb meaning to cut a large mass (see note to preceding story, p. 94); *pèt* adverbial supplement indicating completeness.

Chetàng-tē, "It is not enough": *che*, reflexive particle, *tàng*, verb, to complete, finish; *tē*, negative: literally, "it does not finish our business, it does not do all we want." *Che-hàng-jō: hàng*, to call out, summon; *che*, as before, indicates that they all called out together; *jō* is one of the particles used to indicate plurality; others (which will be found further on) are *jàm* and *krei*. *Làng*, an auxiliary verb which seems to indicate continuousness, to go on being or doing. Observe that *-tē* is used to indicate the two parts of a conditional sentence: "*chainòng ā-òk jòr-dàm-tē, èn-jī làng-tē* "if we go selling cow's flesh, they will go on taking it." In *chainòng-do-ō-pārā*, *ō* is a syllable indicating multitude, perhaps

jòr-dàm-tē, ko-ànsī dohòn kevàn-jī?" Ànsī
if you go selling how much money you will bring?" So

ā-òngmār kòrtē-bāng-theròk ābàng-phu ējòn chainòng
his uncles brothers the six each one one cow

thū-sī ā-òk bahār pòn-sī jòr-dàm-lo, ànsī
having killed, its flesh load having taken, went to sell it, and

jàngrēsō thàn-dun-lo— "Nànglī-tum hālā
the orphan explained to them— "You that (distant)

bāmòn kirī-pō ā-ròng-lē jòr-dàm-nòn: lā-ròng
brahman rich-big's village in go and sell: that village (at) when

lē-lo-tē 'chainòng ā-òk èn-jī-làng-mā' pu-rā
you arrive, 'cow's flesh will (any one) go on taking?' saying

ārju-nòn." Ànsī lātum kòrtē-bàng-theròk chainòng ā-òk
ask." So these brothers six cow's flesh

pònsī dàmlo, hā bāmòn-āròng lē-sī, "Chainòng-
taking went, that Brahman's village having arrived, "Cow's

ā-òk èn-jī làng mā?" pu ārju-lo. Ànsī
flesh will (any one) take more?" saying asked. And

"èn-jī-làng, vàn-nòn," pu nàng-hàng-lo. Ànsī
"we will take more, bring it here," saying they called out. So

bāmòn-pō ā-hèm lē-lo. Ànsī bāmòn-pō
the big brahman's house they reached. Then the big brahman's

ròng-īsī āsànghō che-pàngrum-pèt-sī, lā
village-whole inhabitants, having collected all together, those

chainòng-ā-òk kejòr-dàm-ātum kòrtē bàng-theròk,
cow's flesh bringing to sell-people, the six brothers,

nèp-sī, ā-rī kòk-krei-sī, jāsemèt chòk-sī
having seized, their hands tied firmly having, severely having beaten,

pulo: "Nētum bāmòn-lē: 'chainòng-āòk èn-jī mā?'
said: "We brahmans are: 'cow's flesh will any one take?'

pu nàng nàng-kātirvā-hai?" pu-sī lō-lo.
saying, you here-solicit a customer dare?" saying let them go.

another form of *òng*; *pūrā* is a loan-word from Assamese. *Ābàng-phū*, "each one"; also *ābàng-phū-īsī* (used further on); *phū* means "head," *īsī* "one"; the latter is used in *bāmòn-pō-ròng-īsī* in the sense of "the whole," "as one man." *Ā-rī-kòk-krei-sī*: *ā-rī* "their hands," *kòk*, verb, "to tie with a noose," *krei*, particle of plurality. *Kātirvā*, "to offer for

Lā chainòng-ā-òk kevàn-ātum-tā hèm che-voi-lo, ànsī
These cow's-flesh bringing persons home their own went, and

tovār chingvai-pòn-lo: "Mai! àn-lē ālang
on the way took counsel together: "Oh! how much that

jangrēsō ē-kechōbei! ē-chainòng ē-haidi ē-pā-chi-thū-
orphan us has cheated! our cattle (doublet) *he has caused us to*

koi-làng; āphu-thàk-tā ē-rèng ē-hu ē-kā-
kill all; over and above that our skin (doublet) *to us he has*

pesō. Āpòt-kē kelē-pèn ā-hèm
caused to smart. Therefore immediately on arriving his house

mē-kei-dàm-po-nàng." Ànsī hèm che-lē-lo ànkē jàng-
fire-set-to let-us-go." So home they arrived, and the

rēsō ā-hèm mē-kei-dàm-dut inghoi-lo. Ànsī jàngrēsō
orphan's house fire-setting did. Then the orphan

ātum hīnī chibū-sī hèm mē-kechō āphēlō
baskets-two having woven, house-fire-eaten, devoured (*of*) *ashes*

hum-sī bahār pòn-lo, ànsī hā mèk-kesō
having collected a load took, and that (*distant*) *sore-eyed*

āròng lē-lo. Lābàngsō āròng ārlèng ābàng-
(*people's*) *village went to. That village* (*of*) *men, each one*

phu-tā āmèk-kesō-ābàng àngsē. Ànkē phēlō
of them, sore-eyed folk were only. So ashes (*of*)

ā-bahār-pèn jàngrēsō lātum nàng-thèksī nàng-ārju-lo—
a load-with the orphan they having seen, called out to him—

"Nàng kopī kevàng lādāk?" Jàngrēsō thàk-dèt—
"Thou what for comest thou hither?" The orphan answered—

"Ai nàngtum āròng mèk-kesō ā-vur do-tàng-pu
"Oh! your village sore eyes disease has finished getting, thus

ārju-lòngsī nē mèk-kesō ā-bàp nàng-
having got to hear, I (*for*) *sore-eyed people medicine here am*

sale," a loan-word from Khasi (*tyrwa*). *Ē-ke-chōbei*, "us he has cheated," *ē-* is the pronoun of the first person plural including the person addressed. Notice the doublets—*ēchainòng ēhaidi* "our cattle," *ērèng ē-hu*, "our skins" (*hu*, "hide, bark of a tree"), and observe how *ē-* is prefixed to each part of the sentence. *Ātum chibūsī*: *tum* is here a bamboo basket in which to carry a load on the back; *bū*, "to plait or weave." *Hèm mē-kechō* "the house that had been *eaten* (*chō*) by fire (*mē*)"; *hum*, to pick up, collect. *Phēlō* means both "ashes" and "cotton." *Ārju-lòng-sī*, "having got (*lòng*) to hear (*ārju*)." *Ārju* means both "to hear" and "to ask."

kejòr." Ànsī lātum pulo—" Ai! tàngtē mē-òng-chòt-lo,
selling." Then they said—" Oh! then (that) is very good indeed,

pō-ārnàm-pō!" pusi ròng-īsī āsànghō dohòn
my good sir!" so saying the whole village inhabitants money

chi-rung-sī dohòn-bahār-īsī jàngrēsō nàng-pīlo.
having collected, of money load one to the orphan there-gave.

Ànsī jàngrēsō pulo: "Lābàngso ā-bàp nònkē
Then the orphan said: "That medicine immediately

chi-hī-rī-thā: mō nē tovār ēbèng
do not apply (rub) to yourselves: afterwards I the road a piece

lēlo-tē, 'chi-hī-nòn' pu nē nàng-pupo,
have gone when, 'apply (rub) it' saying I will tell you,

àn-lē chi-hī-nòn." Ànsī dohòn-bahār-īsī phēlō
then (and not before) apply it." Then money-load-one ashes (of)

ā-nàm jàngrēsō lòng-sī, hèm chevoilo. Ànkē lā
price the orphan having got, home to his returned. When he

tovār mē nàng-lē-lo, mèk-ā-vur-kelòng-ātum
road a little had gone eye disease who had got people

jàngrēsō-āphàn 'chi-hī-nòn-tu-mā?' pu hàng-lo.
The orphan-to "shall we apply it now?" saying called out.

Jàngrēsō nàng-thàk-dèt "thā"; tebòk-hèt tik-kē
The orphan answered "wait"; near so long as,

"thā" pu-bòm-sī lā hā hēloving lē-lo; ànkē
"wait" saying having continued, he to a distance arrived; and

"nàng-phō-dun-un-ē-lo" pu māthā-lo,
"here reach to me they cannot" saying he thought, "the

"bàp chi-hī-nòn" pu jàngrēsō nàng-hàng-lo. Ànsī
medicine rub in now" saying, the orphan there called out. Then

mèk-kesō-ātum jàngrēsō-kevàn-āphēlō ā-mèk
eyes the sufferers from pain orphan-brought-ashes on their eyes

che-hī-lo. Lā bàp kāchi-hī-pèn-āpārā, āmèk ki-krū
rubbed. That medicine applying from at once their eyes smarted

pukē māthā-thèk-thē jādi thèk-thē: āmèk kesō
so much, it cannot be imagined (doublet)*: their eyes sore*

Chi-hī-rī-thā, *chi* reflexive particle; *hī*, verb, "to rub in"; *rī* particle for the negative imperative, "do not"; *thā*, ordinary imperative affix, which may be dispensed with when the negative particle is used. *Thā!* "wait"!

tàn-muchòt che-plàng-lo. Ànsī lātum chipulo:
more much became. Then they said to one another:

"Mai! àn-lē ālàng ē-ke-chōbei tekàng: lū
"Oh! so much he us having cheated has left: he

vàng-thu-lo-tē, ā-rī kòk-dòng-rā chòk-nàng." Jàngrēsō-kē
comes-again-if, his hands tying fast let us beat him." The orphan

hēm che-lē-sī āpei-āphàn "nē-òng-ātum āhotòn èn-dàm-
home having come his mother-to "my uncles' basket take-go-

lē-thā" pu toi-lē-lo. Ànsī hèm-ēpī ā-īkmār-ātum
again," saying he sent again. Then the widow her brothers'

ā-hèm hotòn hàng-dàm-lē-lo. Ànsī hotòn nàng-lō-sī
house basket to ask-went again. Then the basket having sent

lātum kòrtē-bàng-theròk chi-pu-lē-lo— "Dā,
they brothers six said again among themselves—"Go,

ākibī, làng-dun-lē-thā; hotòn pi-tòng
youngest, watch again; (with) the basket what in the world

kànghoi-ī-jī-nē?" Ànsī ākibī-ābàng nàng-làng-dun-
is he going to do?" Then the youngest went there to watch

tòn-lē-lo. Jàngrēsō dohòn ketèng nàng-thèk-dun-
secretly again. The orphan the money measuring there he saw

le-lo. Ànke nàng-kelàng-dun-tòn abàng hèm che-voi-sī
again. Then there watching-secretly person home returning

à-īkmār che-thàn-dàm-lē-lo— "Ē-osā chu-
his brothers (to) explained, related, again—"Our nephew than

āphàn-tē nòn dohòn kevàn òng-muchòt lē-lo." Ànkē
last time now money bringing much more has arrived." Then

lātum kòrtē-bàng-theròk jàngrēsō-ālòng dàm-sī ārju-dàm-lo—
they the six brothers the orphan-near going asked—

"Konàt ādohòn-sī nànglī lòng-dām-ō-lo?"
"Where (all) this money you have got so much more!"

Ànsī jàngrēsō nàng-thàk-dun-lo— "Nànglī-tum-mē-nē
Then the orphan there answered them— "(By) you fire my

loan-word from Assamese. *Tàn-mu-chòt*: *mu* is the comparative particle, "more," *chòt* is the constant suffix to *mu*; *tàn*, a verb, to be severe, burdensome. *Chu-āphàn*, "than last time:". *āphàn* is the postposition of comparison = "than." *Lòng-dàm-ō-lo* "have you got *so much* more": *ō* is, as

kekei-pidut ā-hēm ā-phēlō ā-nàm. Nēlī phēlō
applied having house, its ashes price (it is). I ashes
kejòr-dàm-ālòng 'kedòr-dē' pu hàng-jō: 'àn-pin
selling-place (in) 'it is not enough' saying they cried: 'just so much
vàn-thū-thā' pusī pu. Nē-lī hèm-kē bīhèk-sī,
bring again' saying they said. My house being small,
ā-phēlō òng-ē-dèt; nànglī-tum āhèm-kē thē-dung-pārā,
its ashes not much were; Your houses, since they are large,
lālē mē kei-rā ā-phēlō jòr-dàm-tē, dohòn-lē nànglī-tum
therefore fire applying the ashes go selling-if, wealth ye
ko-ànsī kevàn-jī? Kevàn-sī nànglī-tum un-ē."
how much would bring? To bring it you would be unable."
Ànsī ā-òngmār kòrtē-bàng-theròk chi-pulo:
Then his uncles the six brethren said among themselves:
"Tàngtē itum-tā ē-hèm mē chekei-dàm-po-nàng." Ànkē
Then to our also houses fire having applied let us go." Then
hèm mē chekei-dàm-sī, hèm ā-phēlō hum-sī
houses fire their having-set-to, house-ashes having gathered,
kòrtē ābàng-phu-tā bahār-un-tik bahār-un-tik pòn-lo.
the brothers each individually as much as he could carry took.
Ànsī jàngrēsō thàn-dun-lē-lo: "Hā mèk-kesō-
Then the orphan explained to them again: "To that eye-sore-
āròng-lē pòn-nòn; hā ròng-ā-kung lē-lo-tē,
village up to take, carry; that distant village near when you arrive,
'Phēlō èn-jī-mā?' purā-punòn." Ànsī lātum kòrtē-
Ashes will you take?' saying say." So they brothers
bàng-theròk dàmlo. Hà mèk-kesō-ātum āròng pàng-lē-lo,
six went. That sore eyed people's village near arrived,
ànsī ārju-lo—"Phēlō èn-jī-mā?" Ànsī mèk-kesō-
and asked—"Ashes will you take?" Then the people with
àtum "Vàn-thā" pu nàng-hàng-lo; ànsī lātum dàm-sī
sore eyes "Bring it here" saying called out; then they going

before, the particle of multitude. *Kedòr-dē*: *dòr*, "to suffice, be enough"; *dē* negative syllable; *hàng-jō*, "they cried *in crowds*" (*jō*, particle of plurality). *Ong-ē-dèt*; *òng* "much," particle of quantity; *ē*, negative; *dèt* tense-suffix. *Thē-dung* "big"; *ke-thē* great, *dung* particle; on its addition the *ke-* is dropped.

ròng lē-lo; kelē-pèn ārī
the village arrived; immediately they arrived their hands

kòk-krei-inghoi-sī, lā ālàng-tum-kepòn-āphēlō-pèn
tying each, all, having done, those by-them-brought ashes-with

āmèk hī-sī jāsemèt chòklo; ànkē
their eyes having rubbed severely they beat them; then

chòk-thèng-dèt, lātum kòrtē-bàng-theròk
having been beaten and pummeled, those brothers six

hèm nàng-chevoilo. Ànkē tovār nàng-chèngvai-thu-
home returned. Then (on) the road they consulted together

lē-lo—"Mai! àn-lē ālàng ē-kechōbei-rā ē-rèng
again—"Oh! so much he us-having-cheated our skins

ē-kāpesō, āphu-thàk-tā ē-hèm i-rīt
he has caused to smart, over and above that our houses our fields

ē-pā-che-kei-koi; nònkē
us he has caused to set fire to and burn up; now

kelē-pèn ingchin-ārū bèng-rā
immediately we arrive iron-of a cage (in) having firmly secured

làng jòk-thòt-lo-nāng." Ànkē kelē-pèn
(him) water (into) let us throw him." So at once on arriving

jàngrēsō nèp-chèk ingchin-ārū-pèn bèng-chèk inghoi-lo,
the orphan seizing of iron-a cage-in firmly secure they did,

ànsī hābīt làng-bī ākethē-pī ā-kung
and in the jungle a pool very great (deep) on the bank

bī-dàm-kòk-lo. "Mō-lē làng
putting down they placed. "After a little while water (in)

nīm-po-nàng; nònkē kàt-āthai āvē-lo; āpòtkē
let us drown him; now run away-power he has not; therefore

àn che-chō-dàm-sī-nàng" pusī, àn che-chō-dàm-lo.
rice our-eat-go-let-us saying, rice-their they went to eat.

Ànkē ā-òngmār àn chechō-dàm-āphī, konānē
Then his uncles their rice had gone to eat after, some one or other

Hābīt, "in the jungle," locative of Assamese *hābī*, forest. It is noticeable that many, if not most, Assamese nouns borrowed by Mikir are taken over in the locative case (of which the final *t* is the proper ending in Assamese), as here: thus *dèt*, "country" = Ass. *dēh*; *munīt*, "man' = Ass., *muni*; *nòrokòt*, hell = Ass. *nòròk*. *Konānē* "some one or

rēchō-āsōpō òk nàng-kehung vàng-lo, ànsī jàngrēsō ā-dung
King's son deer there-hunting came, and the orphan near

nàng-lē-sī, jàngrēsō-āphàn ārju-lo "Kopī āpòtsī
having arrived, the orphan (accus.) *asked " What on account of*

ingchin-ārū-ārlō nàng-kebèng-chèk-lo?" Ànsī jàngrēsō
iron-cage-inside you are here firmly secured?" Then the orphan

pulo: "Nē-òng-mār-ātum āsōpī kemē pu māthā-thèk-
said: "My maternal uncles a daughter, how fair! as one cannot

thē àn-pin do. Lāsī 'èn-tu' pu nē-phàn
imagine so greatly have. Her 'take to wife' saying to me

nē-kipu, bòntā nē-kē 'èn-ē' pu kipusī,
me they say, but I 'will not take' saying replying,

nē-òng-mār-ātum āning-kithī-sī rū nē-kebèng-
my uncles becoming very angry cage (*in*) *me have*

chèk-lo." Ànsī rēchō-āsōpō pulo—"Chē! tàngtē nē
fastened up." Then the King's son said—"Oh! then I

èn-lòng-jī-mā?" "Lā rū-ārlō-lē nàng
(*her*) *take* (*to wife*) *shall be able?" "This cage into you*

nàng-do-tē, èn-lòng-jī-tē" pu jàngrēsō pulo:
here-get-in-if, you will be able to get her" saying the orphan said:

"ēlòm-tē nē-òng-ātum vàng-po, ànkē—'Ànhēlō-
"in a little while my uncles will come and—'Have you

mā?' pu nàng ārju-lo-tē, 'ànhēlō, èn-po,
anything to say?' saying you if they ask, 'all right, I will take her,

òngmār-lī'—purā punòn." "Tō, tàngtē," pu rēchō-āsōpō
uncles'— saying reply." "Yes, then," saying the King's son

pulo. Ànsī jàngrēsō rēchō-āsōpō-āphàn pulo—"Lā
said. Then the orphan the King's son-to said—"That

other," Ass. loan-word. *Kemē-pu* "she is so lovely!" *mē*, "to be fair, beautiful," *pu*, literally, "saying." *Èn-tu:* here *èn*, "take," has the special sense of "take to wife, marry" (see what is said of *do*, *ante*, p. 95); *tu*, one of the signs of the imperative mood, is perhaps borrowed from the Khasi *to*. *Bòntā*, "but," perhaps a Khasi loan-word. *Àn-hēlo-mā*, a difficult expression to translate: *àn* "so much," particle of quantity; *hēlo* "far"; *mā* particle of questioning; it might be rendered "how are you getting on?" literally "thus-far-what"? But it is also used in the answer to the question: *àn-hēlo* there seems to mean "all right"—"so far so good." *Tō-tàngtē; tō* is a Khasi loan-word: in that language it is

nàng-pē nàng-rī-pèn mamàtlė nàng rū-ārlo nàng-lut-lo-tē,
your coat your dhoti-with bedecked you cage-into here enter-if,
nàng chinī-dèt-po; āpòtkē nē ingpu-nòn:
you they will recognize at once; therefore me let out:
nē-pē nē-rī nàng pīpo, ànkē rū-ārlō lut-nòn."
my coat my dhoti you I will give, then cage-into enter."
Ànsī rēchō-āsōpō rū ingpu-sī jàngrēsō nàng-bār-
So the King's son the cage having opened the orphan there came
lo, ànsī jàngrēsō ā-pē ā-rī rēchō-āsōpō pīlo,
out, and the orphan his coat his dhoti to the king's son gave,
lā rēchō-āsōpō ā-pē, ā-rī, ā-lèk, ā-roi,
that King's son his coat, his dhoti, his necklace, his bracelets
jàngrēsō pī-thū-lo, ànkē rēchō-āsōpō
to the orphan gave in exchange, and the King's son
rū-ārlō lut-lo, ànsī jàngrēsō ingkīr-dun-thīp-lo.
into the cage entered, and the orphan the door made fast.
Ànsī jàngrēsō-tā rēchō-āsōpō ā-pē ā-rī ā-lèk
Then the orphan the King's son's clothes, dhoti, necklace,
ā-roi che-pindèng, āhormu kedo-àn chepindèng-sī,
bracelets, having put on, his things all having put on,
hā āhèm che-dàm-lo. Ànsī jàngrēsō ā-òngmār-tā
away to his house went. And the orphan's uncles also
àn chō-dàm-pèn nàng-che-voi-lo, rū-ālòng nàng-lē-lo,
rice eating-from there returned, at the cage's place arrived
ànsī ārju-lo— "àn-hēlō-mā osā?" "Ànhēlō
and asked— "have you anything to say, nephew?" "All right,
òngmārlī, èn-po" pu jàngrēsō-kethàn-
uncles, I will take," saying the orphan (by) instructed
kàng-āsòn-thòt rēchō-āsōpō pulo. Ànsī ingchin-ārū-pèn
according to the King's son said. Then the iron cage-with
làngbī vār-chuī inghoilo. Ànkē
deep pool (into) throw into water (him) they did. Then
jàngrēsō-ā-òngmār kòrtē-bàng-theròk chi-pu-lo—
the orphan's uncles brothers six said one to the other—

used in answer to a question to express assent = "very well." *Vār-chuī*, "to throw into water," "drown": so also *nīm-chuī*. It seems possible that *chuī* here may be an old word for water, corresponding to the Tibetan

"Àn ālàng ī-duk ē-kànghoi ā-pòt, nòn ànkē
"So much he us-trouble us-causing on account of, now however
ālàng thī-lo"; ànsī hèm che-voi-lo. Ànkē jàngrēsō
he is dead"; and home they returned. Then the orphan
pukē— kithī-jī kālī, rēchō-āsōpō ā-pē, ā-rī, ā-lèk,
as for— dead not at all, the King's son's coat, dhoti, necklace,
ā-roi che-pindèng mēsèn kemàt māthā-thèk-thē
bracelets having put on, beautifully adorned inconceivably,
jādī-thèk-thē-dèt thèk-dàm-thū-lē-lo! Ànsī lātum
unimaginably, they saw again on arrival! Then they
chi-pu-lē-lo— "Jàngrēsō thī-lòt-lo kālī!
said among themselves again—"The orphan is not dead at all!
Hā-lā-lē, kemàt-lèp-rā kā-pàng-ēlim-kē." Ànkē ā-dung
There he is, adorned and strutting in his finery." Then near him
lē-lo, jàngrēsō-āphàn ārju-thū-lēlo— "Osā́! nàmtu-sī
they went, the orphan (accus.) *asked-again—"Nephew! how*
nàngli nàng-kelē-tòng-ròk?" Ànsī jàngrēsō thàk-lēlo—
you here arrived so soon?" Then the orphan answered—
"Chē, òngmārlī, nē-phī-nē-phū-ātum dōlā-
"Oh, uncles, my grandmothers and grandfathers a palanquin-
pèn-sī nē nàng-kāpethòn-dun-kòk-lē; hālī nē-lī
with me here-caused to be escorted back; there I
lē-ròk-pèn-āpārā nē-phī-nē-phū-
from the first moment of arriving my grandmothers and
ātum pē-kemē, rī-kemē, lèk roi nē-kepī:
grandfathers coat-good, dhoti-good, necklace bracelets me gave:
lā làng-nòn! Nànglītum-āphàn-tā pevàng-tu-po-nàng
them look at! You-to also cause-to-come it is necessary
kephā-dun-pār: āsin nàng-kelō, lā sēr ā-tārī-lòn,
they sent word urgently: a sign they have sent, this gold-of knife,
làng-thā!" pu pe-klàng-lo. Ànsī ā-òngmār
look at it!" so saying he showed it to them. Then his uncles

chhu. Che-pindèng "having put on himself": *pindèng,* "to put on," is an Assamese loan-word. *Kithī-jī kālī:* the use of *jī,* the particle of the future, seems anomalous here: possibly the phrase means "he is not going to die, not looking as if he were going to die;" *kālī* is the emphatic separate negative. *Dōlā,* "a palanquin," Ass. loan-word. *Ke-phā-dun-pār: phā,* verb, to send a message: *dun,* verb, to be with: *pār* intensive

pulo—"Kopusī nēlītum kedàm-thèk-po?" "Ingchin ārū́
said— "*How we go shall be able?*" "*Iron cage*

ābàng-phū-īsī che-pòn-rā hā
person-head-one (i.e. *each one of you*) *taking for himself that*

làng-kung lut-dàm-īk-nòn" pu jàngrēsō pulo.
river bank (*to*) *get into it, good sirs*" *saying the orphan said.*

Ànsī lātum ingchin-ārū che-pòn-sī hā làng-kung
So they iron cages having taken that river-bank (*to*)

lut-dàm-lo. Ànsī jàngrēsō ingchin ārū rākdun-
got into them. Then the orphan (*in the*) *iron cages tightly*

hèt-ràkdunhèt-lo. Ànsī jàngrēsō āklèng-sī-ābàng ingchin-
tied up (*each one*). *Then the orphan the eldest one with the*

ārū-pèn làngbī vār-dàm-chuī inghoilo. Ànkē-phòng
iron cage deep pool (*into*) *throw did So then*

làng-ābuk-buruk vàng-jàm-cheplàng-lo; ànkē jàngrēsō
water-bubbles coming up many-continued; then the orphan

pu-lē-lo! "Jā! òngmārlī, làng-thā! nē-òng-ā-klèng-kē
said again! "*There! uncles, look! my uncle eldest*

lā nē-phī nē-phū hòr kipī-sī hòr
him my grandmother my grandfather beer having given beer

kàngrī-sī kā-chèng-òk-lo." Ànsī ādàk-vàn-tā
having drunk is vomiting." *Then the next one also*

làng-vār-lo. Ànkē kòrtē-bàng-theròk-tā làng-
he threw into the water. Then the brothers six having all

vār-klip-sī jàngrēsō hèm nàng-che-voi-lo. Ànsī
thrown into the river the orphan home returned. Then

jàngrēsō-āphàn ā-nī-mār-ātum nàng-ārju-lo—
the orphan (accus.) *his aunts* (*uncles' wives*) *there asked—*

"Nànglī òng-ātum nàmtusī vàng-jī!" "Tòng-tòng
"*Your uncles when will they come?*" "*Quickly*

particle, "urgently." *Nāngkelō* "they have sent": *lō* is a verb, "to send a thing," while *toi* means "to send a person." *Sēr*, gold; it is remarkable that the Tibetan word (*gsēr*, pronounced *sēr*) is used for this object of culture both in Khasi (*ksiar*) and Mikir, and not the Assamese (*sōn*, *hōn*); for silver, on the other hand, the Aryan *rūp* is in general use. *Lut-dàm-īk-nòn*; *lut*, verb, "enter," *dàm*, verb, "go"; *īk*, honorific address = "elder brother" (though he is speaking to his maternal uncles); *nòn* imperative particle. Note the doubling of the verb *ràk-dun-hèt-lo* to indicate repetition of the action in the case of each person.

vàng-vē: àn kāchephō-phē āpòtsī,
they will not come: so long not having met together on account of,

nòn kāchephō-lē-mā?" pu jàngrēsō pulo.
now have they not met at last?" saying the orphan said.

Ansī jō-thòm jō-philī do-sī ākō ā-nī-mār
Then nights-three nights-four having waited again his aunts

jàngrēsō āphàn nàng-ārju-thū-lē-lo—"Nànglī òng-ātum
the orphan (accus.) *asked again there—"Your uncles*

pi-āpòt vàng-vē-rèk-mā?" Ànsī jàngrēsō
what for have not come by this time?" Then the orphan

thàk-lo— "Vàng-dàp-pràng-po." Ànsī jō-nī
answered—"They will come to-morrow morning." Then nights-two

jō-thòm dosī lātum jàngrēsō-āphàn ārju-
nights-three having waited they the orphan (accus.) *asked*

dàm-thū-lē-lo—"Nànglī òng-ātum kopi-āpòtsī nòn-pu-tā
again—"Your uncles for what reason up to now

vàng-vē-dèt-mā?" Ànsī jàngrēsō thàn-lo— "Nòksèk-lē
have not come?" Then the orphan explained—"In the nòksèk

àn dèng-pī-īk-krei-nòn." Ànsī jàngrēsō ā-nī-mār-ātum
rice set on (honorific) *for each." Then the orphan's aunts*

"thī-koi-lo!" pu chinī-sī, chirūlo,
"they are really dead!" saging having recognized, wept,

chērnàp-lo, mòn-duk-lo, mòn-sā-lo. Ànsī jàngrēsō
lamented, and were plunged in sorrow. So the orphan

plànglo-philo, pàk-tā làng-un-ē-ābàng āvē-lo. Ànsī
became rich, any one to look on with envy there was not. So

jàngrēsō rēchō kethē chōsī rèng-mē-rèng-dòk-lo.
the orphan king great becoming, lived a happy and pleasant life.

Nòksèk-lē. The *nòksèk* (see plan of Mikir house at p. 8) is the part of the house where the food (*àn*, cooked rice) is placed as an offering to the *Manes*. *Dèng*, "to place a share, leave a share"; *pī* "give"; *īk* honorific (as above); *krei* particle of multitude = "for each one." *Mòn-duk-lo*, Assamese loan-words (*mon*, mind, heart, *dukh*, grief). *Làng-un-ē-ābàng* "a person who cannot (*un-ē*) look on (*làng*) another (for envy)."

III.

HĀRĀTĀ KUṄWAR ĀTOMO.

HARATA KUNWAR'S STORY.

Harata Kuṅwar kòrtē bàng-theròk,
Harata Kunwar (*and*) *his brothers* (*were*) *six persons,*

ākibī-sī Harata Kuṅwar. Āmehàng-kethèk-pèn-
the youngest (*being*) *Harata Kunwar. From the time of his*

āpārā thijòk, phàk-lèng ke-àp, tiki-kē inghoi-hē;
birth deer, wild pig shooting, he never did any field-work;

ā-īkmār bàng-phòngō-kē sai-kātiki. Ànsī lātum
his brothers, the five of them, laboured in the fields. Then they,

kòrtē bàng-phòngō ā-pō-pèn bàng-theròk chingvai-
the five brothers, with their father six persons, took counsel

lo: "Ālàng Harata Kunwar-kē tiki-kē inghoi-hē òk
together: "This Harata Kunwar doing no work deer

hung-chòt; āpārā ningvē chingvai-nòn." Ànsī
hunts only; therefore at night take counsel together." So

āningvē chingvai-lo. Āpō āsō āklèng-āphàn
that night they took counsel. His father his son eldest (accus.)

NOTES.

This story is a much more elaborate piece of composition than the last, and may be said to exhibit distinct marks of literary style. Its vocabulary is copious and varied, and it makes large use of a device which is employed in Mikir, as in Khasi,* to give amplitude to the phrase by duplicating the leading words; nearly every important term has its doublet, with the same meaning, following it.

Āmehàng-kethèk-pèn-āpārā: *āmehàng-kethèk*, "to see the face," is equivalent to "being born"; *pèn* and *āpārā*, the latter borrowed from the Assamese *parā*, have the same signification, and the latter is really superfluous. *Phàk-lèng*, shortened for *phàk-belèng*, "wild boar"; see the explanation of the term in the notes to No. I, p. 94. *Tiki-kē inghoi-hē*: notice that *both* verbs are given in the negative form; this is unusual.

* See "Khasi Monograph," p. 211.

ārju-lo—"Nàng kopusī àn nē-hī-po?" "Nē-pu-tàngtē
asked— "You how rice me-will-supply?" "As for me,

sārlār plàngsī jō-ārnī mē do-jī;
a headman having become night and day I will hold assembly;

sārlār ā-màn bàng-kevàn āhòr-āhàn-pèn-sī àn-
headman's perquisites by people brought the rice-beer-from rice-

lòk àn-mē hòr-làng hòr-pō nàng pī-jī." "Tàngtē
white rice-good beer (doublet) *to you I will give." "Then*

nàng ādàk-vàm-kē kopusī àn nē-hī-po?" "Nē-pu-tàngtē
you the next, how rice me will supply?" "As for me,

hēmai hànsārī plàng-sī jō-ārnī nokē no-pàk
a blacksmith (doublet) *becoming night and day knives daos*

thīp-jī; lā nokē nopàk nàng-kethīp-ātum
I will forge; by those knives and daos there made by me

kevàn ā-hòr ā-hàn ākovē ābithi pènsī
brought (i.e. *procured*) *beer* (doublet) *betel-nut pān-leaf together*

àn-lòk àn-mē āràk-chidhīr nàng-pījī." "Nàng
with rice-white rice-good spirit (doublet) *you I will give." "You*

ādàk-vàm ādunkē, kopusī àn nē-hī-po?" "Nē-pu-tàngtē
the second next to, how rice will you supply me?" "As for me,

sai-tiki-sī puru phàndār pelòng-sī ànlòk
field-work-doing granary store having got together rice-white

àn-mē hòr-làng hòr-pō nāng-pījī." "Nàng ādàkvàm
rice-good beer (doublet) *you I will give." "You the second*

ādun lē-thòt-kē, kopusī àn nēhīpo?" "Nē-pu
next coming after, how rice will you supply me?" "As for

tàngtē bàng-āhèm do-dun-sī, lābàng
me, (*other*) *person's house inhabiting as a companion, that person*

nē-kepī ā-àn āhòr āhàn-sī nàng pīpo." "Nàng
me given rice and beer (doublet) *you I will give." "You*

ādàkvàm-ādun-lē-thòt-kē kopusī àn nēhīpo?"
the second next coming after, how rice will you supply?"

Màn, "perquisites"; Assamese loan-word.

Kovē, "betel-nut," Khasi *kwai*, Ass. *guwā*. *Chidhīr*, "spirit," the doublet of *āràk* (itself a Hindi loan-word) is perhaps the Khasi *kiad-hiar*. Notice how, instead of using the ordinal numbers for second, third, fourth, and fifth brothers, the father employs clumsy periphrases to indicate the sequence. *Phàndār*, "store," Ass. loan-word (*bhandār*).

"Nē-pu-tàngtē bàng-ābàn āsòt plàngsī nē-
"*As for me, another person's slave* (doublet) *becoming me*

kepī ā-àn āhòr āhàn- pènsī nē-àn nàng pī-
given rice and beer-(doublet) *with, from, my rice you I will*

po." "Tàngtē nàng Harata-Kunwar-kē, kolopu-sī àn nē-
give." "*Then you Harata-Kunwar, in what way rice me*

hīpo?" "Nēpu-tàngtē Ārnàm-āsō Ārnī-āsō
will you supply?" "*As for me, God's child, Sun's child*

èn-sī rēchō kethē plàngsī, inghoi āthàk
having married, a king great having become, throne upon

inghu-āthàk, kāpòt-āthàk kāplèng-āthàk nàng pàngnī-
(doublet) *plank-upon* (doublet) *you having caused*

sī bàn-sòt-ātum nàng-rī nàng-kèng nàng-pechàm-
to sit slaves and maids your hands your feet having caused to

sī, hòr àn āràk-chidhīr nàng-pī-jī." Ànsī chingvai-
wash, beer rice spirits you I will give." *So they finished*

tànglo. Ānērlō sai-tiki-ālòng, Harata-
consulting together. That day, cultivation-place-in, Harata-

Kunwar ābàng-kāvē-āphī, ālàngtum kòrtē bàng-phòngō āpō-
Kunwar not being there, those brothers five, with

pèn bàng-theròk chingvai-thū-voi-phàk-lo. "Ālàng
their father persons-six, began to consult together again. "*That*

Harata-Kunwar Ārnàm Ārnī-āsō èn-sī rēchō
Harata-Kunwar God Sun's child having wedded a king

plàng-jī-sī pu? Konàt ārēchō-sī ālàngkē plàng-jī-mā?
will become, indeed? Where a king is he to become?

āpārā pethī-lòt-lo-nàng. Āpārā ningvē chingvai-thū
so then kill let us (him). So then at night time let us consult

sī-nàng." Āningvē àn-chōdèt jundèt
together again." *That night rice having eaten having drunk*

ālàngtum chingvai-lo, kopusī kāpethī āpòtlo.
they consulted together, how the killing was to be done.

Ā-bàn ā-sòt: in this doublet the second member, *sòt*, properly means "*female* slave"; a similar use of a word of different meaning as a duplicate term will be found below (p. 129), where *ā-mèk* "his eye" is followed by *ā-nō* "his ear," the meaning being "his eyes."

“ Āpārā hèm-thàp kīm-po-nàng; Harata-Kunwar-āphàn-kē
“ So then a field-hut let us build; Harata-Kunwar (accus.)

naidung-āhoi-lē kīm-pī-rā pehòn-po-nàng. Ànkē
clearing-on the border having built it let us cause to watch. Then

ētum ājō dàm-rā chīr-pèn tòk-òt-nàng.”
let us by night going with a spear thrust-and-kill-him.”

Ālàngtum kāchingvai Harata-Kunwar
Them taking counsel together Harata-Kunwar's eldest

ātēpī ārju-dun-lo. Ànsī ādàp àn-chōdèt
sister-in-law overheard. Then in the morning rice having eaten

jundèt ālàngtum kādo-kāvē sai-tiki-dàm-āphī
having drunk they all having gone to work after,

Harata-Kunwar òk-hung-pèn hèm vànglo. Ànsī
Harata-Kunwar from hunting home came. Then his sister-

ātēpī àn pīlo; àn-chōdèt jundet
in-law rice gave him; rice having eaten having drunk

ātēpī pulo— “ Nàng mīsō nàng-
his sister-in-law said—“ (On) you a black ant (here = *louse*) *there*

prōlàng, Harata-Kunwar.” Ànsī ā-rèk pēlo, pē-mā-
let me kill, Harata-Kunwar.” So a louse she killed, while

pē-lo āmèk-krī H. K. ākèng-āthàk nàng-klō-
she was killing it a tear H. K.'s leg-on fell with a

bup. Ànsī H. K. ārju-lo —“ Tēpī, nàng chiru-dèt-
splash. Then H. K. asked —“ Sister-in-law! you are

mā-dā?” Ànsī ātēpī pulo— “ Chiru-rē:
weeping?” And his sister-in-law said—“ I am not weeping:

ārvē ā-mu-sī nàng-ke-klō.” Ākō pē-mā-pē
rain-of a drop has fallen on you.” Again while she was killing,

āmèk-krī nàng-klō-thū-voi-phàk. H. K. ārju-thū-lē-lo—
a tear fell upon him a second time. H. K. asked again—

“ Nàng chiru-dèt āvī, tēpī! nē-thàn-nòn, kopi-
“ You crying are really, sister-in-law! me explain to, for

Kādo-kāvē, literally, “being-not-being,” a periphrasis for “all of them.’ *Mīsō*, “a black ant,” used *verecundiæ causâ* for *rèk*, “louse.” Notice the idiom *pē-mā-pē-lo*, where the insertion of *mā* between the repeated roots indicates the time during which an act is done.

āpòtsī nàng kāchiru-mā." Ànsī thàn-lo: "nē-
what reason you are crying." Then she explained: "my

lòkhai àn-tàngtē nàng-īk-ātum kāchingvai,
father-in-law and also your brethren have taken counsel together,

hèm-thàp nàng pehòn-sī ājō chīr-
a jungle-hut (in) you having made to watch, by night with a

pèn nàng tòk-òt-jī-sī-pu: lāsī nē kā-
spear you will pierce and kill-they say: that is why I am

chiru." Ànsī H. K. pulo— "Pherē nàng-nē; nàng
weeping." Then H. K. said—"You need not be afraid; you

nē-thàn-lo, mē-lo; menàp ā-dàp nàng promàn lòng-
me have told, it is well; to-morrow morning you proof will

jī. Nē thī-thē-tàng-tē, ālàngtum āphī-āphī hèm nàng-
get. I not dead am-if, them after home here

dunsī chilònghē thàm-theròk nē sārnung nàng-
coming, worm-castings clods six I roof (upon) here

vār-po: Lālē sārnung nē-nàngkevār ārkī āvē-dèt,
will throw: that if roof (on) my-here-throwing noise there is not,

tàngtē nē kithī-lo." Ànsī ārnī-kàngsàm āpòr ā-īk-
then I shall be dead." Then day-becoming cool-time his

ātum rīt-pèn nàng-che-voi-lo, ànsī āpō pulo:
brothers from the field there returned, and his father said:

"Ningvē-kē H. K.-tā hèm-thàp hòn-dun nàng-po;
This night our H. K. jungle hut (in) go watching must;

sòk phàk chō-koi-lo; hā naidung-āhoi nētum
the paddy pigs are eating up; there clearing-on border we

hèm-thàp nàng-kīm-pī-koi-lo." Ànsī àn-chō-dèt
a jungle-hut have finished building." Then rice having eaten

jun-dèt, H. K. ā-thai che-pòn-sī hèm-thàp
having drunk, H. K. his bow taking with him the jungle-hut

dàm-lo: ànsī chitū- ā-thē lik-pòn-sī ā-làng
went-to; and (name of a plant) fruit having gathered, its juice

An-tàngtē, "and also," literally, "so much not finished." *Pherē nàng-nē*: *nàng* is the verb of necessity, *nē* the negative particle: "there is no need for fear." *Promàn*, "proof," Ass.

Chitū, the plant called in Assamese *puroi-sāk*, *Basella lucida*; its fruit has a red juice.

phingu-ā-òp-pèn bī-sī, ārlèng ki-ī ā-sònthòt-sī-
plantain-sheath-in having put, man sleeping (of) likeness

āthàk pē pāchàp-sī pi-ī-lo; H. K.-kē
upon clothes having put round he put it to sleep; H. K. himself

sòk ā-sē ārlō chepātu-joi-lo. Ànsī àn-chō-mèk-
rice-arch underneath hid himself quietly. Then after their first

bur ā-pō ā-īk-ātum chingthurlo:— "Vàng-noi,
sleep his father his brothers awoke one another:—"Come now,

H. K. pithī-dàm-po nàng." Ànsī ābàng-phū chīr-ēpàk
H. K. to kill let us go!" Then each one of them a spear-one

chi-vàn-sī, H. K. āhèm-thàp-ālòng vàng-lo. Ànsī
taking with him, H. K.'s jungle-hut-place (to) came. Then

āpō pulo—"Dā-nàng, āklèng! ārlu-rā tòk-dàm-
his father said—"Go you, the eldest, climbing up pierce him

nòn!" Āklèng pudèt— "Kopusī nē tòk-dàm-
through!" The eldest answered— "How I go and pierce

hai-jī-mā? ē-kòr tàng-dèt, ē-mu tàng-dèt-lè;
dare shall? our brother he is, our younger brother he is;

īpī īsī-pèt, ī-pō īsī-pèt; āphūthàk chubòng īsī-pèt
our mother is one, our father is one; moreover nipple one

chithē īsī-pet tòng-ràp-chòm: ākòrtē tàng-dèt, kopusī
breast one we sucked together: brothers-full-being, how

pithī hai-jī-mā? nē hai-hē!" "Dā tàngtē nàng
kill-him should I dare? I dare not!" "Go then, you

ādàkvàm!" Ādàkvàm pu-voi-phàk—"Mai! pātèng-
the second!" The second son rejoined— "Ah! (of a) second

kālī, pāju-kālī: kòrtē-āpòk, mu-tē-
wife he is not (the son) (doublet): *brother of one womb younger*

Ārlèng ki-ī, "a sleeping man": observe that *ārlèng* here evidently means a human being in general (see note, p. 4). *Àn-chō-mèk-bur:* see note, p. 96. *Vàng-noi; noi* is a variant of *nòn*, imperative particle. *Chīr-ēpàk:* "one spear"; notice that the generic class-word for flat things, *pàk*, is used with *chīr*, a spear, referring of course to the head only.

Dā in *Dā-nàng* seems to be a shortened imperative of *dàm*, to go. *Ārlu-rā tòk-dàm-nòn:* notice how *ārlu*, usually a postposition (= up in), becomes a verb when necessary; similarly, further on, in *ē-kòr tàngdèt*, *kòr*, "brother," is furnished directly with the suffix for the past tense; *ē-* and *ī-* are used interchangeably for the pronoun of the 1st person plural inclusive; the second is perhaps employed when the vowel-harmony calls for it. *Tòng-ràp-chòm: ràp*, "to help," is employed as an adverbial supplement to indicate that two persons do the same thing together; *chòm* is a doublet of *ràp*. *Pātèng*, *pāju*, words for a second wife.

āpòk tàngdèt-lē, kopusī pithī-hai-jī-mā?
brother of one womb since he is, how (him) slay should I dare!

nē hai-hē." "Dā-tàngtē nàng ādàk-vām-ādun." Lā pu-
I dare-not." "Go, then, you second-to the next." He re-

voi-phàk—"Kèng-thàm īsī-pèt, kèng-pàk īsī-pèt, rī-dèng
joined— "Our thigh is one, our foot is one, our upper arm

īsī-pèt, rī-pèk īsī-pèt-sī, kethē-ràp-chòm ākòrtē tàng
is one, our hand is one, we grew up together, our brother since

dèt-lē, kopusī pithī-thèk-jī-mā? nē thèk-thē!" "Dā-
he is, how could I possibly kill him? I cannot!" "Go

nàng ādàkvàm-ādun-lēthòt." Lā pudèt—"Mòk ē-bòng-pèt
now you, second-next-next." He said— "Nipple-one (at)

tòng-ràp-chòm ākòrtē tàng-dèt, āphū-thàk-tā bhin
having sucked together brothers fully being, moreover sister

kālī bhā kālī lē, kopusī kāpithī hai-jī-mā? nē hai-hē."
he has none (doublet) *how kill him should I venture? I dare not."*

"Dā-tàngtē nàng ākibī." "Mai! kopusī nēlē nē
"Go-then, you the youngest." "Ah! how me are you

ketoi-mā? Nē dun-tàngdèt, nē-pu-tàng-tē, ākibī-pèn
sending? I being next him, as for me, childhood-from

thē-ràp-ràp: āphūthàk-tā àn ē-vàn-pèt
we grew up together: over and above that, rice (from) one platter

kechō-ràp, hòr hārlung īsīpèt kejun-ràp:
we ate together, beer mug one (from) we drank together:

ābàng-lē nē pithī-hai-jī-mā? nē hai-hē." Ànsī
such a person I to kill should dare? I dare not." Then his

āpō àning-thī-lo: "Tàngtē kopusī 'H. K. pithī-nàng'
father became angry: "Then how 'H. K. must be killed'

pu nàngtum kepu-hai? plàng-plē-plē-lē,
saying ye dared to say? if you cannot bring yourselves to this

nàngtum pinsō plàng-vàngvē," pusī nujòk ārlu-sī,
you male will never become," saying, the post climbing up,

Bhin kālī, bhā kālī: *bhin* is Ass. *bahin*, sister; *bhā* must be Ass. *bhāi*, brother, but is used as a doublet of *bhin*.

Notice the energetic reduplication of the negative in *plàng-plē-plē-tē*. *Pinsō*, male, virile, "worthy of being called men."

chīr-pèn lōbòng-ā-òp tòk-proi-lo; ànsī
with a spear the plantain-sheath he pierced through; then

chitū-ālàng nàng-bu-lo; ànsī "H. K. kàng-
(name of plant)-juice came dropping out: so "H. K. strong

tàng-mā-kàngtàng nònkē nàng-dàn-lo-bō! Ārnàm
though he be, now here he has got his deserts! God

Ārnī āsō ènsì, rēchō kethē peplàng-bòm-
of the sun's daughter having wedded, a great king let him make

lo-nàng nòn-ànkē." Ànsī H. K. nàng-ārju-dunlo: "Kopi-
himself now!" Now H. K. there overheard all this: "What,

kopi tàng-ā, īkmār-lī?" pulo: ànkē "H. K. āthai
what are you saying, brothers?" he said: and "H. K. his bow

do" pu, pherē-sī kàt-lo; chingthu-chērbu-sī
has" saying, fearing they ran away; stumbling and falling

kàt-lo; āhèmthàp kāchilē āning-vàngphàk-
they ran; at their jungle hut their own arriving, they vomited (lit.

vàngphàk, ànsī ājō-pàngthàng bòr-ī-dèt-sī
their breast came up), and night-clearing away with great difficulty

ādàp hèm chevoilo. Ànsī H. K.-tā ālàngtum-
in the morning home they returned. Then H. K. also them

āphī-āphī dun-sī, chilònghē thàm-theròk sārnung vār-dun-lo.
after coming, the worm-casts clods six on the roof threw.

Ànsī àn-chōdèt jundèt ā-īkmār rīt
Then rice having eaten having drunk his brothers field (*to*)

dàmlo; āphī H. K. vànglo. Ànsī ātēpī
went afterwards H. K. came. Then his sister-in-law

àn pīlo. Chōdèt jundèt pulo, "Ai tēpī!
rice gave him. Having eaten and drunk he said, "O sister-in-law!

nē dàk nàng-do-dun thèk-thē-lo: kòrtē-āpòk
I here remain with you cannot: my brothers own

mu-tē-āpòk āphū-thàk ē-pō-āpòk-tā nē-pràn nē-mui-sī
(doublet) *nay even our father own even my life* (doublet)

Kopi tàng-ā "what are you saying?" *tàngā* is only used in this way as a question, as *tànghō* (see above, p. 100) is used in carrying a message, for *pu*, to say.

Bòr-ī-dèt-sī "with great difficulty"; *bòr-ī-bòr-ā*, "by hook or by crook."

nē ārlèn-thuròng : né-pethī-jī nē-pejàng-jī-sī māthā-
me aim at (plur.) ; *me to kill* *me to slay* *they are*

thuròng. Āpòtkē nē chòngvīr-po. Sàng-tèt
plotting (plur.). *Therefore I will go a-wandering. A provision*

sàngtī hīm sàngphēr-lē nē sik-pī-nòn." Ànsī
of rice bread parched rice also to me preparing give." *Then*

ātẹpī pu-tekàng-lo— "Lālē nē thī-dàm-dē
to his sister-in-law he said on leaving—"If I do not die

jàng-dàm-dē-dèt, tàngtē nē-kevàng-āpòr chelònghē
(doublet), *then my-returning-time* (*at*) *worm-cast*

thàm-theròk nàng-vārpo ; ànkē inghoi-inghu kāpòt-
clods-six here I will throw ; then the stools the

kāplèng chàm-nòn." Chiru-ràp-jō-sī chekàk-lo.
planks wash clean." Having wept together they parted.

Ànsī H. K. āthai che-pòn-sī kedàm-mā-kedàm, ànsī
Then H. K. his bow having taken went along, and

ā-phī hèm-ēpī āhèm lē-lo. "O phī ! nàng bàng-
his granny the widow's house (*at*) *arrived. "O granny ! are you*

do ?" Sārpī nàng-thàk-dèt "Komàt-mā ? dàk
there ?" The old woman there answered "Who is there ? as for

putàng-tē, nē-dòn nē-ràp āvēdèt-pīlē : komàtsī kevàng-
this place, to me kith and kin there is not any : Who is

mā ?" H. K. thàk-dèt, "Ai nē phī." Ànsī sārpī
come ?" H. K. answered, "Oh, I, granny." Then the old woman

pulo— "kopi-kevàng-mā, pō ? nēkē hèm-ēpī :
said—"Why have you come, my dear ? I am but a lone widow :

nē hèm āvē nē rīt āvē : chō-hàng chōrèk-chòt-sī
I house have not I field have not : food-begging (doublet) *only* (*from*)

kechō : kopi kevàng-lo ? H. K. thàkdèt—"Nàng-lòng
I eat : why have you come" ? H. K. answered—"With you

nàng-do-dun-po." Sārpī pudèt—
I will remain here as a companion." The old woman said—

Arlēn-thu-ròng, māthā-thu-ròng : ārlèn is "to aim at," *māthā* "to think about"; *thu* a particle meaning "again," and *ròng* one of the affixes indicating the plural. *Chiru-ràp-jō-sī : jō* is an affix indicating the plural.

Nàng-bàng-do ? "are you there ?" lit. "is your body (*bàng*) present ?" *Kopi kevàng mā pō ? pō*, "father," is used as an endearing word in addressing a son, or as here a grandson (see ante, pp. 99, 101).

"Nàngkē rēchō-āthèng kethē-āthèng lē, kopusī nē-
"*You that fit-to-be-a-king, fit-to-be-a-great-man are, how in my*
hèm nàng nàng-kedo-dun-thèk-jī mā? H. K. thàk-dèt—
house you can keep me company? H. K. answered—
"Mē phī: nàng-do-dun-po." Ànsī do-dun-lo
"*Good, granny: here I will stay.*" *So he stayed with her*
thàk-dun-lo. Ànsī āphī hèmēpī pulo—"H. K., nàng
(doublet). *Then his granny the widow said—"H.K., do you*
sòk tē-dun-nòn; nē rēchō-āròng sòk-sàng
the paddy spread out to dry; I in the king's village paddy-rice
rèk-dàm-po. Mo sòk tē-dèt nàng
to beg am going. After paddy you have spread out, you
làng-chinglu dàm-jī-sèt-tā, làng-thàk dàm-rī: lā
in the stream bathe to go if want, up-stream go not: this
ētum ā-hèm ā-lònglē chinglu." Ànsī sòk-tē-
of us two house ground (upon) bathe. Then paddy having
dèt āphī hèm-ēpī rēchō-āròng dàm-lo.
spread out his granny the widow to king's village went.
H. K. sòk pòn-lo: hārlo-dun-lòtsī
H. K. the paddy took: having turned it over frequently
pālòm-pèt pe-rèng-dèt-sī sòk
in a very short time having thoroughly dried it the paddy
oi-sī làng chinglu-dàm-lo.
having collected together in the stream he went to bathe.

Ànsī H. K. māthā-voi-phàk "kopi-āpòtsī nē-phī
Then H. K. thought again—"for what reason my granny
'làngthàk dām-rī' pu nē-kepu-tekàng-lo-mā? Làng-thàk
'*up stream go not*' *saying me telling went away? Up stream*
nàng-dàm-sī nàng-làng-dàm-jī-làng," pusī làngthàk
there going I will go and see for myself:" *so saying up stream*

Sòk is paddy, rice in the husk; *sàng* is rice freed from husk and ready for cooking; *àn* is boiled rice; *tē*, a verb, "to spread out paddy to dry."

"*Hārlo*," a verb, "to turn over" (the spread-out paddy); *rèng*, a verb, of the spread-out paddy, "to become dry"; *oi*, a verb, "to collect into a heap" the dried paddy. *Làng-thàk nàng-dàm-sī nàng-làng-dàm-jī-làng*: in this sentence the word *làng*, which occurs thrice, has three different significations: the first *làng* is a noun, "water, river"; the second is a verb, "to see, look at"; the third *làng* is an auxiliary verb, "to continue doing, or being," used here pleonastically.

dàmlo. Sēr ālàng-thē rūp ālàngthē kephuk
he went. Gold water-vessels silver water-vessels broken

thèk-dàm-lo. "O lāsī 'làngthàk dàm-rī' pu
he, going, saw. "Oh, that was why 'up-stream go not' saying

nē-phī nē-kē pu-tekàng-lē. Ningvē nèng-ārju-jī,
my granny told me when she went away. To-night I will ask her,

komàt-ching ā-lànghē nē." Ànsī hèm nàng-chevoilo.
whose watering-place it is." So home he returned.

Ànsī ā-phī hèm-ēpī-tā rēchō-āròng-pēn ārnī-
Then his granny the widow-also king's village-from in the

kàngsàm hèm nàng-chevoilo. Ànsī ā-ningvē àn-chō-dèt
afternoon home returned. Then that night rice having eaten

jun-dèt H. K. ārju-lo: "Komàt-ching ā-lànghē mā,
having drank H. K. asked: "Whose watering-place is it,

lā làng-thàk? Sēr ālàngthē rūp ālàngthē kephuk
that up stream? Gold water-vessels silver water-vessels broken

oi-chō." Ànsī hèm-ēpī pulo: "Làngthàk dàm-rī pu
are strewn." Then the widow said "Up-stream go-not saying

nē nàng kepu-tekàng: nàng ārju-jē-dèt-sī nàng làngthàk
I you told at parting: you not hearing (obeying) there up-stream

dàm āvī-lē?" Ànsī H. K. thàk-lo— "Dàm-tē-mā, phī:
went surely? Then H. K. answered—"Yes, I did go, granny:

nē-thàn-thā, komàt-ching ā-lànghē mā." Ànsī āphī
explain to me, whose watering place it is." Then his granny

hèm-ēpī thàn-lo: "Bārī-thē Rēchō ā-lànghē;
the widow explained: "Palace-great king's watering place;

āsōmār, kòrtē bàng-theròk, làng-nàng-kāchinglu-ādim:
his children, sisters six, in the water bathing-place (it is):

dàm-rī-nòn āpārkē." Ànsī H. K. māthā-voiphàk—"Nē-
go not now any more." Then H. K. considered again—My

Sēr, rūp, "gold, silver," see note, p. 111, ante. Notice the rare form *nèng* for *nē*, "I"; nasals seem occasionally to be added or dropped at will at the end of words: e.g. *dā* and *dàm*, "go"; *òng* and *ō*, "much, many"; *lā* and *làng*, auxiliary verb. *Komàt-ching-ā-lànghē nē: ching* is a particle strengthening the interrogative *komàt*,—"who-ever?" *lànghē*, a *ghāt* or watering place: *nē* the interrogative particle borrowed from Assamese, = *mā* in Mikir.

Bārī-thē Rēchō, "king of the Great Palace"; *bārī*, "a large house," loan-word from Assamese: *thē*, "great."

phī dàm-rī-thu pusī, nē-pu nàng-dàm-thu-
granny 'go not again' having said, as for me, there going again

jī-làng." . Ànsī làngthàk dàm-thu-lo. Làng-
I will continue." Then up stream he went again. River

kung chipātu-joi-sī nērlo-chitīm Bārī-thē
bank (under) hiding himself quietly, day-middle Palace-great

Rēchō āsōmār kòrtē bàng-theròk làng-nàng-chinglu-
King's children, sisters six, (in) the river for the purpose

jī-sī vànglo. Nàng-klō-èt-jō ākàn
of bathing came. Descending there beautifully their clothes

nàng-chi-bī-kòk làng sun-phit:
there having laid aside into the water they jumped all at once:

īnut ākàn nàng-chibī-kòk làng sun-
each one her clothes having laid aside into the water jumped

phit, kemē-òng chiklō-tur-dèt ārnī tur-dèt lālē
at once, most lovely! moon-splendour sun-splendour (like), there

kāchinglu lālē kāchingthī. Ànsī ārnī ingsàm-
they bathed, there they washed themselves. So the day became

jīn-lo. Āklèng nàng-pinkhàt-lo: "Ai ètmārlī!
cool gradually. The eldest there-admonished-them: "O my dears!

kitun āpòrlo, kedàng āpòrlo, ē-vo chibèng
cooking-time it is, serving-up-time it is, our fowls to house

āpòr, ē-phàk chibèng āpòrlo: ē-pī ē-tàmpo,
time it is, our pigs to house time it is: our mother us will scold,

ē-pō ē-tàmpo, dàm-po-nàng." Ànsī chinglu-tànglo,
our father us will scold, let us go!" So bathing-they finished,

chingthī-tànglo: īnut ākàn nàng-chihijīr-
washing themselves they finished: one her clothes shaking out

Nàng-klō-èt-jō "there they descended beautifully"; *klō*, "to fall or sink down from a height"; *èt* a syllable indicating beauty or charm; Mr. Stack notes that it is perhaps connected with the word *ètpī*, "yellow, golden"; it is also used as an affectionate form of address in *èt-mār-lī*, "my dears!" *jō*, plural affix. *Kàn*, a ceremonious word for clothes; the ordinary expression is *pē* or *rī*. *Sun-phit: phit* means "all at once," "suddenly." *Tur*, "the brightness, splendour" (of the moon and sun).

The syllable *jīn* in *ārnī ingsàm-jīn-lo* indicates the day *gradually* drawing on to evening. *Āpòr-lo*: notice the verbal affix *-lo* appended to the noun *pòr*, "time." *Bèng*, "to house animals for the night." *Hijīr*, "to shake out," as a bird its wings before starting to fly.

phlum-phlum chi-ī-lòk-si ingjār-èt, īnut
so as to flap, having put on flew away beautifully, another

ākàn chihijīr-phlum ingjār-èt,
her clothes having shaken out so as to flap flew away beautifully,

ànsī ākibī-sī-kē āphī ingjār-èt-jō,
and the youngest of all afterwards flew away beautifully

chiklō-ātur ārnī-ātur thēlālàk. Sining
moon's-brightness sun's brighiness just like. The heaven

lut-lē-tik, lālē H. K. kelàng-dun pukē āngphun
not entered-until, there H. K. stood gazing so that his neck (*in*)

chepekèk-koi. Ànsī sining lutkoi-lo,
he got a crook altogether. So the heaven they entered quite,

thèk-dun-dē-lo: ànsī hèm chevoilo. H. K. āning
he saw them no more: so home he returned. H. K. in his mind

māthālo "àn ākemē, àn ākechòk, nàng èn-lòng-lē-tik
thought "so beautiful! so lovely! here until I can get one to wife,

nàng-kīm-lòng-lē-tik
here until I can build the wedding bower (subaud, *I will not rest*);

ningvē nē-phī nàng-ārju-lē-po." Ànsī hèm lē-
to-night my granny I will ask again about them." So home having

ròk àn-chō-dèt jun-dèt H. K. āphī ārjulo:—
arrived rice having eaten having drunk H. K. his granny asked:

"Mai! phī! lā-sòntòt ākemē lā-sòntòt ākechòk nē thèk-lòng-
"*Oh! granny! that-like beautiful, that-like lovely I saw got*

lē-làng; kopusī ke-èn lòng-po-mā? bīdī nē
never; how to take one to wife shall I attain to? a plan to me

thàn-thā!" Āphī pudèt—"Ai H. K.! bàng-kē
explain!" His granny answered—"O H. K.! those ones

Phlum-phlum, onomatopoetic adverb imitating the sound of flapping; *ī*, "to put on one's clothes": *ā-rī kāchi-ī*, "he is putting on his *dhoti*"; *pīnī kāchi-ī*, "she is putting on her petticoat"; in this sense the verb *ī* takes *lòk* as its constant adverbial supplement: when it means "to lie down," "to sleep," it takes *lòt*. Observe how the distributive force of the sentence is expressed by repeating the whole phrase. *Āngphun chepekèk-koi* "he made his neck (*ingphun*) crooked (*kèk-dàng* or *kèk-juk*)"; *koi*, a particle meaning "completely, altogether." *Ēn* "take," and *kīm*, "build," both mean "to marry"; the latter implies the building of a separate house for the newly wedded couple, or perhaps the wedding bower.

ārnàm-āsō ārnī-āsō rēchō-āsō kethē-āsō
god's children sun's children king's children great one's children

kopusī nàngkē ārlèng-āsō-lē ke-èn-
(are): how should you, who are but a child of man, succeed in

lòng-jī-mā?" H. K. pulo—"kālī, phī! èn-lòng
getting one to wife?" H. K. said—"not so, granny! get one

nàng-jī: bīdī nē thàn-nòn."
to wife I must: a plan to me explain."

Thàn-thē tik-tàk ārju-vēr-sī
Did not-explain (she) so-long-as (he) continuing to ask,

thàn-lo: "Nàng ke-èn-jī-pèt-tàngtē, lā làng-kung-
she explained: "You are-bent-on-wedding-one-if, that river-bank-

lē rīt pàn-dàm-nòn." Ànsī H. K. pulo—"Mē-òng-chòt-lo,
on a field to clear go." And H. K. said— "Very good,

phī: menàp-pèn-āpārā pàn-dàm-po." Ànsī
granny: to-morrow-from I will go and clear it." And

ādàp thē-àng thē-àng-ē làng-ding:
the morning dawning not dawning he continued to watch:

ànsī ādàp ing-thànglo. Ànsī nopàk e-pàk
so (at last) the morning dawned fully. Then a dao one

che-pòn-sī dām-lo. Lē-ròk-pèn do-dē,
taking with him he went. Arriving-from he waited not,

sàng-sē, lālē kepàn lālē kepàn, ārnī-sī-pèt
he rested not there clearing there clearing, in one day only

pàn-dèt pī-dèt, ànsī màm thīlo, mē keilo:
he cleared it fully (doublet), *then jungle cut, fire set-to-it:*

lālē kechō pukē, ābèng ākòk
there it (the fire) ate it up so quickly, a piece of wood, a stalk

thī-rok-re chō-èt. Ànsī thèngthē, hànjàng, nòk,
lying-not it devoured. Then maize, millet, sugar-cane,

Arlèng-āsō: notice that here the word *ārlèng* evidently means a human being, opposed to *ārnàm-āsō*, the child of a divine person. *Pàn,* "to cut down and clear the jungle for cultivation." *Làng-ding* "continue to watch": *ding* a particle of continuance (cf. *keding*, tall, long). *Pàn-dèt pī-dèt;* here *pī* has the sense of "to cut down" (a tree, or something thick): so also *thī*. *Màm,* "the jungle." Further on, in *thī-ròk-rē, thī* means "to lie": *Pisī dàk-lē kethī-ròk-mā?* "why are you lying here?" *ròk* is an adverbial supplement.

phingu, ārchē-lo, āphū-thàk-tā mīr phèk-ē,
plantain he dibbled in, over and above also (name of a flower),

tādo, mīr-kādòmphui, āsòn-sòn mīr ē-lo.
white lily, marigold, various kinds flowers he planted.

Ànsī Bārī-thē Rēchō āsōmār làng nàng-chinglu-
Then Palace-great King's daughters (in the) river there-to bathe-

lēlo: nàng-klō-èt-jō kemē thèk-thē-òng
arrived: there they descended beautifully, lovely to impossibility

pukē— chiklō-lē vàng-phlòt, ārnī-lē vàng-phlòt thēlālàk.
so— moon-as-if came down sun-as-if came down just like.

Ànsī chinglu-tàngdèt chingthī-tàngdèt,
Then having finished bathing having finished washing themselves,

H. K. āteràn nàng-thèklo. Ànsī pulo— "Mai!
H. K.'s garden-plot they saw there. So they said— "Oh!

komàt ārīt-mā? mē-òng-hē." Āklèng thàk-dèt—
whose field is it? it is very pretty." The eldest answered—

"Ē-kòrpō H. K. āteràn-lē-mā."
"Our cousin (brother-in-law) H. K.'s garden plot it must be."

Ansī sining chingjār-thū-èt-jō-lo. H. K.
Then to heaven they flew away again beautifully together. H. K.

"nàmtusī ke-èn-lòng-po-mā?" pu māthā-ding,
"how shall I succeed in getting her?" saying continued to think,

ànsī āphī ārju-thū-lē-lo— "Ai phī!
and his granny went and asked again—"Oh, granny!

nàmtu-ching-sī ke-èn-lòng-āpòtlo-mā?" Āphī
when and how am I to succeed in getting one?" His granny

Ārchē is used of sowing or planting many things together, as here: to sow or plant only one thing is *ē*: *thèngthē ke-ē*, "he is sowing maize"; *sòk ke-rīk*, "he is sowing rice broad-cast"; *sòk ke-ē*, "he is transplanting rice." *Mīr-phèk-ē*: *mīr*, "flower," *phèk-ē*, "rice-husks": "a flower that grows out of heaps of rice-husks; has a long narrow leaf and a flower which is red and white mixed" (Stack); *tādo*, "a kind of white lily or arum with a yellow style" (*id.*). *Kemē-thèk-thē-òng pukē*: "so (*pukē*) beautiful (*kemē*) excessively (*òng*) as never was seen (*thèk-thē*)." *Vàng-phlòt*: *phlòt*, a particle indicating suddenness. *Teràn*, an individual plot, as distinguished from the *rīt* or general field. *Ē-kòrpō H. K. āteràn-lē-mā*: *kòrpō*, "cousin (mother's brother's son)," also indicates the relationship between a woman and her sister's husband; here of course it is used in the latter sense, proleptically; it is characteristic of this story-teller that he discloses the *dénouement* of his tale well in advance. Notice the idiom *-lē -mā*, "it must be," an indirect question = "is it not?"

thàkdèt—" Lā-pu-pē-lòng, āsu-pō: hèm-thàp
answered—" That-way-not, grandson-dear: a jungle hut

chi-kīm-thā." Ànsī ādàp hèm-thàp kīm-dàm-
build for yourself." So in the morning a jungle hut he went to

lo. Ārnī-sī-pèt hèm-thàp thēpī kīm-dèt-sī hèm
build. In one day only a jungle hut very big having-built home

chevoilo, ànsī "hèm-thàp tànglo, phī," pu
he returned, and "the jungle hut I have finished, granny," saying

thàn-lo. "Tàngtē pòngsī che-èt-nòn,"
he explained. "Then (in) a flute bore a hole for yourself,"

pusī āphī pinkhàt-lo. Ànsī pòngsī che-
saying his granny advised him. Then flutes he bored several

èt-ō. Ànsī thèngthē-āpòr hànjàng-āpòrlo.
for himself. So maize-time millet-time it became.

Āphī pinkhàt-lo— "Hèm-thàp chehòn-dàm-rā
His granny advised him—" In your jungle hut going to watch

pòngsī but-nòn." Ārīt putàngtē, pālòm-pèt lālē
flute blow." His field as-for, in a very little time there

mīr kàngthu-pukē, māthā thèk-thē-dèt. Ànsī
flowers blossomed-so, it could not be imagined. Then

Bārī-thē Rēchō āsōmār làng nàng-chinglu-lē-lo:
great-Palace King's children in the river there to bathe arrived:

nàng-ingjār-èt-jō īnut ākàn chi-bī-kòk làng
there flying beautifully one her clothes laying aside in the river

sun-phit, īnut ākàn chi-bī-kòk làng
jumped straight, another her clothes laying aside in the river

sun-phit, lālē kāchinglu lālē kāchingthī. Ànsī
jumped straight, there bathed there washed themselves. Then

āklèng nàng-pinkhàt-lē-lo— "Dā, ètmārlī, dàm-po-
the eldest there advised them again—" Come, dears, let us

nàng." H. K. lālē pòngsī kebut pukē, māthā-thèk-
go." H. K. thereupon his flute blew so, it could not be

Pòngsī, Ass. *bansī*, "a flute," made of a piece of bamboo; *èt*, to bore a hole. *Che-èt-ō* "he (cut and) bored holes in a number of flutes"; *ō* seems to be a shortened form of *òng*, many: *hēm kīm-ō*, "they built a number of huts"; *nē vo nàm-ō-lo*, "I have bought a lot of fowls."

thē-dèt. "Mai! pòngsī-kebut-tā ju-mē-òng:
imagined. "Oh! flute-playing indeed is very good to hear:

H. K. ābàng do-āvī: dā ètmārlī, mīr che-hàng-
H. K. a person it is surely: come, dears, flowers to beg

dàm-sī-nàng"; ànsī vànglo. "H. K., nitum mīr
let us go"; so they went. "H. K., we flowers

chilòk-pòn-chòt-làng, chilòk-pòn ning-
for ourselves pluck take a few wish, pluck and take are you

kē-mā, pō?" "Chilòk-pòn ningkē-mā,"
willing that we, sir?" "Pluck and take, I am willing certainly,"

pu, H. K. pulo. Ànsī ābàng-phū-tā mīr chilòk-
saying, H. K. said. So each one of them flowers having

pòn-sī dàmlo, ingjār-pòn-èt-jō.
plucked and tàken went away, they flew away gracefully together.

Sining lut-lē-tīktàk, H. K. lālē kelàng-dun-pukē
In heaven (they) not entered so long, H. K. there continued gazing so,

āmèk chi-pesō-koi, ānō chi-pesō-koi.
his eyes became quite sore, his ears (i.e. *eyes*) *became quite sore.*

Ànsī sining lut-koi-lo: thèk-dun-dē-
So the heaven they entered completely: he-could-no-longer-see-

lo-pu-ànsī, H. K. tā hèm chevoilo. Ànsī āphī
them-when, H. K. also home returned. Then his granny

hèm-ēpī nàng-ārjulo— "Mīnī Bārī-thē Rēchō
the widow there asked him—"To-day great-Palace King's

āsōmār nàng chingkī-pòn-mā?" "Chingkī-pòn-tē;
children with you did converse?" "Yes, they conversed;

mīr-tā nē kehàng-pòn-lànglē." Ànsī
flowers even me they asked to be allowed to gather." Then

Ju-mē-òng, "it is very good to hear": *ju* is shortened from *ārju*; the prefix *ār-* is separable in this word and in *ārnī*, "day, sun," *ārlòng* "stone," and several other words, which appear in composition as *nī* and *lòng*, etc.; it seems probable that it is connected with the Tibetan prefix *r-*, to which the Mikir relative particle, *ā-*, has been prefixed. Notice *nitum* for *nētum*, possibly by vowel-harmony with the following words *mīr* and *chilòk*. *Chilòk-pòn ningkē-mā*: observe that this phrase stands both for the request and its answer—*ningkē*, "willing"; *ning*, "mind";—*mā* is thus not only the interrogative particle, but also indicates its corresponding affirmative reply. *Ā-mèk*, *ā-nō*, "eyes and ears" = eyes only. *Mīnī*, *menàp* (*minàp*), alternative terms for *pinī*, *pēnàp*, "to-day, to-morrow."

āphī bīdī thànlo: "Menàp-tā ārnī kemē:
his granny a plan explained: "To-morrow (*is*) *a day good:*
Bārī-thē Rēchō āsōmār làng nàng-chinglu-lē-jī-
Great palace King's children in the river there to bathe-arriving-
āpòtkē, chipātu-joi-rā làng-dun-tòn-nòn. Lā
on-as-soon-as, hiding yourself quietly watch secretly. Those
āklèng-ātum kòrtē bàng-phòngō-kē āpèngnàn do-àngsē-lo.
elder (plural) *sisters persons five husbands have all got.*
Ākibī-sī dèt-lo, lātu Mòn Rēchō
The youngest only, her Mon Rājā (*King of the winds*)
āsōpō-āphàn kerai-dun; hòrbòng hòrtē
his son-for is asking in marriage; the beer-gourds (doublet)
lē-koi-lo. Bòntā lā-dèt-lo, lā-āpīnī-lē
have all arrived. Nevertheless her only, her petticoat (accus.)
pàngthèk-dun-rā làng kāchinglu-āphī
having carefully singled out, in the river they-have-plunged-after,
dàk vàn-nòn. Nē lā-sòntòt āpīnī ālār-thàk-po:
here bring to me. I it-just like a petticoat in exchange will weave:
lālē pòn-rā ādim-thòt bī-pī-dàm-thū-nòn.
that taking in that same place go and set it down again.
Lā-āpīnī-binòng-kē pātu-joi-po-nàng. Ànsī ālàng ingiār-
Her-petticoat-own hide-quietly-let-us. Then she to fly away
dun-thèk-thē-lo. Lālē āpīnī nàng
with the others will not be able. There her petticoat you
che-hàng-lo-tē, 'īnut-lē-īnut nē-do-nòn' pu-rā
she asks for-if, 'one or other of you become my wife' saying
pu-nòn." "Tō, mē-òng-chòt-lo, Phī," pu H. K. pulo.
say." "Yes, very good indeed, granny," saying H. K. said.
Āphī lābàngsō ābīdī thàn-chèk-pèn-āpārā, H. K.
His granny that plan having explained-after, H. K.'s
āning āròng kedo māthā-thèk-thē-dèt; ājō-tā
mind cheerful became as you cannot imagine; the whole night

Do-àngsē-lo = *do-koi-lo*, "have *all* got."
Mòn Rēchō, probably shortened for *Tomòn-Rēchō*; *tomòn*, "wind." *Kai-dun*, special verb for "to ask in marriage." *Bòng*, "gourd for holding beer"; *tē*, doublet. *Thàk*, "to weave." *Thàn chèk*, "to explain"; *chèk* strengthens verbs for imparting information. *Āning āròng kedo*: *ròng*, "delight," Ass. loan-word.

āmèk jàngthèk-thē ā-nō jàng-thèk-thē māthā-ding.
his eyes close he could not (doublet), *but continued thinking.*
Ànsī ādàp ing-thànglo: àn-chōdèt jundèt
Then morning fully dawned: having eaten rice having drunk
ārīt chedàmlo. "Nàmtu-ching-sī nērlo chitīm-po-mā?"
his field (to) he went. "When day middle will it be?"
pu inghòng-ding; ànsī sàngtī-ārlo chi-pātu-dām-
saying he continued waiting; then sand-beneath he hid himself
joi. Ànkē nērlo-chitīm Bāri-thē Rēchō āsōmār
quietly. So at mid-day Great Palace king's children
vànglo: nàng-ingjār-èt-jō, īnut ākàn nàng-chi-
came: there they flew down gracefully, one her clothes putting
bī-kòk làng-sun-phit īnut ākàn nàng-chi-bī-kòk
aside plunged into the river, another her clothes laying aside
làng-sun-phit, ànsī làngkāchinglu-āphī H. K.
plunged into the river, and they had entered the water after H. K.
thur-joi-sī lā-kibī-sī āpīnī ājīso inghu-
rising quietly that youngest one's petticoat striped cloth stealing
pòn-dèt-sī āphī hèm-ēpī ālòng pòn-phit-lo.
and taking away his granny the widow- to took it straightway.
Ànsī āphī lā-sòntòt āpīnī ājīso thàk-
And his granny it just like a petticoat a striped cloth wore in
thū-lo, pālòm-pèt thàk-dèt. Ànsī H. K. nàng-
exchange, in a very short time she wore them. Then H. K. there
kàt-thū-voi-lo, ādim-thòt-sī pīnī jīso bī-dàm-
ran back again, place-that-same-in petticoat striped cloth putting
thū-sī, āhèm-thàp chevàngsī pòngsī but-lo:
down in exchange, his jungle-hut going into, the flute played:
lālē kebut pukē māthā-thèk-thē jādī-thèk-thē. Ànsī
there he played so that it could not be imagined (doublet). *Then*
chinglu dòr-lo, chingthī-dòr-lo.
they had enough of bathing they had enough of washing themselves.
Ànsī āklèng nàng-pinkhàt-lē-lo— "Ai ètmārlī,
Then the eldest there admonished them again—"O my dears!

Notice again *āmèk ānō* for "eyes" only.

dàm-po-nàng; ketòk-āpòr, kesèt-
let us go; it is (rice) pounding time, it is time for the second

āpòrlo; ketun-āpòr kedàng-āpòrlo; kebē-
pounding; it is cooking-time, it is setting-on time; it is time to

āpòr, kesòr-āpòrlo." Ànsī ākàn nàng-
heat the beer, time to squeeze it out." Then her clothes there

chi-ī-dèt-sī pu-thū-lē-lo— "Dā, mīr che-hàng-dàm-sī-nàng."
having put on she said again—"Come, flowers let us go and beg."

Ànsī mīr chelòk-dàm-dèt ànkē āphràngsī āklèng
Then flowers having gone to pluck thereupon first the eldest

ingjārlo: ànsī ākibī-ātum-tā ingjār-dun-èt-jō-
flew up; then the younger ones also flew up with her gracefully

lo; ànsī ākibī-tā ingjār-dun-lo
all together; then the youngest also tried to fly with them,

ingjār-dun-thèk-thē-dèt: ingjār-tàng-tē, nàng-klō-thū-
but found she was unable to fly: if she flew up, there she fell back

bup; ingjār-dun-chòt, nāng-klō-thū-bup.
again; if she tried to fly with them, there she fell back again.

Ànsī āklèng pulo—"Mai! kopi-ching āpòtlo-mā?"
Then the eldest said—"Oh! what in the world is the matter?"

Ànsī āklèng-ātum-tā nàng-chihīr-thū-voiphàk-lo, ànsī
Then the elder ones also there came down again, and

H. K. ālòng vàngsī pulo—"Ai H. K., nàng sī
H. K.'s place coming said—"O H. K., you it is who our younger

nē-mu āpīnī lār-dèt āvī, āpòt-kē
sister's petticoat have changed without doubt, therefore

vàn-nòn" pu-hàng-lo. Ansī H. K. thàk-dèt—
bring it back" saying they called out. Then H. K. answered—

"Īnut-lē-ìnut nē-do-tē." Bārī-thē Rēchō āsōmār
"One or other of you be my wife." Great-Palace King's children

Tòk, a verb with the general meaning "to thrust, poke"; used already above (p. 116) for thrusting with a spear; here for pounding the rice with a long pestle (*lèngpum*) in the mortar (*lòng*); another sense is "to write" ("to poke with a pen"). *Sèt*, "to give the half-cleaned rice a second pounding." *Dàng*, "to serve up the cooked food." *Bē* "to heat the fermented rice"; *sòr*, "to press out the beer" from the grains, mixed with warm water, which have been put in the conical strainer of woven bamboo, *sī*, by pressing down upon them a gourd, *bòng*.

MIKIR WOMEN POUNDING PADDY.
(Jaintia Hills).

p. 132

pudèt: "Kopusi nàng-kedo āpòtlo? nētum nē-pèngàn
said: "How you to marry is it possible? we our-husbands

kedo-tàng, nē-pèngàn kedo-tàng rèp-lē."
have got already, our husbands have got already married to us."

H. K. pudèt—"Tangtē nē pīnī nàng-pī-thèk-thē:
H. K. said— "Then I petticoat you give up cannot:

īnut-lē-īnut nē-do-mā-sī." Ànsī Bārī-thē Rēchō
one or other of you me must marry." Then Great-Palace King's

āsōmār chepulo: "Tē, nàng-do-nòn."
children said one to another: "Sister (elder), do you marry him."

Āklèng thàk-dèt: "Kopusī nē-lē kedo-jī?
The eldest answered: "How should I marry him!

nē-sō kechàn-jai-lē." "Tàngtē ādàk-vàm, nàng-
I-children several have already." "Then the next, do you

lē do-nòn." "Kopusī nē kedo-thèk-po? nē
marry him." "How I should be able to marry him? I

ningkē nē-sō bàng-philī tàng-dèt-lē." "Ādàkvàm-
myself also my children four have got already." "Second sister-

ādun, nàng-lē do-nòn tàngtē." "Kopusī kedo-
next-to, do you marry him then." "How can I possibly

thèk-jī? nē ningkē nē-sō bàng-kethòm
marry him? I also my children three

tàng-dèt-lē." "Tàngtē ādàkvàm-àdun-lē-thòt, nànglē
have got already." "Then second sister-next-to-next, do you

do-nòn." "Nē-tā nē-sō bàng-hīnī tàng-dèt-lē,
marry him." "I too children two have got already,

kopusī kedo-po?" "Nàng ādàk-vàm-ādun-
how should I marry him?" "You second-sister-next-to-

lē-thòt, nàng-lē do-nòn." "Do-thèk-thē, nē-tā
next following, do you marry him." "I cannot marry him, I too

nē-sō īnut tàng-dèt-lē-mā?" "Tàngtē nàng
my child one have I not already?" "Then you

ākibī-sī-lē do-nòn." Ākibī-sī thàk-dèt—
the youngest, do you marry him." "The youngest answered—

Rèp seems to be a variant of *ràp* (explained above, p. 118), and indicates that *all* of them have been married together. *Chàn-jai*, "to have several children."

"Nē-tu, Mòn Rēchō āsōpō-āphàn nē kerai-dun
"*As for me, Mon Rājā his son-for me is asking in marriage*

tàng-dèt-lē: hòr-bòng hòr-tē nàng-lē-koi-lo; pusī
already: the gourds of beer there arrived all have; how

kedo-thèk-po?" Āklèng-ātum pudèt—"Bòntā
can I possibly marry him?" The elder sisters said—"But

nàng pàngrī-rē-dèt-làng-lē-mā: nàng-lē do-nòn-èt!
you are not married yet: do you marry him, dear!

Ingting-po, nētum dàm-po: hā hèm-tā ē-vo
It will be dark soon, we must be going: there at home our fowls

ē-phàk ingrèng-jō-sī-do-po; āphū-thàk-tā ē-pī
our pigs will all be calling out for us; moreover our mother

ē-pō nàng-làng-phròng-sī-do-po. Nētum-tā
our father there will be looking out for us. We also,

vàng-bòm-jī-le-mā?" Ànsī ākibī-tā
shall we not continue to come and see you?" Then the youngest

pulo—"Pu làng-mā tē-mārlī? do-po,
said—"What is to be done, sisters? I will marry him,

nàng-tum dàm-nòn; ē-pī ē-pō āningthī-dèt-jī."
do you go; our mother our father will be very angry."

Ànsī āklèng-ābàng pulo—"H. K., nàng thàn-
Then the eldest one said—"H. K., you (our) instruction from

bòm-tā ārju-jē-dèt-lo, āpòtkē nē-mu
time to time would not listen to, therefore our youngest sister

nàng-tekàng-po; bòntā āduk pī-rī ālàk
here we are leaving; nevertheless grief give her not, trouble

pī-rī; ketun toi-rī, kedàng toi-rī;
give her not; to cook send her not, to serve up send her not;

Pāngrī-rē-dèt-làng-lē-mā; here again two verbs each have the negative affix, *pàngrī* and *làng*, the latter an auxiliary signifying "to continue to be." *Pàngrī* in the sense "to marry," is the causal of *ingrī*, "to drink copiously of liquor"; the description of the marriage ceremony at p. 18 shows the important part which is taken in it by alcoholic drinks. *Ingting-po*, "it will be dark": observe the impersonal use of the verb, without a substantive: we may say *ājō kàngting-pār*, "the night is very dark."

Nàng-làng-phròng-sī-do-po; *phròng* is one of the particles used to indicate plurality: "they will *all* be looking out for (*làng*) us there (*nàng*)." *Bòm*, one of the verbs indicating continuance may be rendered "from time to time."

āphū-thàk-tā ā-rī su-rī-thā, ākèng su-rī-thā." Ànsī
moreover her hand touch not, her foot touch not." So

ā-mu che-perē-tekàng-sī sining
their younger sister having instructed and left behind to heaven

chingjār-thū-èt-jō-lo. Sining lut-lē
they flew up again beautifully together. Heaven not entered

tiktàk, chi-làng-dun-ding:
so-long-as, they (H. K. and his wife) continued gazing together:

ànsī thèk-dun-dē-lo. Pu-ànsī H. K. pulo—
then they could see them no more. Then H. K. said—

"Ingting-po, ē-tum-tā dàm-po-nàng." Ansī H. K.
"It is getting dark, let us also go our way." So H. K.

āning āròng do-lo, jō-ārnī thījòk ke-àp phàk-lèng
his mind joyful lived, night-and-day deer shooting wild-pig

ke-àp ā-ur krèng-krē ā-ràp
shooting, his platform (for drying flesh) was never dry his shelf

krèng-krē.
was never dry.

Ànsī ningkān isī ingtàng-lo. "Ai phī, nē hèm
So a year one came to an end. "O granny, 'I home

chedàmpo pusī nē-kepulo, kolopu-lo-mā?" pu
I will go' saying I say to myself, what am I to do?" saying

H. K. pulo. "Nàng hèm-tàng-dèt, nàng rīt-tàng-
H. K. said. "You have your own house, you have your own

dèt-lē-mā, chedàm-tā mē; bòntā nàng-pēsō nàng-che-mē-
field indeed, you can go, well; but your wife with you does

mē-làng." "Bòntā," H. K. pudèt, "ningkàn-isī-lo-
not get on well yet." "But," H. K. said, "a year one (whole)

A-rī su-rī-thā, ā-kèng su-rī-thā: this injunction not to touch the hand or foot of the fairy princess has different parallels in other lands; in the Celebes version referred to on p. 72 it is the *hair* that is not to be touched. *Pe-rē*, causal of *rē*, "to be knowing, clever." *Ur*, a platform or screen for drying flesh in the sun; *ràp* includes also a shelf in the house.

Krèng, to be dry, bears the same relation to *rèng*, dry (ante, p. 122), as *klàng* (p. 99), to perceive, does to *làng*, to look at; in both the prefix *ke-* has apparently been incorporated in the root.

Chedàm-tā-mē "You can go if you like": observe the force of *mē*, "well, good." *Che-mē-mē-làng*: the verb *mē* here seems to be the Assamese *mēl*, "agreement," not the Mikir word for "good." Observe the idiomatic expression *ningkàn isī-lo-lē-mā thī*, in answer to an objection:

lē-mā-thī, phī." "Bòntā nàng che-mē-mē-lā."
it is, though, granny." "Nevertheless, you have not hit it off yet."

Ànsī "Ai tàngtē, dàm-thèk-thē-làng-po" H. K. pulo. Ànsī
Then "Oh, then, go I cannot yet," H. K. said. Then

H. K. lālē kātiki lālē kànghoi puru kelòng
H. K. there working in the field (doublet) *barns-full getting*

phàndār kelòng, hèm-ēpī āhèm pukē ingkrō
granary-full getting, the widow's house so cylindrical receptacle

ingtòng ārdung-dung. Ànsī
for rice conical basket were so many (i.e. *was filled with*). *And*

H. K. āsō Ārnàm pīlo, āsō īnut-lo. Ànsī āphī
H. K. a child God gave, a child one only. Then his granny

ārju-thū-lē-lo: "Ai phī nē-pī nē-pō-ātum ā-lòng
he asked again: "Oh, granny, 'my mother my father's place (to)

chedàmpo-sī nē kepu." Hèm-ēpī thàkdèt: "Nàng-
I will go' I say to myself." The widow answered: "Your

pēsō nàng chemē-mē-làng-tī, āsupō." "Kālī
wife (to) you is not yet well reconciled, grandson dear." "Not so,

phī, chemēlo: nē sō īnut tàng-dèt-lo-
granny, she is reconciled: me child one has she not already

lē-mā?" "Dā tàngtē: nàng thàn-bòm-tā, nàng ārju-
given me?" Go then: you I repeatedly advised, you would

thèk-thē-dèt-lo; chedām-nòn; bòntā nàng-pēsō nàng-
not listen to me; go together; nevertheless your wife is not

chemē-mē-làng dē." Ànsī H. K. āpēsō chepulo
thoroughly reconciled, indeed." Then H. K. his wife (to) said

"Ai nàng-pī, ī-lī-tā ē-hèm chedàm-po-nàng." Āpēsō
"O thou dear one, we two to our home let us go." His wife

thàkdèt, "Dā, nàng nē kepòn āling-lo-hē." Ànsī ādàp-
replied, "Go, you me taking wherever you will." So it became

lo: àn-chō-dèt jun-dèt dàmlo. Tovār
morning: rice having eaten having drunk they started. Road

so one says, in reply to a request for payment, *nē nàng pī-tàng-dèt-lo-lē-mā-thī* "but I have paid you *already!*" Observe that in *nàng che-mē-mē-lā* the last syllable = *làng* without its nasal. *Āsō Ārnàm pī-lo*, "God gave a child": possibly this phrase is due to the narrator, who it will be remembered was a Christian. *Tī*, a particle = "not *yet* reconciled." *Dē*, a particle of asseveration, "indeed," probably the Assamese *dēi*.

ē-bèng lēlo. Ànsī āsōpō-pèn āpēsō-pèn āvàm
a piece (of) they arrived. Then his child and his wife his waist

tàmpòng-hèt-sī, poho-pèn
putting between waist and girdle firmly, with his turban

che-vàm-phòng-hèt-lo. Ànsī dàm dàm dàm,
he bound well round his body. So as they went on their way,

vo-hār ālopō inglòng nàng ārkē-dut,
a jungle-fowl male on the mountain (side) there was scratching,

ārlòk nàng-ārkē-dut māthā-thèk-thē jādī-thèk-thē. Ànsī
the precipice was scratching inconceivably (doublet). *Then*

H. K. pulo—"Chī, vohār-ālopō, kopi kācheplàng-mā? nē
H. K. said—"Oh, jungle-cock, what are you doing there! I

hèm kāchedàm-tòng tovār nē pèk-nòn."
home am-going-in-a-hurry, the way to me leave free." The

Vohār ālopō thàkdèt— "Tovār nàng kepèk-jī
jungle cock answered—"The way to you I will leave free by no

kālī: 'minī H. K. āpēsō āsō chevàn-po' tàng
means: 'to-day H. K. his wife his child will bring' so much

pusī ākhàt ākhàt āmàng āmàng nē nàng
saying to myself, the way he is coming (doublet) *I here*

ketòn-lē." H. K. pu-voiphàk—"Chē, pulèm-dèt-rī! ēmōkē
am watching. H. K. rejoined— "Oh, joke do not! hereafter

'H. K. āpēsō āsō hèm rīt chevàn-ànsī nē-pràn
'H. K. his wife his child house field (to) bringing while, my life

nē-mui dàmlo' pu pupā-nā." Vohār ālopō pudèt,
my soul is gone' thus do not have to say." The jungle cock said,

"Pupē. Mīnī nàng-tā-mē nē-tā-mē." H. K.
"I do not say so. To-day either you or I (will prevail)." H. K.

pulo "Sākhit-mā?" "Sākhit." "Dohai-mā?"
said "Is that true?" "Yes, true." "Do you swear it!"

Hèt, a particle used with verbs meaning to tie, bind, in the sense of "firmly, securely." *Dut*, a particle used with verbs of scratching or cutting. *Tòng*, a particle indicating hurry or haste. *Ēmōkē* "in a little time": *mō*, "space or interval of time," *ē*- particle of unity, as in *ē-jòn*, *ē-bèng*. *Pulèm*, "to say in joke: *pu*, "say," *lèm*, "seem, pretend." *Pràn*, Assamese. *Pu-pā-nā* "don't have to say": *nā* Assamese. *Nàng-tā-mē*, *nē-tā-mē*, idiomatic, "it will be well with you or it will be well with me," *i.e.* "either you or I will come off the better." *Dohai*, "an oath"; probably the Assamese *dōhāi*, "call for justice": *semē* (the Khasi *smai*) is also used.

"Dohai." Ànsī H. K. āthai chepāching-kàngsī ābòp.
"I swear." So H. K. his bow having set shot him.

Ànsī dàm-thū-chòt, vo-rèk ālopō tovār nàng-
Then a little further he went, a cock pheasant the way right

pārpàn-pèt inglòng nàng-ārkē-dut, ārlòk nàng-
across the mountain there was scratching, the precipice there

ārkēdut māthā-thèk-thē jādī-thèk-thē. Ànsī H. K.
was scratching in an extraordinary manner. Then H. K.

pulēlo "Chī vo-rèk-ālopō, kopī nàng-cheplàng-mā? nē hēm
said again "Oh, cock pheasant, what are you doing there? I home

kāche-dàm-tòng, tovār nē-pèk-nòn." Vo-rèk
am in a hurry to go, the way leave free for me." The cock

ālopō pudèt—"Tovār nàng kepèk-jī kālī:
pheasant said—"The road to you I will yield by no means:

'mīnī H. K. āpēsō āsō chevàn-po-tàng' pusī ākhàt
'to-day H. K. his wife his son will bring along' saying the way

ākhàt āmàng āmàng nē nàng-ketòn-lē." H. K. pudèt—"Chī,
he is coming (doublet) *I am watching." H. K. said—"Oh,*

pulèm-dèt-rī! ēmōkē 'H. K. āpēsō āsō chevàn-ànsī
don't joke! hereafter 'H. K. his wife his son bringing-while

nē-pràn nē-mui dàm-lo' pupā-nā." Vorèk ālopō
my life my soul departed' don't have to say." The cock-pheasant

pudèt "pupē." H. K. pu-lē-lo— "Sākhit-mā?"
said "I don't say so." H. K. said again "Is that true?

"Sākhit." "Dohai-mā?" "Dohai." Ànsī H. K. āthai
"True." "Do you swear?" "I swear." Then H. K. his bow

chepāching-kàngsī ābòp.
having set shot him.

Ākō dàm dàm dàm, phàk-lèng ālopō kethē pukē māthā
Forward as they went, a wild boar (male) great so as could

thèk-thē jādī-thèk-thē, àngthur àngni pàn-lòk-phòng,
not be imagined (doublet), *his snout his tusks overlapping so,*

tovār nàng-pār-pàn-pèt inglòng nàng-thīmur-phàk ārlòk
road there-right-across the mountain there was rooting the precipice

nàng-thīmur-phàk ābīdī thèk-thē-dèt. Ànsī H. K. pulo:
there was rooting in an extraordinary way. Then H. K. said:

"Chī, phàk-lèng ālopō, kopi nàng cheplàng-mā? Tovār
"Oh, wild boar, what you are doing there? The way

nē-pèk-thā: nē hèm kāpelē serāràk-jī." Phàklèng ālopō
leave free for me: I home want to get quickly." The wild boar

thàkdèt— "Tovār nàng kepèk-jī kālī:
answered—"The road for you I will leave free by no means:

'mīnī H. K. āpēsō āsō chevàn-po-tàng' pusī
'to-day H. K. his wife and child will bring along,' saying to myself

ākhàt-ākhàt āmàng-āmàng nē nàng ketòn-lē." H. K. pudèt
the way he is coming (doublet) *I here am watching." H. K. said*

"Chī, pulèm-dèt-rī! jāsemèt mā-pu-mā?" Phàk-lèng ālopō
"Oh, don't jest! is it true or not?" The wild boar

pulo "Jāsemèt." H. K. pudèt—"Ēmōkē 'H. K. āpēsō
said "It is true." H. K. said "Hereafter 'H. K. his wife

āsō hèm chevàn-ànsī nē-pràn dàm-lo nē-mui dàm-lo'
his son home while bringing my life is gone, my soul is gone'

pupā-nā." Phàklèng ālopō pudēt— "Pu-pē."
don't have to say." The wild boar said— "I don't say so."

"Sākhit-mā?" "Sākhit." "Dohai-mā?" "Dohai."
"Is that true?" "It is true." "Do you swear?" "I swear!"

"Chī, tàngtē"—pu ā-thai chepāching-kàngsī ābòp. Ànsī
"Oh, then"—saying his bow having set he shot him. So

hèm-lē-jī-dòk-dòk-lo, chilònghē thàm-theròk
(*when*) *he had nearly arrived at his home, worm casts clods six*

pàngrum-sī H. K. sārnung vārdàmlo. Ànsī
having collected H. K. the roof (*on*) *went and threw them. Thus*

ātēpī pulo—"H. K. vànglo! Tō inghoi
his elder sister-in-law said "H. K. has arrived! Then the stools

kechàm inghu kechàm." Ànsī inghoi inghu kāpàt kāplèng
wash the seats wash!" So the stools seats planks benches

chàm-lo. Ànsī H. K. phàklèng ē-jòn vàn-sī,
they washed. Then H. K. wild-boar one having brought,

Bòp, to shoot a bird or animal; *àp*, to let off a bow or gun.
Dòk-dòk, particles used to indicate that an event has *nearly* happened (with *jī*, future affix). *Tō*, imperative particle borrowed from Khasi, and *prefixed*, as in that language.

pai-ā-rē nàng-bīkòk-sī hèm vànglo. Ànsī
the hedge beside there having set it down home came. Then

kelēpèn ātēpī hòrlàng hòrpō hīm
on his arrival his eldest sister-in-law beer (doublet) *bread*

sàng-phēr nàng-pī-lo. Āpēsō kemē-òng pukē, ārnī
parched rice gave him there. His wife very beautiful so, sun's

ātur thēlālàk chārsàp un-ē. Ànsī ā-īk-
splendour like, be looked in the face could not. Then his

ātumkē—"pāningvē kopi-ching āhàn-lo-mā?" pu
brothers—"To-night what in the world has happened?" saying

ning-rī-jō. Ànsī H. K. pulo: "Nē mō tovār
were perplexed. Then H. K. said "I a while ago on the way

phàksō nàng-ābòp: jā pai-ārē-sī mē bī-tekàng-
a little pig there-shot: there beside the hedge well I placed and

kòk: lālē chō-phī dàm-nòn." Ànsī ā-īkmār-ātumkē
left it: there scorch it for eating go." Then his brothers,

kòrtē-bàng-phòngō dàmlo; āphàk kethē-òng peklèm-
the brothers five, went; the boar (*was*) *so very big, move it*

àn-tā un-ē: thàngtā chònghoi thèk-thē.
even they could not: anything do by themselves they could not.

Ànsī H. K. dun-lo: ārī ē-hòng rum-dàm-
Then H. K. accompanied them: hand one (*with*) *he lifted and*

kòk: ànsī phī-sī ingthàn-lo, ànsī
brought it away: then having scorched it they cut it up, and

hèm vàn-lo, chō-tun-lo chōdànglo. Ànsī āròng bohòng
home brought, cooked it, served it up. And joyful, noisy,

chingnèk chingnī-sī chō-lo, jun-lo.
laughing and making merry, they ate, they drank.

Ànsī puthòt-ādàplo. "H. K. āpēsō chevànlo"
So next morning dawned. "H. K. his wife has brought"

Pai-ā-rē "beside the hedge (*pai*)" = *pai-ā-kung*. *Chō-phī*; the Mikirs scorch (*phī*) every bird or animal before preparing it for cooking. *Chònghoi*, reflexive form of *inghoi*, "to do," = "to do by themselves." *Ā-rī-ē-hòng*: *hòng* is the generic class-word for a limb (see ante, p. 79). *Ingthàn*, "to cut up fish or flesh, whether raw or cooked." *Chingnèk* reflexive of *ingnèk*, to laugh, "laughing together." *Chingnī*, reflexive of *ingnī*, doublet of *ingnèk*; the verb also means "to sit."

Puthòt-ādàp-lo; *puthòt*, "next": cf. *lē-thòt* in *ādàk-vàm ā-dun-lēthòt* on p. 114 above; the time-affix *-lo* is joined directly to *ādàp*, "morning."

tàng pu ārju-lòng-sī ā-ràt-īsī ādèt-īsī
so much saying having got to hear the whole country-side
nàng kelàng chethòr-prē māthā-thèk-thē
there to see kept coming and going as you could not imagine
jādī-thèk-thē. Ànsī H. K. āpēsō āpīnī binòng, ājīsō
(doublet). *And H. K. his wife's petticoat own striped cloth*
binòng, āsēr ālèk, pòng-ting-kē, làng-pòng
own, gold jewels, necklace, gold-drum (in a) bamboo joint
thàp mēsèn-sī kārdòng ràklòk. Ànsī
putting away carefully, (in the) pitch of the roof tied up. So
H. K.-kē ròng-phū-rī dàmlo, rūp-phū-rī-dàmlo:
H. K. the village people each went to visit (doublet)*:*
āràt ādèt chi-phū-rī dàm: āphī
the ryots, the country in turn came to visit him: afterwards
āpēsō nàng kelàng vàng-prē. Mānē-kē
his wife there to gaze on they kept coming and going. Some
"nī" mānē-kē "nèng" mānē-kē "tē"
"aunt" some "sister-in-law" (*brother's wife*)*, some "elder*
mānē-kē "pīnu" pu-ābàng-tā-dolo. "Vai!
sister" some "paternal aunt" saying each one was. "Oh!
mē-òng-tē-mā?" pu pāsingnàk-jō. Ànsī
is she not beautiful, sister?" saying they all admired. Then
H. K. āpēsō thàk-dun-lo—"Àn-chòt kālī lànghē! Nē pīnī
H. K.'s wife answered them—"So much not yet! My petticoat
binòng, nē jīsō binòng, nē lèk binòng, nē roi
own, my striped cloth own, my necklace own, my bracelet
binòng lē nē chepindèng-lòng-tē, āpārtā sō-sē-làng."
own again I to put on were to get-if, it would not be thus only."

Ā-ràt, ā-dèt, both Assamese loan-words; *ràt* is *raiyat*, "ryots," *dèt, dēh*, "country." *Chethòr-prē, vàng-prē*, are both used for "continually coming and going, of many people"; the former expression indicates greater numbers and frequency than the latter. *Pòng-ting*, "a gold drum, worn on the breast, strung in the middle of a set of strings on which black, coral, and gold beads are arranged in alternate rows six deep" (Stack); in Assamese *mādoḷī*. *Nī, nèng, tē, pīnu*: see the table of terms of relationship on p. 20. *Āpār-tā-sō-sē-làng*: this sentence appears to be made up thus: *āpār*, "greatly, much," *tā*, corroborative particle: *sō*, diminutive particle, negatived by *sē, làng*, auxiliary verb, "continue"; the force of it, then, would be—"the effect would not be only the poor result you see, fine though that is, but ever so much more!"

Ànsī mānē āsārpī pulo—" Chī, tàngtē nàng pī-thā."
Then some old woman said " Oh, then do you give them to her."

Ànsī H. K. āsārpō pulo—" Konàt-tòng lā osō ingchàm
Then H. K.'s old father said—" Where ever (did) that boy mad

bīpīkòk-lo-nē-lē ? kopi āthē-tàng āpīnī jīsō
stow them away ? for what reason her petticoat striped cloth

binòng kepī-pē-dèt ?" Ànsī H. K. āpēsō thàn-lo—
own did he not give her ? Then H. K.'s wife explained—

" Hālā kārdòng-lē keràk-chèk-kē." Ànsī phrī-
" That pitch of roof-in he has tied them in a bundle. Then having

dàm-sī nàng-pī-lo. Ànsī chepindèng-
untied there he gave her (the things). Then she put them on

lō che-sum-pòt-lo. Lālē kemē-pukē māthā-thèk-thē-dèt
herself (doublet) *Thereupon beautiful so inconceivably*

chi-plàng-lo. Ànsī " Ai ! mē-kē mēsèn-tē-mā ! ārnàm-āsō
she became. Then " Oh ! beautiful, lovely indeed ! God's child,

ārnī-āsō pu pai-pē-lo." Ànkēphòng H. K.
the sun's child, called not for nothing is she." Thereupon H. K.'s

āpēsō thur-phlut-sī chehijīr-phlum-phlum-lo,
wife rising up her full height shook out her clothes flap-flap,

ingjār-èt-dàn-lo. Ànkē H. K.
flew away gracefully (thither whence she came). Then H. K.

hā-tovār-pèn nàng-chethèk-dun-sī, thai-pèn
from a distant path there having watched her, bow (accus.)

jō-dun-ràng-ràng-lo. Ànsī āpēsō pu-tekàng-lo,
continually kept bending. Then his wife said on leaving him,

" Thā, thā, mō chiphōjī." Ànsī H. K.
" Wait, wait, hereafter we shall meet again." Then H. K.

chirū chērnàp mòn-duk mòn-sā-sī hèm nàng-lē-lo.
weeping lamenting sad and sorry at his house arrived.

Konàt-tòng = *konàt-ching,* " wherever ?" *Kopi-āthē* = *kopi-āpòt.*
Pai-pē-lo: this idiom is illustrated by the following phrases: *klèm-dùm pai-pē-lo,* " he is not working gratis, for nothing"; *là āklèng pai-pē-lo,* " he is not the elder for nothing"; *i.e.* he can do better than his younger brothers. *Ingjār-èt-dàn-lo:* the element *dàn* gives the force of returning to her own place whence she came. *Jō,* verb, " to bend a bow," *ràng,* particle of continuance. *Thā,* " wait!" Assamese loan-word. *Phō,* verb, " to touch, arrive at," as a boat comes to the shore with *chi,* " to touch one another, to meet" (see p. 112, lines 1 and 2).

Nàng-kelē-pèn chō-chē jun-jē ā-osō
Immediately on arrival, not eating, not drinking, his child
nàng-chi-bu-dèt-sī hā āphī hèm-ēpī āhèm
having taken on his back, to his granny the widow's house
chedàm-phit-lo. Ànsī dàm dàm dàm āphī hèm-ēpī
he started to go. So going along his granny the widow's
āhèm lēlo: kelē-pèn lālē kāchirū lālē kāchērnāp
house (at) he arrived: on arriving there he wept there he lamented
māthā-thēk-thē jādī-thèk thē. Ànsī āphī pulo—"Hākō-
as you could not imagine. Then his granny said—"From
pèn 'Nàng-pēsō nàng-chemē-mē-làng' nàng-pulo-hē;
the first 'Your wife is not yet united with you' I told you verily;
kopusī nòn-lē nàng-kelàng-jī-làng? Nàng sining-lē kopusī
how now will you get to see her again? You heaven-to how
kedun-thèkjī?" Ànkē chirū-pèt àn-muchòt
will you be able to follow her? Then weeping so much the more
chō-chē jun-jē āphī kedàm-āling dun-krī,
not eating not drinking his granny went-wherever following,
bār-pī bār-sō-lē kedàm-tā hundun-krī,
outgoings-great outgoings-little-in going also he kept dogging her,
kethī kejàng-sī kedo-po. Ànsī āphī
one-dying, one-perishing (like) he remained. At last his granny
pulo: "H. K. ākhī lō-du-dèt-lē chō-thā:
said: "H. K., food leaf (in) having wrapped up eat (imper.):
nē mō bīdī nàng-thàn-jī." Ànsī ākhī-lō-
I thereafter a plan to you will explain." Then food-in-a-leaf-
du hīm sàngphēr chō-lo. Ànsī āphī bīdī
wrapped bread parched rice he ate. Then his granny a plan
thàn-lo: "Mīnàp-kē nàng-pēsō Mòn Rēchō āsōpō nàng-
explained: "To-morrow your wife Mon Raja's son there
kāchepàngrī-jī vàng-po. Ākō nàng-hupō
to marry will come. Before that your father-in-law's
àngnār-tā nàng-làng-chinglu-jī vàngpo. Lālē nàng
elephant-also there in the river to bathe will come. There do you

Akhī-lō-du; *ākhī*, "something to eat," *lō*, "leaf," *du*, "wrap up," = "so much food as can be wrapped up in a leaf," a morsel.

sàngtī-ārlo chi-pātu-dàm-joi-nòn; ingnār dàm-jī
sand-underneath go and hide yourself quietly; the elephant to go
dòkdòk-lo-tē, lā-ārmē rīp-hèt-rā nàng-
is-making-ready-when, its tail (to) holding on tightly your-
poho-pèn nàng-sō che-vàm-phòng-hèt-nòn. Lālē
turban-with your child to your waist bind firmly. There
ingnār nàng-ārju-lo-te, 'Nē-tā hā nē-pēsō ālòng nàng-
the elephant you asks if, 'I also to my-wife's place am going
kechedun-jī' pu-rā pu-nòn. Ànkē menàp ārnī-kàngsàm-sī
along with you' saying say. Then to-morrow in the afternoon
nàngtum lē-po. Nàngkē làng-kung-lē dokòk-non. Ànkē
you both will arrive. Do you the-river-bank-on wait. Then
nàng-pēsō làng-kepànglu-jī-āphàn ābàn-ātum
your wife with-water-to-bathe-for-the-purpose her male slaves
āsòt-ātum làng nàng-sòk-po. Ànkē 'osō-āphàn
her female slaves water will-draw-there. Then 'For the child
làng-ējoi-pèt nē pī-thā' purā hàng-dun-nòn. Ànkē
water one draught only me give' saying call out. Then
làng nàng-pī-lo-tē thibuk-ārlo nàng-sēr-ārnàn jòk-dun-
water you-give-if, the water pot-into your-gold-ring drop
thòt-nòn. Ànkē nàng-phàn nàng-hàng-po: ànkē dun-
in. Then for you there she will call: then go with
nòn: kelē-pèn nàng-sōpō ō-dàm-kòk-nòn; ànkē
them: on arriving your child set down on the ground; then
osō āpē-ālòng chedàmpo." Ànsī ādàp
the child its mother-towards will go of itself. So the morning
ingthàng-lo: chōdèt jundèt H. K. hā làng-kung
dawned: having eaten and drunk H. K. to the river bank
dàmsī sàngtī-ārlo chipātu-dàm-joi-lo.
having gone under the sand went and hid himself quietly.
Ànsī ingnār làng nàng-chinglu-jī vànglo. Ànkē
Then the elephant in the river there to bathe came. Then
chinglu-dèt dàmjī dòkdòklo. H. K. ārmē rīp-dun-
having bathed to go it made ready. H. K. its tail holding-on-

Ē-joi, "one draught"; *joi* is perhaps Ass. *jol*, "water." *O*, verb, "to leave, set down."

lòk-sī, āpoho-pèn ā-sō che-vàm-phòng-dèt-lo. Ànsī
tight-to, his turban-with his child tied firmly to his waist. Then

ingnār hā sining ingjār-pòn-lo, ànsī hā
the elephant to heaven flew up, taking him with him, and there

làng-kung ō-dàm-kòk-lo. Ànkē Mòn Rēchō-ātum-tā
on the river bank set him down. Then Mon Raja's people also

H. K. āpēsō-pèn āsōpō nàng-kāpàngrī-jī-sī Bārī-thē
H. K.'s wife-with his son in order to marry great palace

Rēchō āhèm vànglo. Ànsī Bārī-thē Rēchō ābàn-
King's house (to) had come. Then great-palace King's male

ātum āsòt-ātum H. K. āpēsō làng-kāpànglu-jī-
slaves female slaves H. K.'s wife with-water-to-bathe-for-the

āphàn làng nàng-kesòk-jī vànglo. Ànsī H. K. āsōpō-āphàn
purpose water there to draw came. Then H. K. his child-for

làng hàng-pī-dun-lo: "Làng ējoi-pèt nē-pī-thā
water begged them to give: "Water one draught only give me

nē-sōpō-āphàn, pē-mārlī." Ànsī īnut-tā pī-pē
my son-for, good mothers." Then one-even would not give

īnut-tā pī-pē. Ànsī āphī-sī sārpī nàng-
one-even would not give. Then at last an old woman came up

dun-lo: ànsī hàng-dun-thū-lo H. K.—"Làng ējoi-pèt
to them: then called out again H. K.—" Water one draught only

nē pī-thā, pē-ārnàm-pī, nē-sōpō āphàn." Ànsī sārpī
me give, good Madam, my-child-for." Then the old woman

làng pī-lo; thibuk pheroidun pelèm-pelàm-sī, H. K.
water gave him; the water-jar to touch making as though, H. K.

sēr ārnàn jòk-dun-thòt-lo. Ànsī H. K. āpēsō làng-pànglu-
gold ring dropped into it. So H. K.'s wife they bathed with

lo: ā-rī ā-kèng chàm-èt āphī-sī sārpī-
water: her arms her legs washing-beautifully after the old

ālàng-thibuk āphū nàng-dunglo: sēr-
woman's water-jar her head (over) they poured there: the gold

ārnàn nàng-klō-bup. Ànsī H. K. āpēsō pulo—"Ai! nàng
ring there fell out. Then H. K.'s wife said—" Oh! here

· *Mòn Rēchō-ātum*; notice that here *tum* has its original sense of "company"; "*Mòn Rājā*'s company, or following."

chelē-dun-tànglo komàtching ālàng-thibuk mā ?" pu
has arrived to us whose in the world water-jar ?" saying

bisār-lo. Ànsī īnut-tā—"Nē thibuk kālī" īnut-tā
she enquired. Then one— "My jar it is not," another—

"Nē thibuk kālī" pulo. Ànsī "sārpī ā-thibuk"
"My jar it is not" said. Then "(it is) the old woman's jar"

pu-hur-lo. Ànsī sārpī-āphàn pulo—"Konàtsī nàng
they all said. So to the old woman she said—"Where did you

bàngsō ārnàn kelòng-lòk? Lābàngsō ārlèng èn-dàm-nòn!
this ring get hold of? That man go and fetch!

Lā-lē nàng vàn thèk-thē-dèt, tàngtē nàng
Him if you bring cannot, then (it is a matter of) your

pràn!" pulo. Ànsī sārpī chirū chērnàp-sī
life!" she said. Then the old woman weeping lamenting

H. K. ālòng dàm-lo, ànsī hàng-dàm-lo— "Nē-dun
towards H. K. went, and called out to him—"With me be

īk-nòn: kopi-āpòtsī 'Làng nē pī-thā' sī pu-
pleased to come: for what reason 'Water me give' this having

tē nē-pràn nē-mui nē-kāpedàm-jī-lē māthā-thuròng-
said my life (doublet) me to cause to lose did you have it in your

mā?" Ànsī H. K. āsō chibu-sī dun-
mind?" So H. K. his child carrying on his back went with

lo. Kelēpèn osō ō-dàm-kòk-lo. Ànsī
her. On arriving the boy he set down on the ground. Then

osō kàt-tàng-tàng-sī āpē chērbàk dàm-kràp-lo,
the boy running straightway his mother's lap (into) climbed up,

ànsī mòk chu-lo.
and her breast sucked.

Ansī Bārī-thē Rēchō pulo: "Ai! ābidī thèk-
Then the great palace King said: "Oh! a thing never

Pu-hur-lo: *hur* is one of the particles indicating plurality.

Nē dun-ik-nòn: *ik*, "elder brother," used as a respectful form of address; observe its place in the compound imperative. *Māthā-thuròng*, lit. "you had another (*thu*) meaning" (viz. to make me lose my life). Notice how *-sī*, the mark of the conjunctive participle, is affixed to the reported utterance of H.K. *Chērbàk* = *che-ārbàk*; *ārbàk*, the lap or bosom; also a verb: *osō kārbàk*, "she holds the child to her bosom." *Kròp* is said to be used only of a child climbing up into its mother's lap.

the-lo! a-so-si chi-pethe-rap-tang-det-lo-le-ma!"
seen before! a child-even have they got great between them already?"

Ansi Mon-Recho-atum therak-lo ingringlo:
Then Fon-Raja's people were ashamed, were disgusted:

mon-duk mon-sa hem chevoi-lo. Ansi H: K. pen
grieved and sorry home they returned. Then (of) H. K. and

Bari-the-Recho asopi pangri-lo pangdon-lo.
great palace King's daughter they celebrated the wedding

Ansi ningkan-isi ningkan-hini do-dun-si tiki-
So year-one year-two living with them he laboured

lo inghoi-lo, ansi puru-krehini phandar-krehini
in the fields and worked, and granaries-twelve barns-twelve

long-lo. Ansi H. K. apeso aphan chipulo: "Ai
got. Then H. K. his wife-to said privately: "O

nang pi! ili-ta vo-phri ason vo-thung ason e-tar
my dear! we two also sparrows-like doves-like a nest

an-ke do, e-thon an-ke do; apotke chedam-
at least have, a roosting-place at least have; therefore let us go

po-nang: onghai pen anihai arju-non."
away together: father-in-law and mother-in-law ask."

Ansi aningve H. K. apeso ape apo
So that night H. K.'s wife her mother her father

Cherjulo: "Ai pe pen po! nangli osa
asked privately: "O mother and father! your son-in-law

kepu-ke: 'ili-ta vo-phri ason vo-thung-ason e-tar
says: 'we two also sparrows-like doves-like a nest

anke do. e-thon anke do; onghai pen
at least have, a roosting-place at least have: father-in-law and

anihai arju-non: chedam po-nang'— pusi pu:
mother-in-law ask: let us go away together'—so he says:

Nangtum kopi abida-si ne phar-dun-po-ma?" Ansi Bari-
Ye what order me will command?" Then palace-

Ingring, used as homonym of *therak*, "to be ashamed," also means to be afraid, disturbed in mind."

Cherju-lo = che-arju-lo. Phar, "to order"; *nang ne kephar aling-lo*, "as you order me"; *ne phar-dun peme-sen-lo*, "I gave him careful instructions." *Bida = Ass. bidai*, "leave to depart."

thē-Rēchō pulo— "Che pē! lō-thui āsòn
great-King said—" O daughter! a bundle of greens like,

hànthui āsòn ēboi-sī nàng chochòk-pālār
a bundle of vegetables like, once for all you given away, or

chothèng-pālār tàng-dèt-lō-lē-mā. Mīnàp-lē
in exchange (doublet) completely I have. On the morrow

dàm-thā chidun, mīnī-lē dàm-thā chidun." Ànsī āpō
go away together, to-day go away together." Then her father

pu-thū-lo: "Kopisī nàngtum kārī-mā? bàn-mā?
said again: " What do you desire of me? male slaves?

sòt-mā? ārmo-mā? òkso-mā? sēr-mā? rūp-mā?"
female slaves? ryots? husbandmen? gold? silver?"

Ànsī *H. K.* che-thàn-dàm lo: "Ai nàngpō! nē-pē pèn
So H. K. *she went and told: " O my dear! my mother and*

nē-pō kepu-kē— 'mīnī-lē dàm-thā mīnàp-lē dàm-thā
my father say— 'this very day go away to-morrow go away

chi-dun-tā-mē; āphūthàk, bàn-mā? sòt-mā? ārmo-mā?
together if you like; moreover, slaves? handmaids? ryots?

òkso-mā? sēr-mā? rūp-mā? Kopisī nàngtum kārī-mā?
cultivators? gold? silver? What do you desire?'

pusī pu." Ànsī H. K. pulo: "Thàngtā nàngnē." Ànsī
they say." Then H. K. said: " Anything I need not." So

ādàplo. Ànsī H. K. ānīpī pèn
it became morning. Then H. K. his mother-in-law and

āhupō ārdòm-lo ārdī-lo. Ànsī
his father-in-law saluted respectfully (doublet). And

āhupō pulo: "Kopisī nānglī kārī-mā? bàn-mā,
his father-in-law said: " What do you desire? slaves,

sòt-mā, ārmo-mā, òkso-mā, sēr-mā, rūp-mā?" Ànsī
handmaids, ryots, cultivators, gold, silver?" Then

Che pē; notice that *pē*, "mother," is used as an affectionate term of address to a daughter, exactly as *pō*, "father," is used above to a son or grandson. *Lō-thui-hàn-thui*, "a bundle of vegetables, with a leaf wrapped round it." *Chòk* and *thèng* mean literally "to beat," but are here jocularly used for getting rid of a person. *Pālār* causal of *lār*, "to be changed or exchanged," also apparently used jocularly of giving in marriage.

H. K. pulo "Thàngtā nàngnē." Ànsī H. K. ātum
H. K. said "I need nothing." So H. K. and his wife

pèngnànsō tàngtē āsōpō hèm chedàm-lo ànsī hèm
the wedded pair and also their son started for home and arrived

chilē-lo. Rēchō chōlo kethē chōlo, jō-ārnī
there. A king he became, a great one he became, night and

mē, jō-ārnī thē, ànsī ārēchō
day he was happy, night and day he was great, and his kingdom

ākethē thīrlo.
was great and stable.

H.K.-ātum: notice the plural affix used to indicate H.K. *and his wife*. *Chō-lo*, "he became"; this seems to be a different verb from *chō*, "to eat." Notice *ā-rēchō* "his kingship"; *rēchō* stands for *rāj* as well as *rājā*. *Thīr*, Ass. *thīr*, "steady, stable."

Additional Notes.

Divisions of time. On p. 95, note, the divisions of the day are given. To these may be added those of the year, as recorded by Mr. Stack. A year is *ning-kàn* (*cf.* Lushei *kum*, Shö *kun*, "year," and Lushei *ni-kum*, Thado *ningkūm*, Shö *yan-kun*, "last year"). A month is *Chiklo*, "moon"; but the Assamese months, which are solar divisions of the year, not lunations, appear to be followed. The days of the month are not generally counted, and there is said to be no week. (This is borne out by S. P. Kay's English-Mikir vocabulary, which gives *hopta*, the Hindustani *hafta*, as the word for "week," with *nī-thròksi*, "seven days," as an alternative. In the *Mikir Primer* published by the American Baptist missionaries in 1903, however, *rui* is said (p. 21) to be the word for "week.")

Kechung-āpòr (*chung*, to be cold) is the cold season. *Ning-krèng* (*krèng*, to be dry) is the dry portion of winter. *Chung-phàng-òk* (*chung*, cold; *phàng-òk*, hot), is the spring, merging into summer. *Bārlā* is the rainy season, followed by *Chung-jir-jir* ("becoming cold by degrees") autumn. The following are the names of the months, with the corresponding Assamese names, as set down by Mr. Stack:—

Literary form.	*As pronounced in Assam.*	*Mikir names.*
Chaitra	Soit	Thàngthàng
Vaisākha	Boihāg	Thērē
Jyēshṭha	Jēth	Jàngmī
Āshāḍha	Āhār	Āru
Śrāvana	Srābon	Vosik
Bhādra	Bhādur	Jākhòng
Āświni	Āhin	Paipai
Kārtika	Kārti	Chiti
Mārgaśirsa	Mārg	Phrē
Paushya	Pōh	Phaikuni
Māgha	Māgh	Mātijòng
Phālguni	Phāgun	Ārkoi

According to the *Mikir Primer*, however, the Mikir names (which agree with those given by Mr. Stack) correspond with periods earlier by at least a month, Thàngthàng being the equivalent of February, instead of Chaitra (which begins at the vernal equinox), and the other months in ordinary sequence (Thērē, March, Jàngmī, April, etc.). Thàngthàng is said by Mr. Stack to be called *Chànglăchòng-ròng-do*, "the stay-at-home month." Thērē is the month in which the jungle is cut and strewn to dry (this would agree well with the equivalent of the *Primer*, rather than with Boihāg, April–May, when the firing would take place). Vosik ("sprout") should indicate the month of vigorous growth, when the rains have set in. Phaikuni seems to be borrowed from the Sanskrit *Phālguni*, but does not correspond with it. The other names are not explained.

Musical instruments. A flute, *pongsī*, cut from a bamboo, is mentioned on p. 128: *pongsī* is the Assamese *baṅsī*, the well-known instrument of the youthful Krishna (*Baṅsī-dhar*). Other instruments known to the Mikirs are *muri*, a fife; *chèng*, a drum; *chèng-brup*, the small hand-drum used by the *rīsōmār* to accompany their dancing at funeral feasts; and *kum*, a one-stringed fiddle. The last is made by stretching a string made from a creeper, *màngrī*, across a gourd, *bòng*, which provides an air-chamber. It is played with a bow, *kum-ālīsō* (*lī*, a bow, *sō*, diminutive particle) made of bamboo, the string of which is a tough fibre of bamboo. (Compare the one-stringed fiddle, *pena*, of the Meitheis: Meithei Monograph, p. 56.)

VII.

AFFINITIES.

The place of the Mikirs in the Tibeto-Burman family.

SOME idea of the mental equipment of the Arlengs will have been gathered from the two preceding sections. It has been seen that, within the limited circle of their experience, they possess a medium of expression which may be described as adequate to their needs, well knit together in its mechanism, and copious in concrete terms, though, like all such languages, wanting in the abstract and general. Their folk-tales are lively and effective as narratives, and the themes, though probably borrowed from the great treasury of popular story elaborated in Peninsular India, have been appropriated and assimilated to the social conditions of the Mikirs themselves. Little has hitherto been done to enlarge the resources of the language in the direction of higher culture, or to use it for the expression of ideas lying beyond the scope of the tribal life; but there appears to be no reason to doubt that the language of the Mikirs will be found in the course of time to be as capable of development for this purpose as the speech of their neighbours the Khasis.*

The leading feature of the race, in contrast with other hill tribes of Assam, is its essentially unwarlike and pacific character. Its neighbours—Khasis, Kachāris, Kukis, Nagas—have for centuries been engaged in continuous internecine strife, and their tribal individualities have been preserved, and differences accentuated, by the state of hostility in which each unit, however small, lived with all adjacent peoples. The Mikirs

* Reference may here be made to a summary of the Gospel history in Mikir entitled *Birtā Kemē*, "Glad tidings," published by the American Baptist Mission Press, Tika, Nowgong, in 1904.

have always, at least during the last two centuries, been, as Major Stewart described them in 1855, "good subjects." Numbering some ninety thousand souls, they are extremely homogeneous, while other tribes in their neighbourhood differ in an extraordinary manner from village to village, and constantly tend to split up into smaller aggregates, looking on all outsiders as enemies. No such disintegrating influence has affected the Arlengs. Whether in North Cachar, the Jaintia Hills, Nowgong, or the Mikir Hills, their tribal institutions, their language, and their national character are identical, and they pursue their peaceful husbandry in the same manner as their forefathers, raising in ordinary years sufficient food for their subsistence, and a considerable amount of cotton and lac for export to the plains. In these circumstances, surrounded by warring tribes, and still nomadic in their habits of cultivation, they have from time to time found it necessary to place themselves under the protection of stronger peoples. It has been mentioned in Section I. that the traditions of the race show that they were formerly subject to the Khasi chiefs of Jaintia and the eastern states of the Khasi Hills, and that they migrated thence to the territory subject to the Ahom kings.* During their sojourn in Khasi-land they assimilated much; dress (p. 5), ornaments (p. 6), personal names (p. 17), methods of divination (pp. 34, 35), funeral ceremonies (pp. 38–42), memorial stones (p. 42), all come from the Khasis, who have also contributed many words to their common speech. Borrowings from Hinduism are equally manifest in their language, their folk-tales, and their religion. Assamese words are numerous in Mikir; *Ārnàm Kethē* (p. 30) seems to be a translation of *Mahādēva; Jòm-āròng* (p. 28), and the ideas linked therewith of an after-life, are strongly impressed with a Hindu stamp.

Yet they retain, together with these borrowed features, a sufficiently definite stock of original characteristics. Physically they differ much from Khasi and Assamese alike. Their social fabric is based upon clearly marked exogamous groups, with patriarchal principles of marriage and inheritance; they call these by a Khasi name (*kur*), but have no trace of the matriarchal

* This seems to have taken place in or about 1765 A.D. See Gait, History of Assam, p. 181.

family as known among the Khasis. They build their houses on posts, while their neighbours, except the Kukis, build on the ground. Their deities are of the primitive kind which is common to all Indo-Chinese races, well known, under the name of *Nats*, as the object of popular worship and propitiation in Burma.

Ever since the race has been studied, it has been noticed that it was difficult to establish its exact place and affinities in the heterogeneous congeries of peoples who inhabit the mountainous region between India and Burma. This was remarked by Robinson in 1841 and 1849, by Stewart in 1855, by Damant in 1879. At the Census of 1881 an attempt was made to bring the Mikirs into relation with the Boṛo or Kachārī stock; but it was seen at the time that more must be ascertained regarding their neighbours before any final judgment could be arrived at. Dr. Grierson, on linguistic grounds, has classed them in the *Linguistic Survey* as intermediate between the Boṛo and the Western Nagas. It appears to the present writer, in the light of the much fuller information now available, that they should be classed rather with those tribes which form the connecting link between the Nagas and the Kuki-Chins, and that the preponderance of their affinities lies with the latter of these two races, especially those dwelling in the south of the Arakan Roma range, where the Chin tends to merge into the Burman of the Irawadi Valley.

When Robinson and Stewart wrote, it was still remembered that the Mikirs had once been settled in strength in the country (now called North Cachar) to the immediate north of the Barāil Range, and in contact with the Angāmi, the Kachcha, and the Kabui Nagas; and that, exposed as they were in this locality to the inroads of the Angāmis and the oppression of the Kachāri kings, they had migrated westwards to the territory of the Jaintia Raja in search of protection. It was noticed in the Assam Census Report of 1881 that in this region north of the Barāil, where there are now no Mikirs, local names belonging to their language indicated their former presence. When they lived there, they must have been in touch with tribes belonging to the Kuki-Chin stock, who have for centuries occupied the hill ranges to the south of the valley of Cachar, and the mountains between that valley and Manipur.

The institutions of co-operative agriculture by the village lads (p. 11), the bachelors' house or *teràng* (id.), the former custom of ante-nuptial promiscuity (p. 19), and the traces of village *tabu* resembling the Naga *genna*, still characterizing the annual festival of the *Ròngkĕr* (p. 43), all point to a connection with the Western Naga tribes, rather than to affinity with the Kachāri stock. From the Kuki and Chin tribes the Mikirs are distinguished chiefly by their pacific habits, and by the absence of the dependence upon hereditary tribal chiefs which is so strong a feature among the former. The customs of both races as regards the building of houses upon posts, with a *hong* or open platform in front, are identical; in Major G. E. Fryer's paper "On the Khyeng people of the Sandoway District, Arakan," published in the *Journal of the Asiatic Society of Bengal* for 1875 (pp. 39, 99), a Khyeng house is figured which bears a striking resemblance to the Mikir house. The institutions of domestic and individual life among the Khyengs (Chins), as described by Major Fryer, especially as regards marriage, funeral ceremonies, the disposal of the dead (after copious feasting of friends and relatives) by cremation, the rules of inheritance (females being wholly excluded from succession), the treatment of disease, the propitiation of spirits, and the annual festivals in honour of the gods who preside over man's welfare, present the closest analogy to those of the Mikirs as set forth in this monograph. Like the Mikirs, the Chins are divided into exogamous groups and follow the rule of male kinship; but, like the Mikirs also in this, the approved marriage is that between a man and his first cousin on the mother's side. It has been noticed already (p. 21) that the word for *father-in-law* (*òng-hai*, wife's father) in Mikir is identical with that for maternal uncle, *òng*, and that *son-in-law*, *osā*, also means *nephew* (sister's son). The story of "the Orphan and his Maternal Uncles" illustrates the obligation which lies on a lad to marry his mother's brother's daughter (see above, p. 53). Similarly, Harata Kuǹwar, though but a mortal, calls his father-in-law the *Bārī-thē Rēchō ònghai* (p. 147), and is spoken of by him as *osā* (id.), while the fairy princesses call him *cousin*, *kòrpō* (p. 127). The same phenomenon appears in the Kuki-Chin languages. In Shö or Chin

(Khyeng) *apû* means both maternal uncle and father-in-law; so also in Lushei, *pu* has both meanings. The following list of words indicating relationship in Mikir and Lushei (representing the Central Kuki-Chins) shows how closely the two languages correspond in this important part of their vocabulary:—

	Mikir.	*Lushei.*
grandfather	*phu*	*pu*
grandmother	*phi*	*pi*
grandson	*su-po*	*tu-pa*
granddaughter	*su-pi*	*tu-nu*
father	*pō*	*pā*
mother	*pei*	*nu*
aunt:		
father's sister	*nī*	*ni*
mother's sister	*pi-nu*	*nu*
father's brother's wife	*nī*	*nu*

Among all these tribes the most important index to racial connexion is to be found in their languages. No one would now assert that language, any more than religion, is everywhere a conclusive mark of racial unity; immense masses of the people of India to-day speak languages imposed upon them from without, and Aryan speech has extended itself over many millions in whose blood nothing is due to the original invaders from the north-west. Again, the practices of a predatory state of society bring into the tribe slaves and wives from outside; or, as among the Mikirs (p. 33), aliens may be accepted on equal terms as members, thus modifying the unity of blood. On the other hand, it would be equally unreasonable and opposed to the facts to deny that, among such communities as the Tibeto-Burman peoples of Assam, race and language do, constantly and in a general manner, coincide. People who speak a tongue which is unintelligible to their neighbours are necessarily thrown together into a unity of their own. Their ancestral ideas and institutions, secular and religious, their tribal history, must tend to keep them united, and perpetuate the influence of a common origin by the fact that all outside the community are actual or potential enemies. Language, therefore, when it coincides with tribal separateness, is our chief guide in determining the relationship of the hill tribes of Assam one to another.

Here another qualification is, however, necessary. The word-stock of the Tibeto-Burman races is to a large extent identical. The same methods of arranging the elements of the sentence, in other words the same general principles of grammar, prevail throughout the whole family of speech. We must, therefore, in investigating the nearer kinship of one group to another, not be misled by linguistic resemblances which are common to the whole stock to which both groups belong.

In comparing Tibeto-Burman languages it has been usual to choose for examination in the first place the numerals and in the second the pronouns. The vocabulary of nouns, adjectives, and verbs is liable to disturbing influences which do not equally affect the simple ideas represented by number and person. Let us begin, therefore, with the numerals. These, so far as they are necessary for our purpose, are as follows in Mikir:—

one, *isī*
two, *hīnī*
three, *kethòm*
four, *philī*
five, *phòngō*
six, *theròk*
seven, *theròk-sī*
eight, *nĕr-kèp*
nine, *sir-kèp*
ten, *kèp*
eleven, *krē-isī*
twelve, *krē-hīnī*
thirteen, *krē-kethòm*
etc.
a score, *ing-koi*
twenty-one, *ing-koi-rū-isī*
etc.
thirty, *thòm-kèp*
forty, *philī-kèp*
etc.
a hundred, *phārō*

Here the first thing to be noticed is that the three numerals between six and ten are not independent vocables, but compounds; seven is six *plus* one: eight is ten *minus* two, and nine is ten *minus* one. In most of the other languages of the family this is not so; the Boro, the Naga, and the majority of the Kuki-Chin languages all have independent words for seven, eight, and nine. It appears to be only in the Kuki-Chin group that we can find an analogy to the Mikir words for these three numerals. In Anāl, a language of the Old Kuki family spoken in Manipur, seven is *tak-si*, which seems to be identical with the Mikir *theròk-sī*; and in Meithei (the language of the Manipuris) eight is *ni-pān*, "two from ten," and nine is *ma-pān*, "one from ten."

We next notice that *ten* is expressed by two separate words, *kèp* (in ten and its multiples) and *krē* (in the compounds from eleven to nineteen). So far as vocabularies have yet been published, the only other tribes of the Tibeto-Burman family * which have a word resembling *kèp* for ten are Maring Naga, one of the Naga-Kuki languages, where it is *chip*, and Shö or southern Chin, where *gip* is used for ten in the sequence thirty, forty, fifty, etc. (*thum-gip*, thirty, *mlī-gip*, forty, *nghā-gip*, fifty, exactly corresponding to the Mikir *thòm-kèp*, *philī-kèp*, *phòngō-kèp*). The close resemblance of the other numerals in Maring to Mikir forms is noticeable; four is *filī*, five *fungā*, and six *tharuk*. The other word for ten, *krē*, strongly resembles the Angāmi *kerr* or *kerru* and the Kachcha Naga *gārēo;* in the Central Naga group the prefix *ke-* has been replaced by *ta-* or *te-*, and the words for ten are *ter*, *tarā* (Ao), *tarō*, *tarā*, *tarē* (Lhota), etc. In the Naga-Kuki group Sopvoma has *chirō*, Marām *kero*, Tangkhul *tharā*, etc. In the Kuki-Chin group Meithei *tarā* is the same word: in the Central Chin another prefix, *pu-*, *pö-*, or *pā-*, is used, and we have Lai *pörā*, Banjogi *parā*, Taungthā *parhā*. There are no Bo̤ro forms which correspond to *krē*, nor any much resembling *kèp*.

The Mikir word for twenty, *ingkoi*, is made up of the prefix *ing-*, and *koi*, formerly (before the loss of the final *l*) *kol*. Kachcha Naga has the same word, *engkai*, Kabui *choi*, *koi*, or *kol*. The word also appears in Garo (*kol*), Tipura (*khol*), and Deori-Chutiya (*kwa*), of the Bo̤ro group; Angāmi *me-kwū*, *me-khi*, *mekko*, Lhota *me-kwī*, *mekwü*, in the West and Central Naga groups; Marām and Sopvoma (*makē*, *makei*), Tangkhul (*magā*), Phadeng (*ma-kui*), in the Naga-Kuki group, and Singpho *khun*. In the Kuki-Chin languages it is very common (Meithei *kul*, Siyin *kul*, Lai *pö-kul*, Shonshē *ma-kul*, Banjogi *kūl*, Shö [Chin] *kūl*, *goi*). There does not appear to be any trace of this word for a score in the Tibetan and Himalayan languages, where twenty is invariably rendered by "two-tens." † The Northern Indian word *kōṛī*, which has the same meaning, has been compared with it; it is difficult, however, to imagine borrowing on one part or the other.

In the series of tens, 30 to 90, Mikir prefixes the multiplier: *thòm-kèp*, *philī-kèp*, *phòngō-kèp*, etc. The Bo̤ro group prefixes

* Words resembling *kèp* are found for *ten* in some of the pro̤nominalized languages of the lower Himalayas of Nepal; but these do not enter into our present field of comparison.

† Lepcha *khā*, Khaling *khāl*, are probably the same word.

the tens (Garo *sot-brī*, 40, *sot-bonggā*, 50, *sot-dok*, 60, etc.).* The Naga group has both systems; Angāmi prefixes the tens: *lhī*†*-dā*, 40, *lhī-pangu*, 50, *lhī suru*, 60; Lhota and Ao suffix them: Lhota *tham-dro*, 30, *zü-ro*, 40, *rok-ro*, 60; Ao *semur'* 30, *lir'* 40, *rok-ur'* 60. In the Kuki-Chin group the majority of dialects prefix the tens (Thado and Lushei *sōm-thūm* 30, *sōm-lī* 40, etc.), and this is also the rule for Kachcha Naga, Kabui, and Khoirão, as well as for all the languages classed by Dr. Grierson as Naga-Kuki. But the Shö or southern Chins not only have the same collocation as the Mikirs (*thum-gip, mlī-gip, nghā-gip*)—an arrangement which also obtains in Burmese,—*but use the same words.* This coincidence is very striking.

The word for a hundred, *phārō*, bears no resemblance to any word expressing this numeral in the Boṛo languages. It agrees with the Angāmi *krā*, Kezhāmā *krī*, Sopvoma *krē*, and in a remarkable way with the words used by the Southern Chins (Taungthā *ta-yā* = *tarā*, Chinbòk *phyā* = *phrā*, Yawdwin *prā*, Shö (Chin) *krāt*). It will be seen that *phā-* in Mikir, *k-* in the Naga languages, and *ta-*, *ph-*, *p-* and *k-* in the Chin dialects, are numeral prefixes, and that the essential element of the numeral is *rā* (Mikir *rō*) or *rāt*. It appears in this form, without any prefix, in several other Kuki-Chin languages.

Here should be mentioned a custom which obtains in Mikir of counting *by fours;* a group of four is *chekē* or *chikē*, which corresponds to the Boṛo *zakhai* (*jakhai*). This system is used for counting such things as eggs, betel-nuts, fowls, etc., of the same class; *e.g. vo-tī chikē phòngō-rā ē-pum*, 21 eggs (4 × 5 + 1): *chikē phòngō-rā pum-thòm*, 23 eggs (4 × 5 + 3). Possibly one language has borrowed from the other. (This method of counting by fours is common throughout the Aryan languages of Northern India, where a group of four is called *gaṇḍā*.)

Our conclusion from these comparisons is that while Mikir has few coincidences, beyond those common to the whole Tibeto-Burman family, with the Boṛo group, it has many with

* Other Boṛo languages borrow Aryan words for higher numbers than ten.

† *Lhī* is the relic of *krē*, with the prefix *k* dropped and the *r* changed to *l*.

the Naga and Kuki-Chin groups, and especially with the Shö or southernmost Chins.

Before leaving the numerals, something must be said of the prefixes which they exhibit throughout the Tibeto-Burman family. Taking first that member for which we have the oldest materials, Tibetan, the first ten numerals are as follows :—

	As written.	*As now spoken in Central Tibet.*
one	gchig	chik
two	gnyis	nyī
three	gsum	sum
four	bzhi	shi
five	lngā	ngā
six	drug	ḍhuk
seven	bdun	dün
eight	brgyad	gyā
nine	dgu	gu
ten	bchu	chu

Here we observe several different prefixes, once no doubt supplied with vowels, but from the dawn of written record united in Tibetan with the following consonant, and now no longer heard in utterance; in the first three units the prefix is *g-*: in four, seven, eight, and ten it is *b-*: in six and nine it is *d-*: and in five it is *l-*.

In the Tibeto-Burman languages of Assam and Burma we find the same phenomenon of numeral prefixes; but while some languages have the same prefix throughout the ten units, others, like Tibetan, have several different prefixes. In some cases, again, the prefixes have been incorporated in the numeral and are no longer recognized as separable, while in others they may be dropped when the numeral occurs in composition; in others, again, the prefixes have (as in spoken Tibetan) been dropped altogether.

Of the first class the best examples are the Central Kuki-Chin languages :—

	Lai.	*Shonshē.*	*Lushei.*
one	pö-kat	ma-kat	pa-khat
two	pö-ni	ma-nhi	pa-nhih
three	pö-thūm	ma-ton	pa-thum
four	pö-lī	ma-li	pa-lī
five	pö-nga	ma-ngā	pa-ngā
six	pö-ruk	ma-rūk	pa-ruk
seven	pö-sari	ma-seri	pa-sarih
eight	pö-ryeth	ma-rīt	pa-riat
nine	pö-kwa	ma-ko	pa-kuā
ten	pö-ra	ma-rā	shom

Of the second class Mikir, in common with most of the Assam family, is an example; in *one* and *two* the prefix *ke-* (representing the Tibetan *g-*) has been abraded to *ī-* and *hī-*: in *three* it persists; in these numbers the prefix may be dropped in composition, leaving *sī*, *nī*, and *thòm* remaining. In *four* and *five* we have the prefix *phi-* (for *pi-*) and *pho-* (for *po-* or *pa-*), representing the *b-* of Tibetan, but now no longer separable. In *six* the prefix *the-* represents the original *d-*, and has similarly become inseparable. In *ten*, the form *krē* represents an original *kerā*, answering to the Kuki-Chin *pö-rā* and *ma-rā* and the Meithei *ta-rā*. We notice that in Mikir, as in the Naga and Kuki-Chin languages, the hard consonants *k, p, t* (*ph, th*) have replaced the soft *g, b,* and *d* of the Tibetan. In the Boṛo languages, on the other hand, the original soft consonants of Tibetan are retained, as will be seen from the forms below:—

	Boṛo.	*Dimāsā.*	*Garo.*
one	se, sŭi	shī	sā
two	ni, nŭi	ginī	gnī
three	thām	gatam	gitām
four	brè, brŭi	bri	brī
five	bā	bongā	bonggā
six	ro, ḍo	ḍo	ḍok

In these changes Mikir follows the phonetic laws obtaining in Naga and Kuki-Chin, not those which obtain in Boṛo.

It has been pointed out already (p. 78) that generic determinatives are used in Mikir when numbers are joined to nouns. This practice is common to the Boṛo languages and to the Kuki-Chin group (as well as Burmese), but does not appear to be prevalent in the Western Naga group. A list of the words used in Darrang Kachārī is given at p. 13 of Mr. Endle's grammar; for Garo, a list will be found at p. 6 of Mr. Phillips's grammar; it much resembles the Darrang list, but neither contains any forms coinciding with those of Mikir except the Garo *pat*, used for leaves and other flat things, which resembles the Mikir *pàk*. On the other hand, in Kuki-Chin we have in Lai *pum* for globular things,* the same as in Mikir, and in Shö (Chin) we have for persons *pün*, the Mikir *bàng* (*bàng* in Mikir and *pang* in Lushei mean *body*), and for animals *zün*, the Mikir *jòn* (Mr. Houghton's grammar, p. 20). Here again the affinity of the Arleng is with the Kuki-Chin group,

* *Linguistic Survey*, vol. III. part iii., p. 118.

and especially with its southernmost member, rather than with the Boṛo.

Turning now to the pronouns, the Mikir *nē* for the first person singular finds it exact equivalent only in the two Old Kuki dialects Anāl and Hirōi, spoken in Manipur, where the corresponding pronoun is *ni* (Anāl) and *nai* (Hirōi). In Boṛo the form is *āng*, in Angāmi *ā*, in Sema *ngi*, in Ao *nī*, in Lhota *ā*, in Kachcha Naga *ānui*. In the majority of the Kuki-Chin family another stem, *kei* or *kē*, is used. Here Mikir agrees with the two Kuki dialects mentioned and with some of the Naga forms, rather than with Boṛo.

For the second person singular all the Tibeto-Burman languages of Assam have *nàng*, or closely similar forms.

For the third person Mikir now uses the demonstrative *lā*, but, as the possessive prefix shows, had formerly *ā*. In this it agrees with Lai, Lushei, Chiru, Kolren among the Kuki family, and Tangkhul and Maring among the Naga-Kuki group. What the original Boṛo pronoun of the third person was is not now ascertainable; the demonstrative *bi* (Darrang), *bē* (Lalung), *bō* (Dīmāsā) or *uā* (Garo) is now used instead. This seems to correspond with the Mikir *pe-*, *pi-*, *pā-* in the words mentioned on p. 80. In Angāmi the pronoun is similarly *pō*, in Sema *pā*, and in Ao *pā*. In Meithei and many other Kuki-Chin languages another demonstrative, *ma*, is used; this may be connected with the Mikir *mi*, *me*, in *minī*, to-day, *menàp*, to-morrow (see p. 80). But, although *ma* is used as a separate pronoun for the third person in the majority of the Kuki-Chin group, the prefixed *ā-* of relation, usual in Mikir, which (as explained on p. 76) is really the possessive pronoun of the third person, is widely employed throughout the family, as a prefix both to nouns and adjectives, in exactly the same way as in Mikir. This coincidence, again, is striking; the Boṛo languages seem to present nothing similar.

The plural pronouns in Mikir are formed by adding *-tum* to the singular. Exactly the same thing takes place in Tangkhul, a Naga-Kuki language: *i*, I, *i-thum*, we; *nā*, thou, *nā-thum*, ye; *ā*, he, *ā-thum*, they. The plural of nouns, however, in Tangkhul is formed by other affixes, generally words meaning "many" (*cf.* the Mikir *òng*).

Mikir has two forms for the pronoun of the first person plural, according as the speaker includes the person addressed or excludes him, *ī-tum* or *ē-tum* in the former and *nē-tum* in the latter case. The first, it will be seen, agrees with the general word for *we* in Tangkhul. In Angāmi also two forms are used, *hē-ko* for *we* exclusive, and *ā-vo* for *we* inclusive; the former seems to agree in form, though not in sense, with the Mikir *ē-tum*. The affinity of Mikir with the Western Naga and Naga-Kuki languages seems to be exemplified here also. The Boṛo languages have not the double form for this person.

The reflexive pronoun or particle in Mikir, *che* (see p. 80), is represented in Thado Kuki by *ki*, which is perhaps the same word. Angāmi has *the*, Meithei *na*. Boṛo does not appear to possess any corresponding particle.

The interrogative particle *-mā* in Mikir (p. 80) is *mo* in most of the Kuki-Chin languages (in some *-em*, *-am*), while in Angāmi it is *mā*, and in Kachcha Naga *mē*. The same particle (*mā*) is used in Garo and Boṛo for questions.

Two particles are used in Mikir as suffixes to magnify or diminish the root-word; the augmentative is *-pī* (as *thèng*, wood, firewood, *thèngpī*, a tree; *làng*, water, *làngpī*, the great water, the sea), the diminutive is *-sō* (as *hèm*, a house, *hèmsō*, a hut; *làng-sō*, a brook). Boṛo has *-mā* for the augmentative, *-sā* for the diminutive (*dui-mā*, great river, *dui-sā*, brook); but Meithei and Thado have the same particles as Mikir, *-pī* and *-chā* (*ch* is equivalent to *s*).

The Mikir suffix *-pō*, feminine *-pī*, corresponding to the Hindī *-wālā* (see several examples on p. 12 *ante*), seems to be identical with the Meithei *-bā* (*-pā*) and *-bī* (*-pī*), though it has nothing like the extensive use in Mikir which *-bā* (*-pā*) has in Meithei.

The noteworthy separable prefix *ār-* in Mikir, which is probably connected with the Tibetan prefix *r-* (see *ante*, p. 129, note), appears to occur in the Kuki-Chin languages, but does not seem to have any representative in the Boṛo family. The examples in the Kuki-Chin volume of the *Linguistic Survey* are found in Rangkhol (p. 6, *er-ming*, "name"), Aimol (p. 215, *ra-mai*, "tail," Mikir *ārmē*), Kōm (p. 245, *ra-mhing*, "name";

ra-nai, "earth, ground" [*nai* perhaps = Mikir *lĕ* in *lòng-lĕ*]), Kyaw or Chaw (p. 254), and Hirōi (p. 282). All these forms of speech belong to the Old Kuki group, which has already yielded several other analogies with Mikir.

The prefix *ke-* (*ki-*, *kā-*), which plays so important a part in Mikir (see pp. 77, 83, 84) in the formation of adjectives, participles, and verbal nouns, and answers to the Boṛo *ga-* and the Angāmi *ke-*, has for the most part disappeared from the Kuki dialects, perhaps because it conflicts with the prefixed pronominal stem of the first person, *ka-*. It survives, however, in the three Old Kuki languages, Kōm, Anāl, and Hirōi. In Tangkhul, of the Naga-Kuki group, it is used exactly as in Mikir, to form adjectives and verbal nouns, *e.g.*:—

	Mikir.	*Tangkhul.*
to come	ke-vàng	ka-vā (to go)
to eat	ke-chō	ka-shāi
to remain	ke-bòm	ka-pam (to sit)
to beat	ke-chòk	ka-shō
to die	ke-thī	ka-thī

The particles used in Mikir as suffixes to indicate tenses of the verb, with the exception of that for the completed past, *tàng*, which appears to be identical with the Thado and Lushei *tā*, do not seem to have any close analogues in the Kuki-Chin or Naga-Kuki groups; they are also quite different from those used in the Boṛo group. Causative verbs, however, are in many Kuki-Chin languages constructed with the verb *pē* or *pèk*, "to give," as in Mikir; and the suffix of the conjunctive participle in Mikịr, *-sī*, is perhaps the same as *-chū* in Khoirāo. In Boṛo the prefix *fi-*, answering to the Mikir *pi-*, was formerly used to form causatives, as appears from verbal roots in current use; the construction now most common uses *-nu*, which has the same meaning ("to give") as a *suffix*.

The negative verb in Mikir is formed by suffixing the particle *-ē* to the positive root, when the latter begins with a vowel. Similarly, in Boṛo a negative verb is formed by adding the particle *-ā*. In the Kuki-Chin languages different suffixes are employed (*lo*, *lai*, *loi*, *māk*, *ri*), and in a few dialects prefixes. Here Mikir resembles Boṛo rather than the Kuki group. But the remarkable feature of Mikir in reduplicating initial consonants before the suffixed negative (see *ante*, p. 85) has no analogy in either family, unless the isolated example in Kolren (an Old Kuki dialect) quoted in the *Linguistic Survey*, vol. III., part iii., p. 19, supplies one. It is to be observed, however, that in the construction there cited (*na-pē-pèk-māo-yai*, "did not give"), the verb *pèk* has suffixed to it the negative particle *māo*, and that the reduplication alone appears to have no negative force. Other examples seem necessary before the rule of reduplication can be considered to be established. Possibly *loi* and *lai* in Kuki correspond to the separate Mikir negative *kā-lī* (see *ante*, p. 86).

It remains to give some examples of correspondence in general vocabulary between Mikir and other Tibeto-Burman languages. It has been shown above from the analysis of the numerals that prefixes play a large part in all these languages. These prefixes, which to some extent are interchangeable, and also differ in the different members of the family, have to be eliminated in order to find the roots which are to be compared. Again, certain changes in vowels and consonants between different languages regularly occur. Our knowledge is not yet sufficient to enable a law of interchange to be formulated; but the following conclusions seem to be justified. In vowels, Mikir has a preference for long *ō* where other languages have -*ā*, especially in *auslaut*;* on the other hand long *ā* in Mikir is sometimes thinned down to *ē*; the word *rēchō*, answering to the Aryan *rājā*, is an example of both processes. Long *ī* in Mikir often corresponds to *oi* and *ai*, as well as to *ē* and *ei*, in the cognates. As regards consonants, nasals at the end of syllables are often rejected; thus within Mikir itself we have *ō* and *òng*, *dā* and *dàm*, *nē* and *nèng*, *lā* and *làng*. Some languages (as for instance Angāmi† Naga) tolerate no consonantal endings, not even a nasal. In Mikir itself final *l* has been vocalised into *i* or dropped; and in many Naga and Kuki-Chin dialects (as also in Burmese) final consonants have disappeared or have suffered great changes. As already noticed,

* Southern Chin, as will be seen from the word-lists which follow, agrees in this respect with Mikir against Lushei, Meithei, and other Kuki-Chin languages.

† The only exception in Angāmi is *r*, in which a few words end.

the surd mutes *k*, *p*, *t* (sometimes aspirated) have taken the place of the original sonants *g*, *b*, *d* to a large extent in Mikir, though *b* and *d* (not *g*) still survive in a fair proportion of words. Boṛo generally retains the old sonants of Tibetan, and Meithei uses both classes according to the adjacent sounds. The palatals *ch*, *j* of Mikir tend to become sibilants, *s*, *ts*, *z*, in the cognate languages; *j* is also often softened to *y* in Kuki-Chin. *L* and *r* in *anlaut* frequently interchange in Meithei, the interchange depending on the adjacent vowels. These letters also interchange freely in other languages of the family. In Burmese *r* has everywhere been changed to *y*, except in Arakan. *L* and *n* also often interchange. Initial *d* in Mikir seems sometimes to correspond to *l* in other cognates; and it is possible that Mikir initial *s* may occasionally be represented by *h* in the latter, though this is not quite certain. *Th* and *s* often interchange in *anlaut*, some dialects of Kuki-Chin showing the intermediate stage of *θ*, which in Burmese now everywhere replaces original *s*.

Lastly, it should be noticed that Tipura, an outlying member of the Boṛo group, often exhibits a sound system more closely corresponding to that of the Kuki-Chin languages (which are its neighbours) than Boṛo, Dīmāsā, or Garo.

The resemblances in vocabulary between Mikir and the Western Naga dialects are extensive, as will be seen from the list (due to Mr. A. W. Davis) at p. 201, vol. III., part ii., of the *Linguistic Survey*. These need not be repeated here. The following is a list of Boṛo (Darrang), Dīmāsā, Garo, and Tipura words which seem to correspond with Mikir. It will be seen, however, by reference to the columns headed Kuki-Chin and Naga (including Naga-Kuki), that in the case of nearly all these words the other two families, as well as Mikir, have the same roots. They therefore belong to the common stock of the Tibeto-Burman languages of Assam, and do not by themselves prove any close connection of Mikir with Boṛo.

Nouns.

English.	*Mikir.*	*Boro family.*	*Kuki-Chin.*	*Naga.*
nose	nōkàn	*Garo*, nukum, nākung *Tipura*, bukung	*Meithei* nātōl (n) *Thado* nakui *Lushei* nhār	*Tangkhul* nātūng *Angāmi* ā-niki *E. Naga* nākong nātong
eye	mèk	*Boro* mēgan *Dīmāsā* mu *Garo* mik-rēn	*Meithei* *Thado* } mit *Lushei* *Shö* (*Chin*) mik	*Ang.* mhi, mhü *Tangk.* mik *Marām* mek *E. Naga* mik, mek
mouth	ing-hō	*Boro* khū-ga *Dīmāsā* khau *Garo* hō-tom, ku-sik	*Lushei* kā *Khāmī* khā *Shö* khō	*Ang.* thā, mē-thā *Rengma* màng-khòng
tooth	sō	*Boro* hā-thau *Dīmāsā* *id.*	*Andro* sho *Sengmai* shoa *Thado* *Lushei* } hā *Shö* haw	*Ang.* ho, hu *Sema* a-hu
ear	nō	*Garo* nā-chil, nā-kāl	*Meithei* *Lai* } nā *Shö* a-nhō	*Ang.* nü *Lhota* en-nō *Maring* ka-nā
face	me-hàng	*Boro* makhàng *Garo* mikkang *Tipura* muk-hàng	*Meithei* māe *Lushei* hmai	
belly	pòk	*Dīmāsā* ho *Garo* ok, pī-puk *Tipura* bahak	*Meithei* puk *Andro* pūk *Shö* puk *Lai* paw *Thado* wai	*Ang.* vā *Sema* ā-pfo *Lhota* o-pòk
father	pō	*Boro* *Dīmāsā* } fā *Garo* pā, bā *Tipura* bā	*Meithei* *Lushei* } pā *Thado* *Sengmai* *Khami* } pō *Shö*	*Ang.* pō *Sema* pā *Ao* ta-bā *Lhota* o-pō
son	sō-pō	*Boro* f'sā *Dīmāsā* pasā, sā *Garo* sā, pī-sā *Tipura* basā	*Meithei* *Thado* } chāpā *Khami* chōpo *Shö* chō	*Lhota* o-tsöe *Maring* chā *Hatigoria* chāpā
daughter	sō-pī	*Dīmāsā* pu-su	*Meithei* cha-(anu)-pī *Khami* numpui-chō	
cat	mèng, mèng-kālū	*Garo* mèng-gō *Tipura* ā-mīng	*Thado* meng-chā *Rangkhol* meng *Shö* min	
iron	ing-chin	*Boro* shurr *Dīmāsā* shēr *Garo* sil, sar *Tipura* sir	*Andro* sēn, sēl *Lushei* thīr *Thado* *Shö* } thī *Khami* sing	*Ang.* the-zhī *Yachumi* inchi *Thukumi* īsē

ADJECTIVES.

English.	*Mikir.*	*Boro family.*	*Kuki-Chin.*	*Naga.*
big	kethē	*Boro* gadet		*Ang.* kedī
small	kibī, bi-hèk	*Boro* gahai	*Meithei* ā-pīsek	
bitter	kehō	*Boro* gakhā	*Lushei* khā *Meithei* khā-ba *Thado* a-khā	
cold	ke-chung	*Boro* gazang	*Lushei* shik	
beautiful	mēsèn, mē	*Boro* mozang	*Lushei* moi	

VERBS.

English.	*Mikir.*	*Boro family.*	*Kuki-Chin.*	*Naga.*
go	dàm	*Boro*, *Dīmāsā*, *Tipura* } thàng		*Ang.* tā *Sopvoma* tā-o *Maring* tā-so
come	vàng	*Boro*, *Dīmāsā*, *Tipura* } fai		*Ang.* vor *Kwoireng*, *Marām* } pā-lo
eat	chō	*Boro* zā *Dīmāsā* jī *Garo* chā, sā *Tipura* chā	*Meithei* chā-ba *Khami* chā (*Burmese* chā, tsā)	*Ang.* chi *Kwoireng* tyū-lo *Tangkhul* ka-shāi
beat	chòk	*Dīmāsā* shu		*Tangkhul* ka-sho
die	thi	*Boro* thoi *Dīmāsā* tī, thei *Garo* tī, sī, tai *Tipura* thai	*Meithei* sī-ba *Thado* thī *Lushei* tī *Khami* dēi	*Ang.* sā *Sema* ti *Sopvoma* thiyē *Marām* tei-lo *Tangkhul* ka-thī
run	kàt	*Boro* khāt *Dīmāsā* khai *Garo* kat	*Meithei* chatpa (?) (to go) *Andro* kat-e *Tangkhul* ka-chat	
say	pu	*Boro* bung		*Ang.* pu
do, work	klèm	*Boro* khlàm		
think	māthā	*Boro* mithi		
be necessary	nàng	*Boro* nàng *Garo* nàng	*Lushei* ngai	

The above list exhibits all the coincidences which could be found on a search through the vocabulary appended to Mr. Endle's Kachāri grammar, and it will be seen that the agreement is not extensive.

The words in which Tibeto-Burman languages agree most widely with one another are perhaps those for *water* and *village;* for the former *dī, tī, tui, dzü, zu, jī, chī,* and other similar forms, all apparently identical with the Tibetan *chhu* and the Turki *su*, run through the whole family: for the latter *khul, khu, ku* (Turki *kū, kūi*) are similarly widespread. It is somewhat surprising to find in Mikir an exception to the general rule. *Water* is *làng*, and *village* is *ròng*. Searching through the tribal vocabularies, Tangkhul Naga (a Naga-Kuki form of speech) appears to have, in *ta-rā*, the corresponding word to *làng* (*r* = *l*, and *ta* a prefix). Nowhere else in the neighbourhood is there a trace of a similar word until we come to Burmese, where *water* is *rē* (now pronounced *yē*). Similarly, it appears to be only in Burmese that we have a word for *village*, *rwā*, corresponding to the Mikir *ròng*. These coincidences, like others already mentioned, seem to point to the south for the affinities of the Mikir race. At the same time it is to be observed that Mikir appears once to have had, like the Kuki-Chin languages generally, the word *tī* for *water*. This survives in the word for *egg*, *vo-tī*, which must mean "fowl's water," and corresponds in sense to the Boṛo *dau-dui*, Chutiya *du-ji*, Garo *do-chi*, Shō (Chin) *a-tui*. In Angāmi and Lushei "fowl" is omitted, and the word for "egg" is merely *dzü, tui*, = water.*

It would be tedious to enumerate the coincidences in vocabulary which are found between Mikir and all the Kuki-Chin dialects. We have had reason to expect that these coincidences will be found to be most numerous with the Chin languages spoken in the Southern Hill tracts to the west of the Irawadi Valley; and the following list of similar words will show that this expectation is borne out by the facts. In most cases the forms in Lushei, a leading language of the Central Kuki-Chin group, are added; where they are wanting the Mikir word does not appear to have any corresponding form in that language.†

* This seems to make it improbable that, as suggested on p. 109, *chuī* in *vār-chuī* and *nīm-chuī* (to throw into water, to drown) is connected with the Tibetan *chhu*.

† The Chin words are taken from Mr. B. Houghton's *Essay on the Language of the Southern Chins and its Affinities* (Rangoon, 1892). In transcribing them *h* has been substituted for ' to indicate the aspirate, but the spelling has not been otherwise varied. The Lushei words are from Messrs. Lorrain and Savidge's *Grammar and Dictionary of the Lushai Language* (*Dulien dialect*) (Shillong, 1898); here too the spelling of the original has been retained.

NOUNS.

English.	*Mikir.*	*Chin (Shö).*
male (of man)	pinso	pa-tho (*Lushei* pasal)
female (of mankind)	-pī suffixed	-nü * suffixed (*L.* nu, and pui)
body	bàng	ā-pün (*L.* pàng)
corpse	āru	ayö (*L.* ruang)
face	mehàng	hmoi-san (*L.* hmai)
nose	nō-kàn	hnut-tō (*Meithei* nā-tōn, *L.* hnā)
ear	nō	a-hnō
eye	mèk	a-mī, mik (*L.* mit)
[tear	āmèk-krī	a-mī-khlī]
tongue	dē	lē (*L.* lei)
mind, breast, heart	ning	a-mlüng (*L.* lung)
[angry	ā-ning-kethī	a-mlüng-thö (*L.* thi-n-lung-sha)]
back	nung	a-hling (*L.* hnung)
arm	phàng	bawn (*L.* bawn)
foot, leg	kèng	khön or khö (*L.* kē, *Burmese* khyè)
stomach	pòk	pük
[stomach-ache	pòk-kesō	pük-thō]
hair of body	àng-mī	a-hmaw (*L.* hmul)
bone	rē-pī	yo'' (*Lushei* ruh, *Angāmi* ru)
tail	ār-mē	ho-mē (*L.* mei)
old man, chief	sār, sārpo	hsan, hsan-bo
son	osō, sō-pō	hsō (*Burmese* sā [θā])
tiger	te-kē	ā-kyē (*L.* sa-kei, *Burmese* kyā)
cow	chainòng	hsaw-nü (*L.* sē-bawng)
pig	phàk	wök, wō (*Burmese* wak)
squirrel	kārlē	a-hlē (*L.* the-hlei)
rat	phijū	pha-yü (*L.* sa-zu)
bird	vo	wu (*L.* vā)
kite	vo-mū	a-hmū (*L.* mu)
parrot	vo-kèk	a-kyē (*L.* va-ki, *Burmese* kyē)
bat	vo-ārplàk	phalau*h*
crayfish, prawn	chekung	kyē-khön (*L.* kai-kuang)
scale of fish	lip	lit (*L.* hlip)
louse	rèk	hèk (*L.* hrik)
land-leech	ingphàt	a-wot (*L.* vang-vàt)
sun	ār-nī	kho-nī (*L.* annī, nī)
moon	chi-klō	khlō (*L.* thlā)
night	ā-jō	yan (*L.* zān, jān)
rain	ār-vē	yō-ō (*L.* ruah, *Burmese* rwa)
fire	mē	mē (*L.* mei)
[a flint for striking fire	mē-chèt ā-lòng *i.e.* fire-spark-stone	mē-khā-lün (*L.* mei-lung), fire-spark-stone]
smoke	mihi	mē-khū (*L.* mei-khu)
steam	hi	a-hū (*L.* hu)
stone	ār-lòng	a-lün (*L.* lung)
rice	sàng	saung

* In Mikir this root is perhaps found in *pi-nu*, mother's sister, *nimso*, a virgin, and *chai-nòng*, cow. *Chainòng* is now used for both sexes, but the cognate languages point to *chai* (for *chal*) being the original word for the bovine species.

English.	*Mikir.*	*Chin (Shö).*
vegetables	hàn	awn (*L.* an)
house	hèm	in (*L.* in, *Burmese* im)
wood, tree	thèng, thèngpī	then″ (*L.* thīng)
leaf	lō	law (*Meithei* lā, *Thado* nā, *L.* hnā)
fruit	ā-thē	thē (*L.* thei)
seed	ā-thē	sē
cotton	phēlō	phoi
broom	ār-phèk	phā-phē
iron	ingchin	n'thi (*L.* thīr)
arrow	thai	ā-thaw (*L.* thāl)
bow	thai-lī	ā-lī (*L.* thāl-ngul)
boat	tē-lòng	hmlū or hmlü (*L.* long)
earring	nō-thèngpī	nā-thong
basket	tòn	tawng
dream	màng	maung (*L.* māng)
name	mèn	a-mín (*L.* hming)
matter, affair	hormū	a-hmū (*Burmese* id.)
heap	bui	ā-pün (*L.* vūng, būm)
place	dim	awn-dün
edge, border	ā-prē	ā-pē
rope	ā-rī	a-yöh (*L.* hrui)
handle	bē	bī″ (to take, seize), (*L.* bèng)

VERBS.

to pour out	bu, bup	bauk, bō (*L.* bua*k*,* bun)
to put	bī	bī (to clap, pat)
to jump	chòng	dong (*L.* zuang)
to die	thī	dü, dī (*L.* thī)
to kill by cutting	thū	thük, tük
to pound	tòk	dut″
to open	ing-pu	hü
to sleep, lie down	ī	ī″ (*Burmese* ip)
to hinder	khàng	khā
to fall	klō, klī	klauk (*Burmese* krā, *L.* tlā, tlā*k*)
to grind	koi-ī	kluk
to be bitter	hō	khō (*L.* khā)
to bend	kekèk	kòk-lök, khü-ī
to tie, fasten	kòk	khun
to laugh	ing-nèk	hlek ; *also* noi (*Meithei* nok, *L.* nui)
to arrive, hit	lē	leng
to be distant	hē-lō	hlō (*L.* hlā)
to get, obtain	lòng	lö-ē
to lick	ing-lèk	m-lē-ē (*L.* lia*k*, hliao)
to be happy	mē	moi
to extinguish	pe-mèp	hmyit (*L.* ti-mit)
to smell	ing-nim	nan (*L.* hnim)
to be yellow	èt	oi (*L.* eng)
to speak	pu	pauh (a word, language)
to give	pī	pèk (*L.* pèk, pē)
to be full	plèng	plē

* A final mute italicised in Lushei words indicates that it is formed with the vocal organs, but not pronounced.

English.	*Mikir.*	*Chin (Shö).*
to reach, touch	phō	phō (*L.* paw*h*, phā*k*)
to pull out	phu	phuk (*L.* phoi)
to work, labour	sai	sai*h*
to wash	chàm	shau (*L.* shu*k*)
to beat	chòk	shö
to pierce	chàng	shün, hsün (*L.* chhun)
to begin	chèng	sī
to explain	thàn	hsin
to be wet	chàm	sō
to know, perceive	thèk	thàk, thē
to be fat	ing-tu	thau (*L.* thao)
to itch	ing-thàk	thauk (*L.* thāk)
to rise, get up	thur	thö, thü (*L.* tho, thaw*h*)
to send	toi	thō
to weave	thàk	tō-tàk (*L.* tah)
to rot	thu	thü (*L.* toih)
to be sweet	dòk	tü-ī
to cover, veil	up, òp	ün'' (*L.* hup)
to throw	vār	wo'' (*L.* vorh)
to hear	ār-ju	yauk
to sell	jòr	yi'' (*L.* zuar)

A few words from Lushei may be added, for which Southern Chin does not appear to possess corresponding terms :—

English.	*Mikir.*	*Lushei.*
buffalo	chelòng	cheloi
bear	thòk-vàm	sa-vom, vom *
deer (*sāmbhar*)	thi-jòk	sa-zuk
snake	phi-rui	ma-rul, rul
monkey	me-sàng	zawng
frog ("the jumper")	chòng-hō	chung-u
mosquito	timsik	tho-shī
water-leech	ing-lit	hlit, sai-hlit
crab	chehē	chak-ai
devil	hī-ī	huai

These close and numerous correspondences between Mikir and the Kuki-Chin family appear to warrant the conclusion that the former is intimately connected with the latter. The institutions of the southern tribes, as already pointed out, confirm this conclusion; and it may be asserted with some confidence that no such extensive affinity can be proved between Mikir and the Boṛo family. As regards the Western Nagas, while the institutions largely correspond, the coincidences in language, though more numerous than those with

* *Sa* in Lushei means *animal*, and we see that the prefix *te-* (in *tekē*, tiger), *thi-* (in *thi-jòk*, deer), or *thòk-* (in *thòk-vàm*, bear) has the same meaning in Mikir.

Boro̩, are much fewer than those with Kuki-Chin. The Southern Nagas, and especially the Tangkhuls, who form the group intermediate between Naga and Kuki, have a considerably closer affinity with Mikir. Possibly if the inquiry were pushed further into Burmese than is within the power of the present writer, more correspondences with Mikir might be discovered in that language.

BIBLIOGRAPHY.

1. *A descriptive account of Asam, with a sketch of the local geography, and a concise history of the Tea-plant of Asam, to which is added a short account of the neighbouring tribes, exhibiting their history, manners and customs,* by William Robinson, Gowhatti Government Seminary: Calcutta, 1841. Account of the Mikirs at pp. 308–312.

The facts stated agree generally with those recorded by Mr. Stack. The chief deity of the Mikirs is called *Hempatin.* This may be a mistranscription for *Hemphu,* but is more probably a mistake due to a confusion between Mikirs and Kukis; *Pātīn* (or a closely similar form) is the word for God in a number of the Kuki dialects (Khongzai, Thado, Lushei, Rangkhōl, Aimōl, Kōlrēn, etc.). Of course if the name *Hempatin* was ever actually used by the Mikirs for their chief tribal god, this would be an additional important evidence of a connexion between them and the Kukis.

2. *Notes on the languages of the various tribes inhabiting the Valley of Asam and its mountain confines,* by Wm. Robinson, Inspector of Government Schools in Asam. *Journal of the Asiatic Society of Bengal,* vol. xviii. (1849).

The Mikir language is treated at pp. 330–336. It is probable from certain indications that the Mikir words were written down for Mr. Robinson in Assamese characters, and transliterated by him into Roman. There are a great many misprints. The declension of nouns, the distinctions of gender, and the position of adjectives are in general correctly explained; but the important prefix *ā-* is not noticed, nor its original force understood. The omission of the plural affix *-tum* is remarkable. The numerals agree with those of the present day, save that *ch* is used (as in Assamese) to indicate *s.* The use of determinative class-words with numerals is mentioned. The personal pronouns are in part correctly, but often wrongly given; the demonstrative pronouns are wrongly stated, and so are the interrogatives. The absence of a relative pronoun, and the substitute for it, are noticed. In the verbal forms there are many errors, unless the particles used to indicate time have greatly changed since 1849, which is improbable. Thus, *-ye* is given as the future suffix instead of *-jī*, and *-bō* instead of *po*. The participle in *ke-*, *ki-*, *kā-* is omitted, and the much-used conjunctive participle in *-sī* is misrepresented as the present participle. There is no mention of the past in *tàng; āyok* (possibly a mistranscription of the Assamese) is given instead of *āpòt* as the particle indicating purpose. The form of the negative verb is altogether misunderstood. There is no mention of the causative in *pe-*, *pi-*, *pā-*.

One interesting point in Mr. Robinson's grammatical sketch is that words borrowed from Assamese, which now end in *-i* as a substitute for Assamese *l*, as *hai* for *hāl*, *tāmoi* for *tāmol*, *pītoi* for *pītol*, are all written with *l;* and in the following cases final *l* appears in Mikir words now written with final *i*:—

ingkol, a score, now *ingkoi*
inghol, to do, now *inghoi*
sāl (field-) work, now *sai*
āphel, afterwards, now *āphī*
phurul, snake, now *phirui*

It seems possible that this represents a real change in pronunciation, since *l* was certainly the original ending in the borrowed words, and most probably (from the similar forms in the Kuki-Chin languages) was the original ending in the Mikir words. This vocalization of final *l* is quite common in the Kuki dialects, and is an additional argument for their connexion with Mikir.

3. *Travels and adventures in the Province of Assam*, by Major John Butler: London, Smith, Elder & Co., 1855. The Mikirs are described at pp. 126–139. Major Butler was in charge of the district of Nowgong, and visited the Mikir Hills in 1848. His notes on the Mikir people are not very detailed, but indicate that their condition sixty years ago was much the same as it is now. On the question of polygamy (see *ante*, p. 19), he writes (p. 138): "Polygamy is not practised, and they reproach their countrymen of the plains for having adopted the Assamese custom."

4. *Notes on Northern Cachar*, by Lieut. R. Stewart. J.A.S.B., vol. xxiv. (1855), pp. 582-701. This treatise is an excellent account of the various tribes inhabiting the tract. The Mikirs are dealt with at pp. 604–607. There is a full and useful comparative vocabulary at pp. 658–675 of more than 400 words, besides verbal and adverbial forms, in Manipuri, Hill Kachāri (Dīmāsā), New Kuki (Thado), Angāmi Naga, Arung Naga (or Ēmpēo), Old Kuki (Bētē), and Mikir. This is much the most important evidence of the state of the language half a century ago, and is superior in several respects to the materials collected a little earlier by Robinson (to which Stewart does not refer). The Mikir words are generally recognisable as identical with those of the present day, and it is noticeable, with reference to the change of final *l* to *i*, that Stewart gives the forms now in use (*pitoi*, brass, *pheroi*, snake, *ingkoi*, a score *in(g)hoi*, to do). The verbs are chiefly given in the imperative, with *nòn* (often wrongly printed *not*), sometimes as the bare root, and sometimes with *-lo* added. There are some good measurements and other physical characters of Mikirs at pp. 690–693, from which it appears that in Lieut. Stewart's time most of the Mikir men shaved their heads, with the exception of a large tuft of hair on the scalp.

5. *Descriptive Ethnology of Bengal*, by Col. E. T. Dalton: Calcutta, 1872. There is a brief section on the Mikirs at pp. 53–4, which however contains no information that is not in Robinson or Stewart. The race is not among those figured in the volume.

6. *Specimens of the Languages of India*, collected by Sir George Campbell: Calcutta, 1874. The specimens of Mikir are at pp. 205–217; they are full of misprints and misunderstandings of what was desired, and are worthless for linguistic purposes.

7. *A Vocabulary in English and Mikir, with sentences illustrating the use of words*, by the Rev. R. E. Neighbor, of Nowgong, Assam: Calcutta, 1878.

A most useful publication.

8. *Notes on the Locality and Population of the Tribes dwelling between the Brahmaputra and Ningthi Rivers*, by G. H. Damant. *Journal of the Royal Asiatic Society*, vol. xii., 1880, pp. 228 *ff.*

A posthumous work (Mr. Damant was killed in the Naga Hills in 1879). The Mikirs are mentioned on p. 236, and there is a short vocabulary on p. 254.

9. *A Statistical Account of Assam*, compiled by J. S. Cotton under the direction of W. W. Hunter: London, 1879. Contains an article on the Mikirs at vol. ii., pp. 188–190.

10. *A Gazetteer of India*, by Sir W. W. Hunter, London. First edition 1881, second edition 1886. Article on the Mikir Hills and their inhabitants.

11 to 13. The next occasions on which the tribe was dealt with were in the Reports of the Censuses of 1881, 1891, and 1901 (Assam Province):—

11. *The Report on the Census of* 1881 (Calcutta, 1883) contains a chapter (VI.) on *Castes and Tribes*, written by Mr. Stack. The Mikirs are described at pp. 77–82. The inquiries on which these paragraphs were based were followed by the more detailed investigations which afforded the materials for the present monograph.

12. *The Report on the Census of* 1891, by Mr. E. A. Gait, reproduces part of the matter of the previous report relating to the Mikirs, and adds the detailed list of *kurs* or exogamous divisions already referred to (*ante*, pp. 23 *ff.*). It also contains an interesting comparison of the Mikir language with those of the Naga tribes, by Mr. A. W. Davis (reproduced in the *Linguistic Survey*, vol. iii., part ii., pp. 198–202). At pp. 254–256 there is an account of the Mikirs in North Cachar by Mr. E. C. Baker, sub-divisional officer, which states that their principal deity is called "Pertart Rijie." This is correctly *Pirthàt Rĕchō*, the first word being the Khasi *Pyrthat*, "thunder," and indicates a borrowing by the small remaining Mikir population in North Cachar of the ideas of their Khasi neighbours.

13. *The Report on the Census of* 1901, by Mr. B. C. Allen: Shillong, 1902. A few remarks on the religion of the Mikirs will be found at pp. 46–47, which however require correction by the more accurate data contained in this monograph.

14. *The Tribes of the Brahmaputra Valley*, by Lt.-Col. L. A. Waddell, I.M.S.: J.A.S.B., vol. lxix., part iii., 1900. This account is chiefly based on anthropometrical data. The facts stated concerning the Arlengs at pp. 29–35 appear to be taken

from Dalton and the Assam Census Reports of 1881 and 1891. The measurements taken by Col. Waddell (see *ante*, p. 4) are at pp. 78–79. The tribe is not figured in the plates appended to the paper.

15. *Linguistic Survey of India*, vol. iii., part ii., compiled and edited by Dr. G. A. Grierson, Calcutta, 1902. The Mikir language is dealt with at pp. 380–410 and 432–448.

16. *An English-Mikir Vocabulary, with Assamese Equivalents, to which have been added a few Mikir phrases*, by S[ardoka] P[errin] Kay: Shillong, Govt. Press, 1904. An extremely useful book by an educated Mikir (see Introductory Note, p. viii.). Sardoka was Mr. Stack's chief authority on the Mikir language. The phrases (388 in number) are very important illustrations of the structure of the speech. The vocabulary is an enlargement of Mr. Neighbor's work (No. 7).

A Mikir-English dictionary or vocabulary is still a desideratum.

The following is a list of all the publications in the Mikir language which have come under the notice of the writer. They are all due to missionaries.

1. *Dhorom Ārnàm āphràng ikithàn:* First Catechism, in Mikir (Assamese character), pp. 13. Anon. Sibsagar, 1875.

2. *Ārlĕng Ālàm*, a Mikir Primer, by Miss E. Pursell, 1891.

3. *Ārlĕng Ālàm (Plīplī-ākitàp)*.* A Mikir Primer. Anon. Published by the American Baptist Mission, Tika, Nowgong, Assam, 1903.

4. *Ārlĕng Ālàm, Āngbòng ākitàp.* Mikir Reader, second book, by the Rev. J. M. Carvell and Thengkur Pandit. Published by the Government of Assam, Shillong, 1904.

5. *Ārlĕng kālākhā ākitàp.* Mikir Primary Arithmetic, by the Rev. P. E. Moore and the Rev. J. M. Carvell. Published by the Assam Secretariat Press, Shillong, 1904.

6. *Birtā Kemē*, "Glad Tidings," in Mikir, by Mosendra Pandit and Missionaries to the Mikirs. Published by the American Baptist Missionary Union, Tika, Assam, 1904. A summary of the Gospel history and teaching.

(All except the first are in the Roman character.)

* So called from the figure of a butterfly (*plī-plī*) on the cover.

INDEX

THE END

ASSAM SHOWING AREA OCCUPIED BY MIKIR TRIBES.

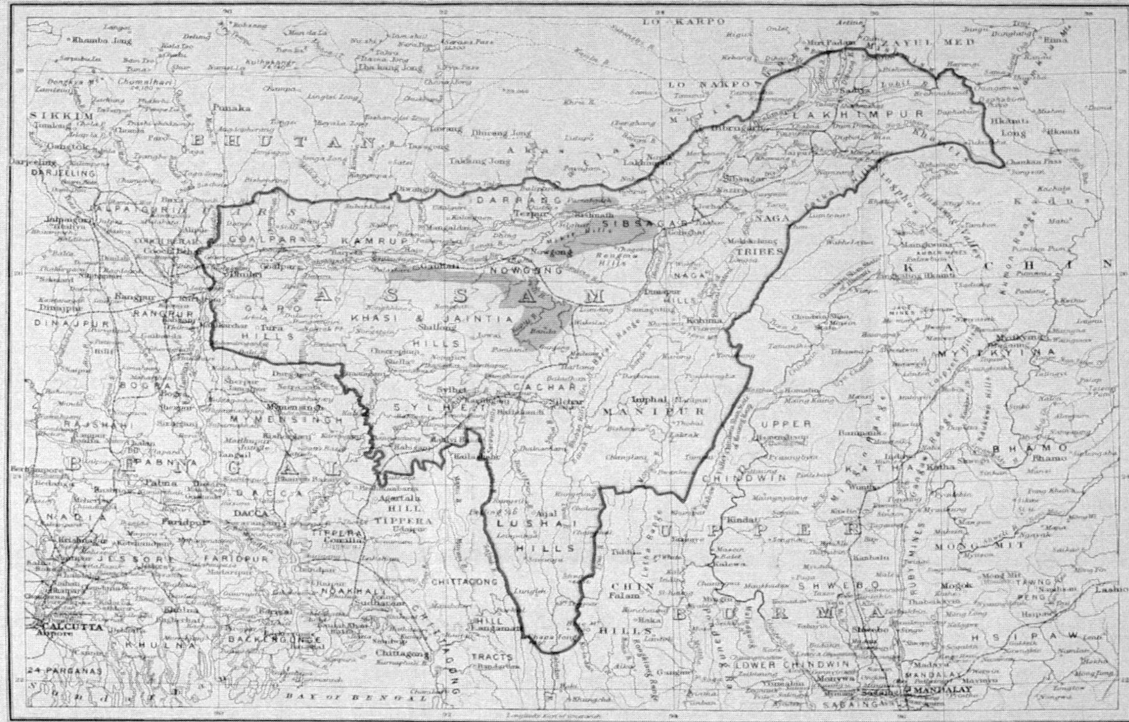

Mikir Tribes coloured thus